D1109755

THE SHADOW OF GOD

THE
SHADOW
OF
GOD

*A Journey
Through Memory,
Art, and Faith*

CHARLES SCRIBNER III

DOUBLEDAY
New York   London   Toronto
Sydney   Auckland

PUBLISHED BY DOUBLEDAY
a division of Random House, Inc.

Copyright © 2006 by Charles Scribner III

All Rights Reserved

DOUBLEDAY and the portrayal of an
anchor with a dolphin are registered
trademarks of Random House, Inc.

Book design by Jennifer Ann Daddio

Library of Congress
Cataloging-in-Publication Data
Scribner, Charles.
The shadow of God : a journey through
memory, art, and faith / Charles Scribner III.
p. cm.
I. Scribner, Charles. 2. Catholic converts—
United States—Biography. I. Title.
BX4668.S37 A3 2006
282'.092—dc22
2005051903

ISBN 0-385-51658-4

PRINTED IN THE UNITED STATES
OF AMERICA

1 3 5 7 9 10 8 6 4 2

First Edition

IN MEMORIAM PATRIS MEI

Lux perpetua luceat ei

ACKNOWLEDGMENTS

I wish to offer heartfelt thanks to my friend and pew mate at St. Vincent Ferrer, Joan Cuomo, who was the first person to read my manuscript—in unedited weekly installments—and who offered a quality of persistent encouragement impossible to resist. Every writer should have such an angel, in or out of church. At Doubleday, my publisher and editor, Michelle Rapkin, took over with that rare combination of faith and expertise that makes her a publisher's publisher, an editor's editor, and an answer to an author's prayers (for the way they were answered, I refer the reader to Friday the thirteenth of December in this journal!). I want also to thank, in the editorial department, Jen Kim and Darya Porat, who have been unfailingly helpful at every stage; Doubleday Religion's editor-in-chief, Trace Murphy; and its publisher, Bill Barry, who saw the book through to publication with grace and skill. I am especially grateful to Bette Alexander for finding the virtuoso copy editor Chuck Antony, who with eagle eyes and superior knowledge left no page unimproved. The elegance of those pages is due to the designers, Jennifer Ann Daddio and Maria Carella. Finally, I owe Baroque thanks to a former colleague, graphic artist John Fontana, who after several years of making Scribner titles look enticing moved on to Doubleday and together with Kathleen DiGrado designed the uplifting cover by which I hope this book will be judged.

THE SHADOW OF GOD

Two years ago, at my parish church of St. Vincent Ferrer in Manhattan, I was arm-twisted by the pastor to give a talk in his Lenten series titled "The Role of God in My Life." I never wrote the talk. The title was impossible, so instead I chose to wing it—on the wing of the Spirit, I prayed. It yielded an outline of my spiritual journey through an Episcopalian childhood and schooling on through a college conversion to Catholicism—and beyond. I used as my guideposts passages from books, plays, and poems that had fed my spiritual life, and works of music that resonated into faith. When it was done I thought: This is the oil sketch for a bigger canvas, composed of art and music and books that have illumined faith—and vice versa. I had long taken for granted that spirituality could generate great works of art—from the Gothic cathedrals to Handel's Messiah—yet it struck me that the opposite is equally true: works of art nourish religious faith and spiritual growth. It's a two-way street. Art—art of all kinds—shapes the way we view our world, ourselves, even God. As Shaw put it, "You use a glass mirror to see your face; you use works of art to see your soul."

My dad used to say, "No rush, just do it immediately." On the Feast of Epiphany I decided to follow his formula. I started a spiritual journal, a yearlong journey "back to the future." I've always had a special fascination for those Wise Men following their star. In the middle of this journey my son Charlie happened to ask why I ever became a Catholic. I told him I was writing this book to find the answer. The philosopher Montaigne wrote, "I have no more made my book than my book has made me." This journey through memory, art, and faith shaped the year as it passed from season to season, from Epiphany through Lent, Easter, Ascension, Advent, Christmas, and back to Epiphany. It wasn't a year in Provence, or a year in Tuscany. Most of the time I stayed close to my lifelong zip code I hope to die within. But by the end, I felt I'd been traveling with the Magi.

SUNDAY, JANUARY 6, 2002
—FEAST OF THE EPIPHANY

Today the three Magi, Wise Men, Kings—thank God no longer the "astrologers" of the first New American Bible translation—presented their legendary gifts of gold, frankincense, and myrrh to the Christ Child in Bethlehem two millennia ago, and here I sit to begin writing a book I meant to begin months ago. I care nothing for birthdays or for the symbolism associated with those mounting numbers. Yet recently, on turning fifty, I felt a gnawing dissatisfaction with the prospect of another half century ahead of me. My father, at this milestone, while I was a junior at Princeton, confided to me, "I feel as though my life is almost half over." He added that Jack Hemingway, the eldest son of his most famous author, had remarked, "I've spent the first fifty years of my life being my father's son, and will spend the next fifty being my daughters' father." That story came back to me last year while I was having breakfast at the Ivy Club in Princeton during a visit to my freshman son. Hearing my name mentioned, a girl looked up from her reading and asked with all the eagerness of youth, "Oh, are you Charlie Scribner's *father*?" I burst into laughter, explaining that for four years at that very table I had been "Charlie Scribner's *son*" (my father was the real one, a university trustee); and now I come back to be "Charlie's father." Independent identity remains elusive.

I told that story at Jack Hemingway's memorial service at the Explorers Club a few weeks later. I felt a kinship with Jack—well beyond the fact that my grandfather and Ernest Hemingway had been best friends, or that my father had been his final publisher. No, it was that I had always felt that Jack's amusing comment was leavened with love for both his father and his children. It was a love I shared with him and with most of fortunate humanity, the love for one's parents and for one's children, and the pride—the good pride, not the deadly sin—that goes with it. But if truth be told, of the two roles I have always felt far more qualified for the first, that of a professional son. It is one I have played for most of my life, and one develops comfort, not to say confidence, with decades of practice.

Up until that breakfast, I had been able to prolong that role for more than five years beyond my father's death, in 1995. I am still not ready to retire from it: I like being his son, first and foremost. But in doing so, especially during his final years of illness and then in the flurry of activity that followed—estate, memorials, and the excavation of memories—I had slipped into neglecting two key activities in my life, two keyboards in fact: the piano's and this laptop's.

Music has always been my first love. Writing came later, although inescapable through birth, profession, and even surname (originally Scrivener, until the late-eighteenth-century change to Scribner), which means "scribe." Within the past year, I bought three pianos for our new apartment: a baby grand for the living room, an electric one for late-night practice, and finally a new Steinway grand for what I have since dubbed the Music Room. Here I finally face this silent keyboard and the book I now know I must write. Its outlines are dim; the mists have not yet risen as it is late at night, with only twenty-some minutes left in this Feast of the Three Gift Givers.

My books on Rubens and Bernini were easy to tackle: I had both their lives and their (illustrated) works as instant structures. But now I have only a theme—if not a title—"The Shadow of God," taken from an inscription my father gave me to post on my study carrel in Princeton's Marquand Library, my senior year, as I faced writing my thesis. *Lux Umbra Dei*—light is the shadow of God. It seems to fit Epiphany, the feast illumined by the light of that wondrous star and following, by a few weeks, that more ancient festival of lights, Hanukkah.

Last evening, during the Epiphany homily, the priest at St. Gertrude's in Bayville, Long Island, noted that this feast is really about taking a risk for faith. The Magi followed their star for a long journey, but with no guarantee that they would achieve their goal; nor even, after they reached the manger and delivered their gifts, that they would be able to return home as planned. We never learn what happened after they received a warning in a dream and returned home "by another route." Were they able to go home again? Were their lives forever changed in other ways?

Tomorrow I shall begin the journey toward the next Epiphany. WQXR has just played the midnight chime. Time to rest until daylight may reveal the path to take.

MONDAY, JANUARY 7, 2002

The workweek having begun, already I find myself breaking a writing habit that served so well in times past—to write early in the morning, then reflect at night and plan the next day's work. That's what it *was* all about—having a good plan. My father's driving motto—his recipe of marital success, at least in an auto—was "No new routes." (They often lead to getting lost, and spousal consternation.) How did the Magi fare? They went home "by another route": was it a new one? In some ways, it could not have been otherwise. The world was renewed by a baby's birth, but would they have known that? They had left behind the most precious of gifts in a rude hovel. How could that have seemed anything but reckless extravagance?

Perhaps that very extravagance gives this feast its special allure—like a High Mass celebrated with solemn splendor in the simplest surroundings. I should like to visit the Cave of the Nativity someday; it's the very contrast of the royal trappings and the rustic place that gives those paintings of the Magi at Bethlehem their majesty, as in Rubens's at the high altar of King's College Chapel, Cambridge: it's the world upside down, kings paying homage to a poor baby on a straw bed. "Contrast" is too weak a word, "juxtaposition" too technical; the Italians come closer with *contrapposto* and *chiaroscuro*—if it were music it might be "divine dissonance"—the convergence of metaphysical opposites.

Walking home tonight from work, I was saddened to see men already beginning to dismantle the base of the great Rockefeller Center tree. Didn't they know that the Christmas season still has six days to go, until next Sunday, the Feast of the Baptism of the Lord? At least it still stood and shone with its colored lights, this year all red, white, and blue—a patriotic response to the tragedy of 9/11. Then, along Park and Lexington Avenues, all those sad discarded trees—like Shakespeare's "bare ruined choirs"—to be picked up and disposed of in the earliest morning hours. Is there a sadder sight? There was.

Just as I felt melancholy dispersed by the still brightly lit manger outside my parish church, St. Vincent's (those wise and wily Dominicans know better than to close up the stable early), a woman on the corner asked softly for help. I thought she wanted directions, but she asked for a dollar. I was stunned: she was dressed simply, but with a dignity that was reinforced by her voice and manner. She said she lived at the women's shelter across the street, at the Armory. I asked if she knew about the help to be had at St. Agnes Parish, about a mile away. No, she said, she had a place to stay, but she needed some money for another woman in special need, "and it's so hard to ask for money."

I was so struck by the unlikelihood that such a lady would be in such need that I pulled out the largest bill I had and was grateful that she didn't look down at it before she gave a blessing in return. How many epiphanies have yet to be had before the manger, even a miniature one with plastic figures? There are so many such encounters on the streets of New York. What made this one seem so different?

When I got home I pulled out a Christmas card from the pile. It was a poem written by Father Andrew Greeley.

> We live in a cosmos that is oddly forgiving.
> It is never too late to begin again.
> There are always second chances and more.
> Like Ulysses it is possible to go home again.
> We will all be young again and laugh again.
> Love is always and necessarily renewable
> And life is stronger than death.

How can a whole city full of discarded trees negate the joy promised in these verses? Greeley's words literally saved the day. And the book that accompanied them, his prayer journal *My Love*, which he had published so that readers might be encouraged to keep their own journals—well, that has saved me from my worst instinct: to second-guess myself and abandon a project before it is hardly begun.

I am not ready to write to God, but I'll take up the good Father Greeley partway and keep a journal until Epiphany, to follow that star back to its rising again. My father's favorite saying was "The secret of a happy life is to do a little work every day" (to which I, the wise-guy college student, replied, "OK, Dad, I will . . . as little as possible!").

TUESDAY, JANUARY 8, 2002

This morning, after the 9 A.M. mass at St. Vincent's, I stopped at the Rosary Altar, which I had restored in the millennium year as a memorial for my father; it's now in the midst of a plywood construction site of church renovation, which added a certain ambience to the manger scene set up behind the prayer rail. I knelt and took in the carved figures of Magi and shepherds and animals and the Holy Family, with the Babe aglow in his crèche. Three Charleses came to mind. First, my father, whom I now associate in a very vivid way with this richly carved altar of saints. "For all the saints, who from their labors rest" was one of his favorite hymns, a staple of Episcopalian funerals. I like to think of him in their company now. The second is my son Charlie, a sophomore at Princeton; when he was two, I showed him this altar and crèche on Christmas Day. He studied it, and then suddenly sang, "Ee—eye—ee—eye—oh!" (Nothing problematic about the iconography for him.) The third is Charles Ryder, Evelyn Waugh's narrator of one of my favorite novels, *Brideshead Revisited*, whose magnificent translation to film my wife and I watched weekly on PBS television soon after son Charlie's birth. In one early, idyllic summer scene on the terrace of Brideshead, Charles challenges his eccentric and much-beloved new friend Sebastian over the latter's troublesome convictions as a Catholic. Charles dismisses it as "an awful lot of nonsense," but Sebastian replies, "Is it nonsense? I wish it were. It sometimes sounds terribly sensible to me."

> *"But, my dear Sebastian, you can't seriously believe it all."*
> *"Can't I?"*

"I mean about Christmas and the star and the three kings and the ox and the ass."

"Oh, yes, I believe that. It's a lovely idea."

"But you can't believe things because they're a lovely idea."

"But I do. That's how I believe."

And then I thought: What has brought me to this manger, time and again? To Mass? To faith? What is the basis of personal belief? Or, put another way, how far back can we trace the roots of faith? How deep are they? How were they fed? And—dare we ask—who planted the seedling? The questions themselves point toward a journey back to childhood and from there (as in one of my favorite films) "back to the future." With no DeLorean, equipped with flux capacitor, to take me to that very place in time—the mid-1950s—I'll have to rely on flickering memory alone to power the time travel, and this manual machine for the words to unlock doors.

WEDNESDAY, JANUARY 9, 2002

That recollection of Sebastian and Charles discussing the Magi while on summer holiday from their Oxford colleges brought back to me the image of the great Rubens *Adoration of the Magi* in King's College Chapel, which I had first seen as a teenager on summer holiday and which, as a scholar of Rubens, I have pondered and admired more knowingly for the past three decades. But it is only now that I finally realize the appropriateness of its modern relocation at that high altar (it was originally painted for a Belgian convent). The connection between its subject and its final home had never dawned on me: the three kings . . . in King's College! It's so obvious. But then, as my father once said in a talk about Hemingway, "The obvious is these days often much neglected."

What about Sebastian's claim to believe something because it is a "lovely idea"? Is this nothing more than the intellectual equivalent to his teddy bear, Aloysius (named after a young Jesuit saint)? Is truth more likely to be lovely? A theological argument might be made in favor of this "lovely idea" based on the claims of St. John's gospel that God is both absolute Truth and absolute Love—an equation (as it were) that supports Sebastian's point. But how does it ring in our own secular, skeptical, scientific age? Soundly, or merely quaintly? It's astonishing to read among contemporary cosmologists that so often the persuasiveness of a scientific theory is based on the *beauty* of the theory—its elegance and economy in accounting for the ultimately unknowable. On the front page of today's *New York Times* I read under the heading "Hints of a Cosmic Starburst" that "based on the Hubble Space Telescope data, some astronomers believe that light from the first stars emerged from a dark cosmos like a fireworks spectacular, not in the slow manner long assumed." I thought at once of the simple Genesis formula "And God said, 'Let there be light,' and there was light"—and then I heard those thunderous, shimmering chords of Haydn's *Creation*: "The heavens are telling the glory of God, the firmament proclaims the wonder of his work." Art and science and faith never seemed more in tune.

Then, in the next section of the paper, a touching article on an eighty-seven-year-old Catholic priest who holds the record in this city for tenure at one parish—sixty years at St. Helena's in the Bronx—ended with another echo of Genesis: "My eyes are dimmed . . . but this is the idea I hold to now: Everybody is a person, made to the image of God. And for that I love them all." Light is but the shadow of God, yet humankind in all its imperfection and frailty is fashioned in God's image. That surely must be harder to grasp, much less believe, than our Lord's myriad miracles, which pose stumbling blocks to skeptical humanity two millennia later.

A very witty—and ultimately tragic—English teacher at school, James Greaves, once told me, "We can't be sure whether God made man in his image, but we can be certain that man makes God in *his* image." Beneath his cynical banter lay a central truth: our images of God are, from the beginning, molded by human images, beginning with our parents. I don't remember the first time I said the Our Father, but I can be sure that by that time it was easy, for I already had at hand a loving father as a reference point, a model for projection into the heavens. How terrible it must be for a child with a cruel parent even to consider a paternal image of God.

Memory is elusive, but three stories my father liked to tell me about my earliest days provide glimpses of a very literal and pragmatic child's grasppling with the notion of God. That I survived my baptism, at age two, in St. Bartholomew's Church, is itself something of a miracle. While everyone was focused on the font, this toddler wandered a few steps away and was seen tugging at the cord of a large steel fan on a ledge overhead and was grabbed just before bringing it down to crash on his head!

Before I understood the meaning or use of the word "why," my endless questions usually began, "What happened that . . . ?" My father, a historian of science by avocation, said that I had an exclusively causal view of everything. Is that the basis of faith? A need for a First Cause? The Cosmological Argument, as theologians call it? "In the beginning, God . . ." Has any story had a better—or as Sebastian might say, lovelier—beginning?

A second tale has me crossing Park Avenue with my father—I picture it near St. Bartholomew's. The tike is swinging his clenched fists wildly about.

"What are you doing, Charlie?"

"You told me God is everywhere, right?"

"Well, yes, but what does that have to do with it?"

"I'm hitting God." (Not a promising start.)

And finally my early, overheard bedtime prayer for my three-year-old younger brother was not much better: "Dear God, make Blair good . . . and keep me good."

THURSDAY, JANUARY 10, 2002

I never knew my grandfather Charles Scribner, grandson of the firm's founder. Everything I have heard or read about him makes me regret this fact. All the writers he published were devoted to him—above all, Hemingway, who called him "my best friend." Hemingway also wrote that my grandfather knew "a good deal about horses, as much as a man probably should be allowed to know about the publishing business, and, surprisingly, something about books." Classic Hemingway. But it clothes in wit a sadder truth: my grandfather took over the thriving publishing house—founded by the first Charles Scribner in 1846 and built up by his father, the second Charles—not by choice but by birth. His early inclination as a child toward art—a talent he inherited from his maternal grandfather, the clergyman/portraitist Jared Flagg, and shared with his uncle the Beaux Arts architect Ernest Flagg—was soon erased by his alarmed parents, who took away his drawing tools.

We moved into the New York apartment at 31 East 79 Street that my grandfather had given my parents as a wedding present. My first memory of that apartment is of the front hall, lined with bookshelves, and, opposite them, a large, dark portrait of two Dutch children painted by the seventeenth-century portraitist Jacob Gerritsz Cuyp. From my earliest days I believed the picture—despite those Thanksgiving pilgrims costumes—to be of myself with my Irish governess, Mollie.

My most vivid memory at this time is of standing before the kitchen sink to test the birthday present I had just received on my mother's twenty-eighth birthday, four days after my fourth, in 1955: a miniature top-loading washing machine complete with motor and draining hose and the means of making real suds. I was entranced by the mechanics of this modern marvel, and in the coming months—at the house my parents rented in Darien, Connecticut, for the summer—I played equally with that machine and a toy John Deere tractor large enough to ride (perhaps that was my own birthday present). My father took stereoscopic photos of that summer place in Darien, and looking at those color-drenched and almost tangible 3-D images through a viewer persuades me that time travel may yet be possible. Every time I pass the Darien exit on the turnpike, four and a half decades later, I renew my determination to find that house with the long driveway (if indeed it ever was long) and revisit the first "country" I can recall.

FRIDAY, JANUARY 11, 2002

That summer in Darien was punctuated by two dramas of nature. The first was small but frightening; the second, the opposite. First, a menacing hornets' nest, looking like a gray football, wedged in the corner of the house, was removed from outside a second-story window near the landing and my room. An exterminator had been called in to perform the delicate operation, accompanied by silence and awe from those of us inside, watching through the safety of glass. To this day I have had an unnatural aversion to hornets and wasps—I'd prefer to discover a live bomb in my backyard. I don't ever recall being stung by one, which may account for the irrational intensity of this fear of the unknown.

The second was the great hurricane of 1955, which did extensive damage and was, unlike the hornets, a true threat to life and limb. But I found it utterly entrancing—Shakespearean, in hindsight, a thundering tempest that compelled us to spend an entire night in the house by candlelight alone. I loved every minute of it. I can still see my infant brother's nurse walking through the kitchen carrying a single taper with apprehension worthy of Lady Macbeth.

The reason for the candlelight became clear at first light: the electric power line to our house had been hit by a branch and had severed and fallen across the driveway. My father frantically called the power company several times to come and repair this live wire, while I was kept confined to the house without understanding why. The hurricane had devastated the entire state, and we were clearly low on the list of emergencies. So my father took a different tack. He called them back and in the calmest, most casual voice he could muster he apologized for having troubled them with his earlier request for help and explained that the power line across the driveway really didn't look that dangerous after all; it was just sparking a little and "dancing about." He said he'd just go and move it to the side of the road himself. The voice on the other end ordered him not to move and to stay indoors; they would be there immediately. And so they were.

I wish I could recall the most eventful evening of that summer, the dinner my mother had to cook and serve for Colonel and Mrs. Lindbergh. At the age of twenty-eight, with two young children, my mother found it a daunting prospect to be entertaining the first man to fly across the Atlantic solo, the very year she was born. Lindbergh's book about that flight, *The Spirit of St. Louis*, had been published by my father two years earlier, during his first year at the helm of Scribners, and had recently won the Pulitzer Prize. My father later said that Lindbergh was the fussiest author he'd ever had to deal with; he would measure the spaces around punctuation marks, and to him every detail had as much significance "as if it were a moving part in his airplane." So my father was aghast to discover that in the first printing of the Book-of-the-Month Club edition two entire pages had been rendered as gibberish by a typesetting error; it was so bad that he felt he had to call Lindbergh himself and brace him for this catastrophe. But Lindbergh just brushed it off, saying that the mistake would make the first printing more valuable!

My mother found the colonel aloof, icy, impossible to talk to; he never said a word throughout dinner; but Anne Morrow Lindbergh was warm and delightful. That experience must surely have provided my mother instant training in entertaining authors, something she and my father did with natural ease and grace for decades to come. As I write these words, a young editor has just come by with a copy of *The Spirit of St. Louis*, telling me that this year is the seventy-fifth anniversary of the Atlantic flight and that the publishers upstairs are planning a special commemoration of it. Next year, it dawns on me, is the golden anniversary of our book—soon to turn fifty. What are the probabilities, I ask him, that he would appear with that book the very moment I was recalling the author's one visit to my parents' home? Perhaps a beautiful mind like John Nash's could explain it away mathematically; but I prefer to believe that there are no mere coincidences: coincidences, someone once told me, are those moments when God chooses to remain anonymous.

SATURDAY, JANUARY 12, 2002

I have yet to know a child—at least in my own family—to refute the notion that all young children are endowed by their creator with supernaturally strong wills. Still, mine must have tested even the most patient and understanding parents. I can still picture myself standing midway along that Darien driveway, rubbing my legs with a leaf of poison ivy as though giving myself a sponge bath. My horrified governess asked me what on earth I thought I was doing. "Daddy told me never to go near that poison ivy and I'm not going to let him tell me what to do!" On another occasion, I slipped into the downstairs study while my parents were out to dinner, went over to the stack of 78 rpm lacquer Victrola records—the precursors of the LPs that to my CD-attuned children are now equally antique and quaint—and methodically unpeeled from each label the antiskid stickers that my father had carefully applied to prevent sudden lurches in pitch during playing. There must have been dozens of them, lying strewn over the floor like candy wrappers after a movie lets out. I think my father always assumed that this was an act of retribution for some punishment I had suffered. It may be so; I vaguely sense that the room had been closed off to me at the time. Yet I still can see those brown stickers as offending my sense of propriety: they were an unseemly and unnecessary blot on the pristine labels of these magnificent records—like training wheels on a bicycle. Who was my dad to second-guess RCA, Decca, and Columbia?

It was at this time that my love affair with the phonograph began—the first musical instrument I mastered (never to be surpassed by my study of several others). It combined my fascination with household machines and an early passion for music. Our home was always filled with music. My mother often played the Chilton baby grand in the living room; she had studied piano throughout her childhood with an extraordinary teacher who was to transform my own life years later. Mom was naturally musical, something she inherited from her mother's family (I have long attributed the musical gene to my Kissel forebears, for surely in this arena of the arts the Germans trump the English and the Dutch).

My father was no less an influence. He involved me in his dedication to listening via the phonograph to a wide variety of great music—from Jerome Kern's *Show Boat* (a lifelong favorite of his, which was to be, forty years later, the last music he ever heard this side of the angels) to the symphonies of Beethoven and Mozart. The first piece of furniture inside the living room was a massive cabinet of blond wood housing a Fisher phonograph and radio tuner, each in its own compartment, above a huge central speaker, all covered by cupboardlike doors with large brass rings to grab at concert time. To my eyes it was magical. I had my own, portable, child's version in my room—a small gray top-loading machine for my 45s and 78s. But the real excitement—and the real music—sounded in the living room, in "high fidelity."

SUNDAY, JANUARY 13, 2002

Today, the Baptism of the Lord, marks the end of the Christmas season; our tree finally had to come down and go out to join the others remaining on the sidewalk to be picked up by the city's sanitation brigade—but not before leaving most of its scented needles on the dining room floor. How strange that the evergreen scent is strongest and most evocative of the season at that very point when it is dying—the aromatic equivalent, I suppose, to the golden hues of leaves in autumn, or a sunset in all its glory before night falls. It seems appropriate that January finds me looking back to beginnings, for the month is named after the Roman god Janus, who had two faces: one looking back, the other forward. I find consolation and peace in looking back at this time, especially after all the death and sadness of this past September. Perhaps by next January I'll be ready to look forward again.

Our first family celebrations of the Thanksgiving and Christmas feasts began in earnest in 1955, when my younger brother, Blair, then one and a half, was able to sit at table. My mother went all out, and my father captured it on film—he was as avid and talented an amateur photographer as he was a music lover. His portraits of children were so good that eventually a neighbor in Far Hills gave him a one-man show in her gallery. Thanksgiving found my brother and me at a table bedecked with a paper tablecloth (my mother was as practical as she was imaginative) adorned with turkeys; before us she set small pilgrim figures in wax (candles, in fact, but not to be lit) and chocolate, foil-covered turkeys. Christmas Eve found Blair and me sitting in front of our respective felt stockings hanging from the marble mantelpiece; on its top was our spartan offering to Santa of two red apples. A few years later, I was to augment this snack with a vodka and tonic for Santa—at my father's direction.

My passion for machines took a new, creative turn. I started making washing machines, dishwashers, televisions, vacuum cleaners, and phonographs out of cardboard boxes and pipe cleaners. I have no idea what inspired this fascination: my father, after all, made books, not appliances. Perhaps it was that with an infant brother at home I invariably spent much of my time watching the real contraptions in action. There was no nursery school to keep me busy. But I soon started classes in eurythmics—singing, dancing, and musical games—at the Dalcroze School of Music, which I loved from the start.

What I remember most about this school is the image of two grand pianos fitted together like giant pieces of jigsaw puzzle, end to end, so that the two pianists faced each other across this giant instrument. Against such a backdrop, musical chairs—the only activity I can recall with any clarity—took on a new intensity, especially for a high-energy child.

Meanwhile, thanks to my mother, eurythmics were translated to another, more exotic arena: the skating rink. She took me for the first time, and with new black figure skates, to her rink at Iceland, over the old Madison Square Garden, where the Rangers practiced for their hockey games when my mother and her colleagues from the New York Skating Club were not claiming the ice. She had skated at this rink since she was seven, and now she was taking lessons, practicing, and performing in exhibitions alongside Olympic medalists and aspirants. She could have had such a career of her own—but then I might not have been with her that day. Her teacher, Fritz Dietl, took me out for my first turn on the ice. Once around the rink, holding his hand, with wobbly tentative steps, I announced I was ready to take off on my own. The gliding was exhilarating. But even more, it was an extension of the endless music. There was never any silent ice; someone was always putting his or, more usually, her practice record on the turntable. I have as vivid a picture of that elaborate phonograph booth, with its stack of records (many privately pressed for the skaters), as I do of the upper-level cafeteria where we got hot chocolate and watched the rink through its glass wall during those intermissions while new ice was made or a special session—such as dance or school figures—took over the rink.

My mother never stressed the gymnastic side of skating; for her, skating meant interpreting the music with the most graceful of lines. A lieder singer might call it "legato" skating—it was all tied together, all of a seamless piece: the music, the spins, the spirals, and the jumps. I never developed either the discipline or the competitive urge to get beyond the elementary stages of figures (it was a rare boy who did), but I always loved going to the rink with my mother and skating long and fast, with rusty spins and jumps, enough just to

enjoy the music in motion. But then, sitting was never my forte: two years earlier I had had to pose for a pastel portrait by Jean Plunket, only to earn a cap-
tion decades later in her book: "Never relaxed for more than two seconds!"

MONDAY, JANUARY 14, 2002

Last evening my mother gave me the photo album that begins with my parents' wedding in 1949 and covers the next twenty years, providing me at last
with some visual control for the fleeting images of memory. Pages and photos have fallen out; time has not been kind to this book. But I have now
completed the task of restoration with rubber cement and plastic tape,
rather than follow my first instinct—to scrap the scrapbook and transfer
the photos to a new one. Something held me back: perhaps the realization
that the original binding and pages, with my mother's inscriptions, are an
integral part of the record and the tactile experience of poring over these
(literally) familiar pages. I am not a rare-book collector. But this one is different. It is inscribed as a wedding gift and must be preserved as it is. It reminds me of my favorite bedtime book, *The Velveteen Rabbit*, about a boy's
favorite stuffed animal that eventually gets taken away during a bout of
scarlet fever. The rabbit's heart is broken until by the best of fairy-tale miracles he becomes "real" through the power of love—and is given a new life
with other animals. I could never hear that story enough. It touched something deep within, and instilled a sense of nostalgia that has never left me.

I stumbled upon a Zenith table radio on eBay; it was made the year of
my birth—the same one, down to the metallic gold cloth covering the
speaker, that my mother later kept on her desk for many years until it was
replaced in the late 1960s by the KLH still there today. The classic Zenith
is now mine, the auction having just ended in my favor. And so I can look
forward to a visual, tangible, and audible memento of half a century ago.
The strangest thing of all is that this very morning, passing the NBC television windows in Rockefeller Center, I was suddenly taken back to that

very time by a picture window display of the first *Today* show, which this week celebrates its golden anniversary. The set was a perfect replica of the broadcast booth of January 1952, complete with newspapers hanging on the wall and a stack of books, including a Scribner novel—*From Here to Eternity.*

Upstairs in the office, I soon found myself invited to join a small reception for Hugh Downs, one of the most impressive television journalists in the industry. He is here to participate in the fiftieth-anniversary broadcast of the *Today* show, and is also doing a book for us on what it means to be an American. Like my late father, he developed a deep interest in post-Einstein physics; in his case, his avocation and his vocation (in communications) have been reconciled by the latest findings in quantum mechanics and physics. The universe, it seems, on the most basic level—that of the electrons—all boils down to "information"; it may all be reduced, in the end, to pure mathematics—which is to say, to "communication." I told him that, to my mind, these findings were already anticipated by the evangelist John, whose gospel account begins with "the Word." Downs replied that when the scientists push to the top of the highest of all peaks, that final ascent, "they'll probably meet a bunch of theologians waiting for them!"

The priest celebrating midday Mass at St. Patrick's announced that today marks the beginning of "ordinary time" in the liturgical calendar. Some ordinary time! But then, all time is God's time, and ultimately it is both as simple and mysterious as the simultaneity of past and present in the mind's eye. Perhaps therein lies my attraction to that tabletop Zenith, which still receives fresh signals and transmutes them into living voices and the music of composers long dead.

TUESDAY, JANUARY 15, 2002

The photo album, now restored, except for a few loose photos that need an extra dose of rubber cement to keep them in place for another generation, documents many visible firsts around this time, 1955–1956, such as my first pony ride—at my horsy cousins' farm in New Marlborough, Massachusetts—and my first electric train, set up by my father on the dining room floor on Christmas Day. I wonder how my mother felt about having to navigate around the track to set the table. But while horses and trains were to assume important places in my imagination and recreation for years to come—perhaps confirming that I was born in the wrong century—a more memorable first was the time my father took me to see a movie. It was *Around the World in Eighty Days*, so it must have been in 1956—there's nothing like beginning with a panoramic epic. Upon returning home, I announced to him that it was the best movie I'd ever seen. One scene, however, lingers in memory; it bothered me then—and still does. It was the episode in India when our hero rescues a young Indian widow about to be consigned to a funeral pyre, a fiery bed on which her husband's body lies. Only a couple of years ago did I finally learn the correct term for this ritual (from Hemingway's son Patrick): "suttee." But at age five, I saw it not as an ancient ritual but only as incomprehensible cruelty.

That scene, and my reaction to it, was overshadowed a year or so later by the final scene of *Rigoletto*, the first opera I ever saw—in our living room, of all places. The stark black-and-white of the live broadcast added to the horror. How could such beautiful music play against the backdrop of this poor hunchedback father opening a sack to find—to his horror and mine—his young daughter inside, stabbed by a hired assassin, and now dying in his arms? It might have been less upsetting to see it in performance, at a safe distance, in a grand theater surrounded by an audience. But television gave it an immediacy and verisimilitude, as though it were a segment of the evening news, which the composer could never have envisioned. What, I wonder, would Verdi think?

There would be other similarly troubling scenes of cruelty or suffering on television that haunted me for a long time, especially since I had watched them alone and had no one to answer my questions. One was of Mary Queen of Scots going to her beheading; another was of a Revolutionary War soldier being hanged and struggling against his executioners' attempt to cover his head with a sack (the hanging itself seemed less menacing than that black hood); a third was the opening scene of a movie about Lincoln, showing his mother's difficult labor. Of course, I did not know that then; at the time it was just a woman in bed, writhing in pain and screaming while her husband rammed the side of it with a wheelbarrow. Do such images—tame by modern standards—fuel a child's desire to understand what C. S. Lewis called "the problem of pain," the mystery of evil and suffering? I wonder whether I would even remember them if someone had been there to explain them to me. Was it those incomprehensible details that burned them in memory—or rather the fact that I had indeed grasped the underlying message of suffering? Ours is the first generation to be reared on television; we may never know the end of its influence.

WEDNESDAY, JANUARY 16, 2002

My father liked to tell the story of how, on their honeymoon, my mother watched him unpack a pile of books and asked, with some concern, why he had brought them along. "That's my business," he replied, and then, seeing her expression, quickly added, "I mean, I'm in the book business." It seems strange that, growing up in such a family, I do not have any clear memories of when I learned to read. Both parents read to me regularly from the start, and the earliest books have a voice other than my own associated with them. (When we read in silence, it is, of course, not the author's voice we hear but our own—as much as when we think, or daydream.) Before the world of Dr. Seuss opened up to me—beginning with *The Cat in the Hat, The Cat in the Hat Comes Back*, and *Yertle the Turtle*—I was already captive to the musical, rhyming meter of Virginia Kahl's *The Duchess Bakes a Cake*, which my father brought home from the office as soon as he had published this whimsical tale set in the world of knights, damsels, and castles—my first taste of the Middle Ages, which would be my age of choice many years later in college. "A lovely, light, luscious, delectable cake" was its refrain good enough to eat.

The first thing I recall reading for myself—or was it merely memorizing?—was an election pin I picked up at President Eisenhower's campaign storefront downstairs in our apartment building: "I like Ike." There were tables full of these lapel buttons, in various shapes and sizes. The campaign was in full swing as I entered my first daily classroom, kindergarten at the Town School, a few blocks away. It was an assemblage of two or perhaps three adjacent town houses, and we reached our large classroom overlooking the large back courtyard by following a rabbit warren of winding hallways of ever-changing levels.

I was a decided failure at nap time when all the blankets were laid out on the floor. Too boring: I preferred the blanket equivalent of table hopping for a social life. Why should I be sent to school to sleep on the floor? It made no sense. At certain times the class broke into two groups; in the back room, around a table, students were taught to read. Learning to read was optional. I opted out. I preferred to play with blocks, trucks, and figures in the front room. Fortunately, I don't think my father was ever aware of the elective nature of reading, nor of my election.

One Monday morning at the beginning of school, two girls—inseparable best friends—came to class with one of them holding her head and moaning: one end of an arrow protruded from each temple. Her friend explained that there had been a terrible accident in archery practice: she had been shot through the head and they couldn't get the arrow out. It was totally convincing and horrifying—until the victim removed the joke headband from beneath her hair. We boys were no matches for such theatrics. But before that nonacademic year was over, a sudden event at home was almost as dramatic and mysterious as the stray arrow: in April, coming home from school, a month shy of six, I was told I had a new brother—a small bundle in my mother's arms as she sat holding him in an easy chair. I had had no idea he was on the way; no stork had been seen circling over Seventy-ninth Street. So now there were three of us, each exactly three years apart—my mother always explained to friends that my father's hobby was mathematics.

THURSDAY, JANUARY 17, 2002

The Zenith radio was waiting in the front hall when I got home; I unpacked the bubble wrappings and carefully lifted this relic of my earliest childhood. It was just as I had remembered it. I plugged it into a kitchen wall outlet and turned it on: nothing. I unplugged it and tried again: still nothing. I moved it to another outlet: no sound at all. Had it been dropped in shipping? Had a tube broken? As I pondered the possibilities, a faint hum came from the speaker. I turned up the volume all the way and heard the faint echo of music that gradually and mysteriously swelled into full sound. Only then did I realize my folly: there had been nothing wrong with this radio. But four decades of transistors had caused me to forget that in 1951 there was no instant sound in a tube radio—or a tube anything. Tubes have to warm up: so do memories, a reminder that patience is part of the process of retrieving what may only be thought to be lost.

My dual life as a Gemini was to begin that summer of 1957, when for the first of many summers in Far Hills, New Jersey, my parents rented a large house for the three months from Memorial Day to Labor Day. The "Ewing house" was owned by the head of Abercrombie & Fitch; he took his family north to the Cape for the summer while we considered inland New Jersey resort enough. It was a revelation to this city boy—a vast three-storied colonial house, with a screened sleeping porch off my parents' bedroom, separated from mine at the other end by a long corridor of endless bedrooms; a large playroom on the third floor, whose attraction was tempered only by occasional menacing wasps. Lawns, patios, fields, and apple orchard, a playground, and a long winding driveway made the outside no less a marvel. But the playing wasn't confined to this place, for I soon began a summer day camp a few miles away—Camp Red Ram. A yellow school bus picked me up at Larger Cross Road, a bus that took many of the other campers to their local schools; they all knew the driver, Mike. But for me, who was walked each day to and from school by a parent, this first experience of the yellow bus was an adventure in independence. As one of the dozen or so six-year-olds, I was in the youngest group, the Chickadees (from which one graduated to become, the next year, a Wren, then an Owl, then a Falcon, next an Eagle—and finally, the birds having been exhausted, a "senior camper"). Singing was a big part of the day—usually after lunch, to bide the time that had to pass before it was deemed safe to go swimming (according to the prevailing theory of digestion). "We are the Chickadees, and we are busy bees; we like to play and sing, and do most anything; we are the smallest group, but such a merry troop; we smile from ear to ear, we're glad we're here!"—surely the silliest song ever lodged in memory, no doubt from so many repetitions, and perhaps equally by association with something new and altogether happy.

Three of the teenage counselors were from the same large Irish-Catholic family, the Egans. The name came back to me with the papal appointment of our new archbishop of New York last year: Cardinal Egan. I remember being shocked that one of them said she had to give herself a shot every day for something called diabetes. Far less ominous, but no less mysterious, was talk by the eldest sister, Pat, about her plan to become a nun after high school. My limited experience of nuns in New York was of seeing women disguised as penguins walking in pairs down the street; they had nothing in common with this fun sixteen-year-old. I wonder whether she pursued her pre–Vatican II dream.

The most dramatic event of the summer was the announcement that our well had gone dry and we had no more water at the Ewings'. "That's impossible" was Mr. Ewing's repeated response from the Cape. In the spirit of Curious George, one of my favorite literary characters at the time, I tried all the faucets for myself: at first a trickle, finally nothing. We had to pack up and move.

FRIDAY, JANUARY 18, 2002

Our house for the rest of the summer was a century-old white farmhouse facing Lamington Road, complete with front porch, picket fence, and in the back, a large red barn and silo and fenced-in fields with decorative cows—something much more picturesque than any farm I'd seen in black-and-white at dawn on the NBC television show *The Modern Farmer.*

My favorite book that summer was a picture book comparing farming equipment and techniques a century apart; it had the splendid graphic device of showing the same farm scene and activity juxtaposed on opposite pages. I loved the experience of going back and forth in time. I also had a more citified variation on the theme that I read even more avidly. It was Hildegard Woodward's *Time Was* (published by my grandfather in 1941), set at the turn of the century, with four stories about an Edwardian family getting their first bathtub with running water, their first sewing machine, their first roller skates, and their first automobile. Both books sparked an enduring fascination with the past and its artifacts, with nostalgia (an odd trait in a six-year-old), and with what my parents and I called "the olden days." Most of all, I loved studying the pictures; perhaps my unexpected choice of art history as a college major and postgraduate pursuit may be traced to that half summer at the farm after the well went dry.

Since we did not have a swimming pool, we visited several friends who did—among them, the Frelinghuysens, who lived a couple of miles up the road and who had added one to my grandparents' former estate Dew Hollow, which they renamed Merrybrook. There was also the Lake Club, a swimming and boating club built on the shore of an artificial lake that bordered a narrow twisting road, with incessant honking of horns, and was—to my surprise—named after my brother: Blair Lake. Well, almost. It had belonged to a Blair first cousin of my great-grandfather Scribner. (We were all descended from John Insley Blair, father-in-law of the first Charles Scribner and, more to the point, the biggest railroad magnate of the previous century: he owned even more miles of track than Commodore Vanderbilt, on my mother's side.) Up in the trees, atop what looked like a Norwegian fjord, was his grandson Ledyard Blair's huge neo-Renaissance mansion, looming like the House of Usher, though now a convent. The founding Blair, who survived well into his nineties, always lived in a simple farmhouse and with a Scottish frugality rivaled only by his vast philanthropy in New Jersey (which encompassed Blairstown, Blair Academy, and Blair Hall at Princeton). Once he was asked why his grandson planned to live in so grand a mansion and he didn't. "Well, you see, he has a rich grandfather—and I don't."

SATURDAY, JANUARY 19, 2002

Blair Lake is most notable for its murky water. One could see the bottom only in the shallowest, sandy part of the roped-in area for the youngest swimmers like me. Beyond the ropes, the bottom fell out from our feet and, if touched, was forbiddingly soft and slimy. Rumors of snapping turtles did not increase the urge to explore deeply. Older children went out in rowboats, sometimes with fishing rods. I never caught anything then or in years later, but I didn't mind. I wouldn't have known what to do with the fish anyway—God forbid I should have to eat it. Fish made me gag—I was always finding bones in my mouth—as did liver, both of which I was often served because they were "good for me" (since I was allergic to starch: potatoes, white bread—all the things children like).

My father shared my distaste for fish; on a trip to Norway with my mother, he learned to say only one thing in Norwegian—"*Ikke fisk*" (no fish). Yet, paradoxically, the one "reading story"—as distinct from picture books—that I recall from a hefty book of folktales is "The Fisherman and His Wife." It was about a fisherman who caught a magic fish—one that talked—and set it free, only to be sent back by his avaricious wife, who wanted him to have her wishes granted by that prince-turned-fish. First, she wanted a nicer cottage (they were living in a hovel), then a castle, then to be king, then emperor, then pope. Each time the fisherman returned, the waters became more agitated, the winds stronger, reflecting the growing outrage of Nature herself at the woman's hubris. Finally she sent her husband back to ask the exasperated fish—amidst a full gale and churning waves—to grant a final wish: she wanted "to be like God." The fish returned the couple to their original hovel.

Today I went to the library to see whether I could find this tale. I had no luck amidst the books, but revelation came via the Internet: first, that the authors were the brothers Grimm; then, that the description of the presumption of her wanting to be pope made it clear how sacrilegious this wish was. As a six-year-old Protestant, I really had no idea what a pope was, but I remember assuming that it was way above being a king or emperor—and that the drawing of the wife in papal regalia with her triple crown looked both ridiculous and ominous. The Grimm brothers described the incense and procession and acolytes that surrounded this greedy woman once she became pope. Was this my first subliminal experience of the papacy I was to acknowledge as supreme spiritual office, some thirteen years later? I don't know. But I am certain that I never grasped the point and beauty of the tale. I had always taken the ending to be a harsh if deserved punishment for asking for the unaskable—to be like God. It was the grasp for ultimate power that, for that foolish woman, literally brought down the house. Back to square one—something a child used to board games could readily appreciate.

What had never occurred to me until today was that she simply got her wish: "to be like God"—the God who dwelt not in a castle, but who chose to be born in a manger, in a shack. And that is where the fisherman and his wife found themselves once again. (He had, in fact, protested her first wish: it was unnecessary, since they already had all they needed; but he gave in reluctantly to keep domestic peace.) The fish had done no more than to take her at her word. Her wish was granted—she just didn't know what she was asking for. In other words, be careful what you pray for, you may get it.

SUNDAY, JANUARY 20, 2002

What is it that makes endings more memorable than beginnings? Is it possibly that each ending, each farewell or last night contains the promise of commencement—the start of something new? What I remember most of that first summer at Camp Red Ram (the name of its founder, Marder, spelled backward) is the last-night cookout, with campfire and prizes and farewells lit by torches on the shore of the pond. Soon afterward we packed up and returned to New York, something that was to remain the highlight of each summer—not only for me but for my equally citified brothers as well. Years later, my youngest brother, John, would echo, in his own idiom, my sentiments about the return to Manhattan Island: after taking a deep breath upon arrival, he exclaimed to our mother, "Ah, smell the fresh air!"

That September of 1957 marked the beginning of a new school for me, Buckley, which was to be my academic, social, and—later—musical base for the next eight years. In hindsight, it was the most challenging school I ever experienced: the doctoral program at Princeton was a snap by comparison. I was to be a slow bloomer, to put it mildly. Reading was no longer optional, yet I tried my best to prolong the fun and games. Forty years later I ran into my first-grade teacher, Miss Ward, outside my son Charlie's dorm at St. Paul's, where she had a great-nephew. She confirmed my early recollection of standing atop a desk and announcing to the class, "I am the Statue of Liberty—bow down to me." The usual consequence of such disruptions was to be banished to the bathroom; I spent a lot of time in that small room. Sometimes classmates would come in and cheer me up with invitations to their homes after school.

That year the laborious task of mastering perfect penmanship along with the Mae Carden method of phonetic reading began. Across the hall was the school library, where an ancient librarian would read to us from a long adventure novel about a boy named Hal or Tal; I never followed his travels, for instead I took off on my own daydreams each library period. I was no better a listener the following year, when we were read C. S. Lewis's classic *The Lion, the Witch and the Wardrobe.* I followed no farther than the passage through the closet door. Once the children were off to Narnia, I was off to my own dreamscapes, with the soft voice of the teacher providing the background music.

My mental wanderings had a physical counterpart. Once we joined the next-door class for calisthenics supervised by the phys ed teachers: we were all supposed to stand by a desk and run in place. I recall being the lone electron orbiting that nucleus of obedient students until the "sports sir," as we called him, called me out. Perhaps my year at Dalcroze playing musical chairs had something to do with my penchant for perpetual motion.

MONDAY, JANUARY 21, 2002

Musical chairs seemed to be a leitmotif of this national holiday. I took
Ritchie to the dress rehearsal at the Metropolitan Opera of Mozart's *Marriage of Figaro*, which has been my favorite opera ever since I studied it in college. I have listened to it more than any other in the intervening thirty years;
I never tire of it. Once we had played musical chairs in the parterre box,
which was less than half full, to find the best seats, we were transported to
eighteenth-century Seville, where the teenage Cherubino scurried around a
wing chair in Figaro's room as he sought to hide from his master, Count
Almaviva—all to the effervescent music of Mozart. The production by
Jonathan Miller accentuates the humor and wit and poignancy of this original musical version of *Upstairs Downstairs*. At one point I thought, as if for
the first time, This is the perfect work of art. It never stales; there are always new treasures to be found within. For all its social satire and good fun,
it's really about grace and reconciliation and forgiveness—not bad themes
for Martin Luther King Day.

The epiphany today was the anticipation, indeed prefiguration, in act
two when the philandering count, after curses and threats and tantrums, has
falsely accused his wife of faithlessness and asks her pardon. She replies
that someone who cannot forgive others cannot expect forgiveness. I was so
caught up in the music and theatrics that this exchange had previously
passed unnoticed; but today it shone like the jeweled ring the countess ex-
tends to her husband at the end, two acts later—the ring she has tricked
from him by exchanging clothes with her maid, Susanna, to whom the
count believed he had given the jewel as an adulterous bribe during a night-
time rendezvous in the garden. He meantime thinks he has caught his ser-
vant Figaro and the countess (really Susanna in disguise) in flagrante—or
almost. He absolutely refuses their entreaties for forgiveness—"*Perdono, perdono*"—with his curt "No, no," when, like a deus ex machina, the real countess emerges radiantly gowned in white from the garden pavilion. Now the

table has been turned, and recognizing his own ring on her finger, he must do the begging: *"Contessa, perdono, perdono, perdono."* Her reply? *"Più docile io sono, e dico di sì"*—"I am kinder and say yes"—she sings in the most heavenly absolution ever pronounced through music.

Every time we pray the Lord's Prayer and ask that we be forgiven our trespasses "as we forgive those who trespass against us" we acknowledge the equation the countess cites in act two: you cannot be forgiven unless you yourself forgive. But then, is that what we really pray for? Don't we instead ask, in our heart of hearts, for much more from God the Prodigal Father— namely that in his extravagant generosity he might forgive us well beyond what we have merited by our own paltry acts of forgiveness to each other? This is of course what, in the end, the countess does: she forgives the one who refuses to forgive. It is this act of grace—unearned, unmerited, a gift pure and simple—that transfigures this comic opera with a spiritual aura. So it seemed only fitting that the countess, in a dramatically implausible costume change, should reappear in a bejeweled gown, resplendently white—like an angel. When I first saw this new production, a couple of years ago, the implausibility of that gratuitous gown bothered me: why didn't director Jonathan Miller simply follow the usual convention of having her appear dressed as before, in Susanna's clothes, so that all would immediately grasp the trick she played on the count to trap him in his own deceitfulness? No doubt because the words and music elevate her to a heavenly plane, and what we see must harmonize with what we hear—and feel.

TUESDAY, JANUARY 22, 2002

The costume changes in *Figaro*—especially those of the youth Cherubino, who is amusingly dressed up as Susanna in act two, then awkwardly disguised as village girl in the next act—conjured up my own first experiences onstage as a Buckley first-grader. I had two walk-on parts in Nativity pageants that Christmas. The one at St. Bartholomew's Church was very stately and grand, choreographed to the ecclesiastical pomp and circumstance by the resident organist and choirmaster, Jack Ossewaarde. The event itself, staged in the huge domed Byzantine basilica, was overwhelming. Yet I was decidedly underwhelmed by both my superfluous role—one of two train-bearing pages of one of the Three Kings—and by my understitched costume: silk pantaloons and a mini vest worn over a bare torso. I felt I was being paraded down the endless aisle of this "grown-up" church in skimpy pajamas I never would have worn in front of visitors at home. I have often, over the years, had a recurring dream of finding myself naked in church—perhaps its source was this unforgettable debut.

At Buckley School the first grade each year puts on a Nativity play. My son Charlie decades later was to be cast as an angel with a great line—"for unto you is born this day a Savior which is Christ the Lord"—and, still later, his brother Christopher was to be a bespectacled Virgin Mary; yet their father had been but a lowly, mute shepherd. The costumes were bargain basement compared to those of St. Bart's, but I didn't mind: at least I was at last fully covered. But then, this shepherd never made it to the manger, for on the day of the performance I came down with the measles and stayed in bed.

These false starts onstage were soon followed by something magical. My mother enrolled me in a production of Shakespeare's *A Midsummer Night's Dream*, produced by a semiprofessional children's company, the King-Coit Theatre. It was a showcase for aspiring child actors (or perhaps children of aspiring stage parents). I had no stage mother, however, hovering over me; mine simply thought that this would be a fun after-school activity for her theatrical son. And so it was.

I was one of the tradesmen and the only line I recall learning—and saying—was "Will not the ladies be afeared of the lion?" I cannot count the times I was marched out with my fellow members of Bottom's crew to sit in a semicircle, crossed-legged, until the moment came for my line. I assumed that our scene was the entire play, for when we were not onstage, we were kept in a small green room with a floor littered with worn—and very boring—comic books of Mickey and Donald; how I would have loved a dose of Superman.

The payoff was the dress rehearsal. When not onstage, we were now permitted to sit in the balcony and watch the rest of the play. It was a revelation, an epiphany of another realm: the godlike older boys playing The-

seus, Lysander, Demetrius, Oberon, Puck; the girls Hippolyta, Titania, Helena, Hermia. The enchanted staging, the resplendent costumes, and the
surprise of music from the heretofore empty orchestra pit—all worthy of
a dream to remember. If its details have long since vanished in mist, the
memory of that first impression of real theater remains indelible, and still
enticing.

Just today I discovered that the composer of the incidental music was
Frank Lewin, who later became a professor of music at Yale and Columbia;
included in the list of his vast oeuvre is the scoring of over a hundred
episodes of one of my favorite television series as a child, right after Perry
Mason: *The Defenders*, with E. G. Marshall. He also was to go on to compose a Requiem Mass for the late Senator Robert Kennedy, commissioned
by the Aquinas Institute, the Catholic chaplaincy at Princeton University,
the very year I enrolled there—1969. I never heard that Mass, but I recall
seeing a phonograph record for sale my freshman year in the University
Store, and it sparked an interest in that Catholic community at Princeton,
which I was to join within the year. How strange that only now, as I try to
piece together that seminal theatrical experience as an almost seven-year-old
in 1958, another surprising piece falls in place. Now I must seek out the
music of the German-born Frank Lewin. Perhaps I may yet hear again the
music played at the King-Coit Theatre, melodies of a vanished dream.

WEDNESDAY, JANUARY 23, 2002

This morning I called Demeter Music in Princeton, which is listed as the
publisher of Lewin's theater music, and a gentleman answered with a slight
German accent. I took a chance: "Mr. Lewin?" "Yes, this is Frank Lewin."
And so began a wonderful adventure in music. I explained that I was hop-
ing to get a recording of the *Midsummer* music, along with the LP of the
Kennedy Requiem I wished I had bought three decades ago in Princeton.
He confirmed my dim recollection that there had indeed been an orchestra
playing his music during the King-Coit performances: he had conducted all

four performances. He added that it was an extraordinary coincidence that I should be calling at this moment, after those forty-four years, since that music had never been recorded and he was just now looking into having it revived for a CD.

Lewin explained that he has been blind for several years, so that preparing the music for recording, even with the help of assistants, might take some time. I now felt certain that I had to hear this score, originally played by strings, flute, and harp at the small theater—just a mile from where I now live, it turns out. So much for my impression that it was a large theater, but then I was half-sized at the time. I offered to take the score to my friend and musical mentor Mason Senft, who in addition to being Flicka von Stade's vocal coach and accompanist—that is how I met him a decade ago—is a one-man orchestra on his synthesizer and a brilliant recording engineer. And so I find myself, quite unexpectedly, in a new project, and I plan to go down to Princeton next month to visit Lewin at his home. As for the extraordinary coincidence he mentioned—well, I have abandoned any residual belief in accidents. To quote the most famous Princeton physicist (also a German refugee and musician), "God does not play with dice."

THURSDAY, JANUARY 24, 2002

At St. Jean Baptiste this evening for a performance of Mozart's *Coronation Mass*, my mother and I sit in the front pew since I have been assigned to do the readings during the Mass. It turns out to be the most dramatic vantage point of the elaborate, Baroque sanctuary and the soaring dome above: as one couple from Italy remarks with pleasure later, a miniature St. Peter's, Rome. My mother tells me that this was the church her governess—and later mine—Nora Collins, attended. But she doesn't recognize it. In fact, it was given a major gilding and repainting a few years ago that transformed it from a drab bluish gray to a multihued jewel, like a reliquary turned inside out. The setting is perfect for Mozart's *Coronation Mass*, my favorite Mass by my favorite composer. In the organ loft the soloists and choir, directed by Maestro Somary, now organist and choir director of St. Patrick's Cathedral, are accompanied on period instruments played by musicians from St. Petersburg (Russia, not Florida).

As the soprano sings the hauntingly beautiful Agnus Dei, I hear in the mind's ear Mozart's countess from Figaro: her poignant aria in act three, *"Dove sono i bei momenti?"*—Where have the sweet moments of love gone?— is, in fact, a reworking of this Agnus Dei. So much for the myth that Mozart recycled bits of opera for his church music; here it was the opposite. Both begin sorrowfully (as befits the "Lamb of God, who takes away the sins of the world") and then are suddenly transformed into a joyful conclusion. For Mozart, clearly, the peace of *"dona nobis pacem"* ("grant us peace") is not a passive one; this is not peace as the absence of conflict or pain, but the consummation of joy.

But pain is inescapable in our world—especially here in New York after September 11. At the dinner following the Mass, my mother and I sit with Archbishop Martino, the pope's representative at the U.N., and Maestro Somary. During a discussion of the pope's travels planned for this year—Bulgaria and Canada—we urge the archbishop to persuade him to stop by our city and visit Ground Zero. It is, after all, not just a disaster site, but also a giant cemetery. He assures us that just as he persuaded the pope to come here in 1995, he will make the case for a return visit to the U.N.—and Ground Zero—at this precarious moment in history.

The day ends, as it began, with music. Somary mentions that he is auditioning new cantors for the weekday Masses at St. Patrick's—he wants to retire the "ex-vaudevillians," he explains. I cannot resist the temptation to apply. I promise I will not warble.

FRIDAY, JANUARY 25, 2002

Today I walked by the apartment house where my oldest friend, John Powers, lives. We have known each other since that year in first grade, and gradually we became best friends. He was an usher at my wedding, and is godfather to son Charlie. He has been a devout Catholic as long as I have known him—forty-four years—and, now a Knight of Malta, is hoping to be ordained a deacon in the Church. John was the first Catholic boy I remember meeting at school. During one first-grade visit to his family's apartment in Manhattan House I recall him showing me his crucifix: I'd never seen one before. Is this a real memory, or a symbolic reconstruction? I telephone him to find out. He confirms the event—and more—asking me, "But do you remember what you said?" No, I confess, I do not. "You said, 'Let's throw it out the window and watch Jesus fly.'" Needless to say, he did not comply; in fact he still prizes that childhood crucifix, while he has given his godson several others over the years—just in case? Fortunately neither of my sons ever showed such a sign of confusing our Lord with Superman.

SUNDAY, JANUARY 27, 2002

Television played a crucial role in my early religious life. I had been going to St. Bartholomew's Church for Sunday school. Picture books of the Bible and sitting on the floor in a circle cover the extent of my memories. The children's services were held in the side chapel, an Italian Renaissance gem, modeled on the Church of San Miniato in Florence, with a trussed timber ceiling and marble columns and, at the altar, a magnificent painting of the Epiphany, where the Madonna outshone the kings in regal bearing. An uninformed visitor might easily mistake this chapel for the most exquisite Catholic church in New York. Only the absence of a corpus on the radiant gold cross on the altar might provide a subtle Protestant clue to its true identity.

But for me the real interest lay next door in the main church, which I had visited as a page of one of the Magi earlier that year. Easter 1958 was dramatically and irrevocably to alter my perspective, both on that church and churchgoing in general. That morning my father got me up painfully early to accompany him to the seven o'clock Easter service while my mother and brothers slept. He was newly elected to the vestry of the church, and among his more visible duties was passing the silver plate during the collection, a task for which he donned a morning suit with swallowtails and gray ascot with pearl stickpin—right out of the Ascot Races in *My Fair Lady*. It was exciting to go down Park Avenue to that huge church while most of the city still slumbered indoors. But nothing prepared me for the instant revelation inside the church once we took our seats in my father's assigned pew, in front of the pulpit in the right transept. The sanctuary was filled with lilies, the pews filled with worshipers, the vast interior of barrel vaults and Byzantine dome filled with thunderous chords from the organ: I could feel these triumphant Easter tones in my bones; the whole edifice seemed to reverberate.

Yet my epiphany was not at the altar or even in the pulpit; it was off to the side, right in front of me: a network cameraman perched behind a huge television camera. Why was he there? To capture the Resurrection on camera for CBS news? Something big was certainly about to happen, I was sure. My father whispered that the entire service was being televised. I had never seen a church program on TV, so to me it simply meant that I was right where CBS thought the action was that day. I watched the cameraman throughout the entire two-hour service, to be sure that I missed nothing he was broadcasting. I knew right then that I wanted to keep coming back there; as it turned out, the television crew never returned—but I did, for many Easter dawns thereafter. It never seemed too early.

MONDAY, JANUARY 28, 2002

My forebears have worshiped at Princeton longer than in any one church; the first Charles graduated in 1840, his son Charles in 1875, his grandson Charles in 1913, and his great-grandson, my father, in 1943. Someone in the family kept the Yale diploma of Matthew Scribner, grandfather of the original Charles, from 1775; it hangs today in my basement, near the circuit breaker. But ever since the defection from native Connecticut—where the family first settled in 1680—to New Jersey for higher learning, Princeton has remained something of a family pew, if not house of worship. I found a photo of my parents and me sitting and smiling on a warm spring day in Princeton in June of 1953, at my father's tenth reunion, a year after his father had died and we had moved north from Washington. It must have been a bittersweet time, for my grandfather had been even more closely attached to the university than my father had been. My father's experience had been far less collegial, and far more academic: he had graduated a term early in 1943 owing to the war and the need for him to begin work as a naval code breaker at the earliest possible moment. He had graduated with highest honors and, as class salutatorian, had given his commencement address in Latin. The graduating seniors all had codebooks of their own indicating when to applaud, when to groan, when to laugh—all of which mystified my grandmother, who was amazed at their comprehension of that dead and unintelligible language.

After the war my father, along with Princeton's future president Goheen, had been invited back to pursue graduate studies as a Woodrow Wilson Fellow, and his real calling was as a scholar, first as a classicist (like Bob Goheen), but probably as a theoretical physicist or mathematician eventually. But this is all speculation, since he declined the invitation to academe, knowing that it would break his father's heart if he did not follow into the family publishing business. So here he was, the new head of the house, revisiting the place that might have been his home as a professor. I wish I could claim to recall my first trip there, but the best I can do is to take solace that it is buried somewhere in the subconscious.

My first retrievable memory of Princeton dates from five years later, at the end of my first-grade year, in June of 1958, when my father drove me down from Far Hills for the Saturday of his fifteenth reunion. We joined the long line of the P-rade toward the end (only the fifth, tenth, and senior classes were behind us). Early on in the procession, I needed to bow out for a brief moment; the next thing I recall is being led up a long staircase in the tower of Blair Hall—I was impressed, and a little envious, that my four-year-old brother, fortunately absent, was so honored: it looked like a medieval fortress, with turrets, arches, everything but the archers on the roof defending it from the invasion of a seven-year-old looking for a bathroom.

We rejoined the P-rade and marched our way to the end, at which point we went to watch the baseball game from the bleachers behind Palmer Stadium. It was very hot in the open sun. After fifteen minutes or so, the end of the first inning (though that term would have meant nothing to me then), my father announced: "It's time to go; the game's over; each side has had its chance." It made perfect sense to me, my first dose of live baseball. I loved my initiation into the place I was later to spend more than my then total seven years of age. The one question I had asked Dad upon arriving was whether the homework was hard at Princeton. I am sure his answer must have been reassuring, for I never doubted, from that moment on, that someday this would be my home as well. What I never imagined was how spiritual a home it would eventually become. Nor could I ever have allowed myself to imagine how much I would associate Princeton with the memory of my father after his death. It is now more a touchstone than the one at our family plot in Woodlawn Cemetery. Perhaps someday it may become my university, or my son's; today it still belongs to my father.

TUESDAY, JANUARY 29, 2002

Yesterday, at the nine o'clock Mass at St. Vincent's, on my way to work, we celebrated the Feast of St. Thomas Aquinas, the greatest of the Dominican theologians and one of the most influential theologians in all of Catholic Christendom. Father Keitz reminded us of how much exchange St. Thomas had with Islam: he owed his study of Aristotle to Muslim scholars who had preserved the Greek classics. It is something to reflect upon in this time of neo-Crusades. But even more surprising was the observation that no miracles have ever been claimed to have been performed by this saint—either before or after his death. In fact, at the time of his canonization, this usual requirement for proof of sanctity was waived by Pope John XXII on the grounds that everything St. Thomas wrote was a miracle. It seemed an especially apt and encouraging word on the way to a publishing house.

It took me back to one of my favorite childhood books from the first grade, when I could finally read on my own, Marcia Brown's *Stone Soup*. Marcia was one of the all-stars of our Scribner children's program, author and illustrator of countless award-winning classics. I have on our walls today some of her illustrations inscribed to my father or to me—the third Charles in her career, she often reminded me. But *Stone Soup* stands apart from all her other books probably because it's about a miracle—a very witty and sly miracle, to be sure, performed by three French eighteenth-century soldiers who arrive in a village looking for something to eat and a place to spend the night. The suspicious and frugal villagers immediately hide all their food and provisions and claim they have no accommodations; for these three too there is "no room in the inn."

But the soldiers take it in stride, explaining that they quite understand and know how to make a delicious soup out of three smooth stones. Does anyone know where to find some and a large kettle to fill with water? The peasants are intrigued and immediately oblige them. Once the stones are boiling along, the soldiers announce that if only someone had salt and pepper to add, the soup would be even better—though it is quite fine as is. Someone runs off to get the seasoning. Then they say it's too bad there are no carrots and cabbages around, for that would add an extra touch of perfection. So someone runs off to fetch vegetables; it seems the least one can do for soldiers who teach how to make soup with stones. Then some meat is suggested—and supplied. Finally the whole village is so caught up in the excitement of their discovery that they set up tables and trimmings for a huge feast, at the end of which the grateful villagers provide the soldiers with the three best guest rooms in town before they depart as heroes the next day. The villagers are profuse in their thanks: they will never go hungry since they have learned to make stone soup. The soldiers smile and wink to each other as they walk away.

This wonderful tale of trickery has continued to resonate for four decades and more; it strikes a deep chord. It is about a miracle—creating something from nothing. A village is transformed. Stinginess and selfishness give way to generosity and, in the end, a feast. I have, of course, no idea how the miracle of our Lord's feeding of the five thousand took place. The gospel author tells us only that once the few loaves and fishes were blessed and distributed, everyone was filled and a large surplus was gathered at the end of the meal. I feel no need to rationalize the gospel miracles. Yet I must confess that reading *Stone Soup* at age seven has provided an enduring hint of an explanation.

THURSDAY, JANUARY 31, 2002

Today I went to the noon Mass at St. Patrick's and sat up front so that I could practice singing the hymns and responses in full voice without scaring my fellow, soft-singing, congregants. This marks the beginning of my makeshift preparation for being a Tuesday noon cantor at the cathedral once Lent begins. I passed my audition yesterday with Maestro Somary. It was an ecclesiastical adventure.

First, upon entering the cathedral and seeking the music office, I was directed to a tiny elevator in one of the rear stone pillars to take me above the organ loft. I asked the guard whether I would ever be found if the elevator didn't make it. "Oh, you've got a phone inside." I said I'd take the stairs next time. Once I arrived and met Johannes in his office, he took me out to the choir loft for the magnificent view of the vast nave from above. I felt like Jimmy Stewart in Hitchcock's *Vertigo* and was grateful I was not auditioning for the choir. Instead, we went back down and walked to the far end of the cathedral to disappear through a door in the St. Louis Chapel and down to the crypt level, where we entered an ancient choir room with a piano and a small chamber organ, a space tailor-made for the Phantom of the Opera, I thought. He played and I sang a couple of hymns—so far so good. Then he called his assistant organist on the phone and made the schedule arrangements for my slot, and then I sang Bach's (pace scholarly attempts to assign it to a lesser composer) "Bist du bei mir," since this is what I had been practicing on the walks to and from work. Maybe down deep I wanted to give him a chance to reconsider his decision, especially since I would be replacing an operatic cantor of many seasons. I realized then that I hadn't tried out for a singing role since I was a boy at Buckley School, when I had a considerably higher range.

It is just past midnight, and on WQXR I hear Tchaikovsky's orchestral version of Mozart's "Ave verum corpus," reminding me that I recently told Johannes that this choral gem of Mozart's was the very music I would choose if I had to give up all but one piece.

FRIDAY, FEBRUARY 1, 2002

The summer of 1959 found us sharing the rented house with a host of construction workers each day. The place was strewn with tools, two-by-fours, and nails—all of which provided novel possibilities for my brothers and me, along with some photo ops for our father, who there took some of the best pictures of us ever, especially of my brother John, then all of two years old, hammering nails, carrying planks, even playing with an awl.

Now, as an overly apprehensive parent looking backward, I am startled that my parents would have let John play alone with such dangerous tools—until it dawns on me that he was not alone: our father was at the other end of the lens. There is something about certain photographs that erases any consciousness of another human presence. Perhaps that is what gives them the power to transport the viewer into another time and space, their immediacy, their seeming spontaneity: it is art concealing art, or at least concealing the artist, the invisible photographer. But now, realizing that my father was not only present but determining and capturing the moment reflected in each image, I enjoy imagining the vanished dialogue between us. The photos take on a new personality, a paternal imprint. They also remind me of my father's role in developing the pictures, and I can see again that small maid's room at 31 East Seventy-ninth which became his darkroom after it had briefly served as a nursery: a black light, trays of chemicals, negatives and photos hanging in a row to dry. As I stood and watched my alchemist dad perform the ritual ablutions, the black-and-white images gradually, miraculously came into view in that eerie half-light, just as these recollections do now, more than four decades later. Yet now I am alone in seeing them—or am I? *Lux Umbra Dei*: light is the shadow of God.

SATURDAY, FEBRUARY 2, 2002

The main event of that last summer of the 1950s was taking place back in New York, out of sight, but never out of my mind: we were moving to a new apartment. I was appalled by the news. I had been moved from room to room several times before: first, from my original bedroom to a maid's room when my brother Blair and I ceased to cohabit it quietly; then to a daybed in the dining room after the arrival of our baby brother, John, who claimed one maid's room while the baby nurse, Pearl, got the other. (That exile I really enjoyed, for it meant that each morning I awoke to watch out the window the Borden's milk truck pull up to the market facing us across Madison Avenue, twelve floors below.) Finally, I was again back in the maid's room, in solitude off the kitchen wing—with only the occasional problem of sleepwalking or nightmares to send me across to my parents' bedroom for safety. I remember once being utterly terrified by the Cuyp portrait in the hall while only half awake: it took on a Dorian Gray, horrific, menacing aspect that I have never been able to reconcile in daylight with those two plump, rosy-cheeked Dutch children. Another time I reached up to the goosenecked standing lamp beside my bed and, having forgotten to replace a missing bulb, inserted my fingers into the bare and live socket, to be successfully awakened by 120 volts.

My mother had decided to move one day while standing in the cold on Park Avenue, waiting for my school bus to arrive. It was the first stop, only five blocks (one quarter mile) from the school, but that was little consolation to her. The new apartment she found was on the same block as Buckley: we wouldn't have to cross a street to get to school. My enthusiasm was under control, to say the least. I was panicked by the thought of leaving the only home I knew. Even now, even in the hindsight of how much more lay ahead, I am reluctant to pack up those memories of Seventy-ninth Street and move on: the children's Christmas parties given by the kindly spinster Miss Hoyt on the second floor; the view out the window of those small

Christmas trees along Madison, facing the Carlyle Hotel; my grandmother
Sunderland arriving to take me to Liberty Music Shop to pick out a new
phonograph for my sixth birthday; the massive French château of the art
dealer Duveen at the Central Park end of our block, which we passed each
day on the way to the playground; the crystal radio my father built and set
up next to the TV in the living room—which miraculously picked up stations over its headphones without any batteries or plug; the light shows I
used to give with my portable planetarium globe, transfiguring my bedroom
ceiling into a starry sky; that same bedroom transformed into a photographer's studio by my father, complete with blinding flood lamps, to take our
portraits; the album of *My Fair Lady* on top of the record cabinet in the living room, my absolute favorite listening, which was finally brought to life
by a matinee of that musical for my eighth birthday, just before we left that
apartment for good—I'd grown accustomed to that place.

SUNDAY, FEBRUARY 3, 2002

Today is the Super Bowl; in ten days Ash Wednesday will be upon us; yet
this evening a reflection of Christmases past, and a herald of more to come,
greeted me when I arrived back in New York from the country—if indeed
the North Shore of Long Island may be called country. But to a city boy
it is country enough. My favorite illustrated book, dating back to 31 East
Seventy-ninth and forward to our new apartment at 791 Park, has arrived
from a West Coast rare-book seller: *The Tall Book of Christmas*, published
when I was three years old and brought home by my father. I cannot recall
a book that lasted longer as a perennial favorite of mine all the way through
childhood. A selection of Christmas tales, poems, carols—all fancifully illustrated—it is a tall, slender treasure, bound in hard covers, with a colorful jacket and bright endpapers of Christmas friezes of candy canes, angels,
Santas, trees, and antique autos. Back in 1954, it cost a dollar; today it cost
me almost a hundred times as much to have it back in my hands. The flap

copy proclaims: "To the little child, the magic of Christmas endures the whole year through.... Children will turn again and again to the book and the enchanting pictures and each time discover something fresh and new."

Forty-eight years later, I can vouch that this was no hyperbole. It opens with the gospel story of the first Christmas—from Matthew and Luke—and a radiant Epiphany with a golden star at the top of the page casting its rays over the type right down to the Three Kings kneeling before the Child at the bottom. I flipped through the pages to find the favorites I had remembered—"Babushka," "The Story of the First Christmas Tree," and above all, "Granny Glittens and Her Amazing Mittens" (what made them amazing was the fact that children could eat them)—and then a surprising number I had forgotten, such as "A Christmas for Bears," "Giant Grummer's Christmas," and "The Puppy Who Wanted a Boy." Within this cornucopia is a small poem by Eugene Field, credited to his publisher, Charles Scribner's Sons—which finally explains how it happened that the fourth Charles Scribner brought it home to his son. My father had evidently received it as a courtesy permission copy. I am quite certain he never foresaw its future place in my early literary pantheon—right up there with *The Velveteen Rabbit* and *Stone Soup*—and I suspect he would be bemused by my efforts to reclaim it half a century later.

I have no knowledge about the illustrator, Gertrude Elliott Espenscheid, except that her hundred-plus "delicate and fanciful" drawings have an evocativeness unmatched for me by any children's illustrator. I spent countless hours over the years poring over them, as though I might pass through them and enter the worlds and distant times that they captured in a few, direct glimpses and that the text brought to life. I wonder now whether that Christmas book is perhaps the "first cause" of my choosing art history as my major field of academic study many years later. For me, art was never to be for its own sake, but rather to serve as a mirror—or even window—on history, on worlds past, and on faith. It was always about illustration, whether of texts or of beliefs. For children of all ages the magic of Christmas endures the whole year through; perhaps, if we are fortunate, a whole life through.

MONDAY, FEBRUARY 4, 2002

From our new apartment, there was no longer a long walk to begin each day. My father just stood on the corner of Seventy-fourth Street and watched me proceed twice the length of our apartment and then disappear into the door. I was now in third grade, or "junior one." Playtime was over; we now had homework and were taught to write in cursive script—no more printed block letters. This was also to be the last year of female teachers in those days. Mine was a wonderful woman named Louise Parker, who exactly twenty years later was to welcome Ritchie, my new bride, as a new teacher at Buckley a month after our wedding.

Music class at school was still conducted by the lower-school teacher Matilda Cascio and centered on singing songs and playing single-pitch instruments—a triangle, tambourine, rattle, or drum—in a rhythm band. More than forty years later, after her retirement, she is now back at Buckley giving private piano lessons to the boys after school. She has taught both our sons, and she remains my last link at the school to a happy past. How appropriate that my one unbroken tie there is through music; although perhaps it is really not so surprising as I first thought: music, I suspect, is the one proven elixir of youth. Musicians never age.

That year was to mark the beginning of my life at the keyboard. I started piano lessons with a young Juilliard graduate, Ellen Pahl, who came each week to our home. I was a most willing pupil, impatient to move as quickly as possible through those embarrassing children's pieces and on to the classics. The first piece was a five-finger exercise to the words "Buy a broom, buy a broom; buy a broom and sweep the room." But fortunately young Mozart, who composed some simple, exquisite minuets—serious music, to my ears—at the ripe age of six, soon came to the rescue.

TUESDAY, FEBRUARY 5, 2002

My obsession with Mozart was given a big boost just before Christmas, when my school put on a book fair. We were supposed to pick out books to be given us by our parents at Christmas—all in the interest of stimulating reading in this new TV age, and generating some profit for the school library, where the sample books were laid out on long tables. It was there I discovered Charles Schulz's *Peanuts*. Long on pictures, short on text—just the way I liked my books. I bought every one of the series. At home, I found in them my alter ego: Schroeder. Always sitting at his diminutive piano, playing Beethoven, often with the composer's bust resting on the top, like a votive statue. I could not hope to rival his devotion to Beethoven, but I could claim Mozart. So I soon went to G. Schirmer's music shop with my father and bought an idealized metal bust of Wolfgang on a marble base—I still have it, and it still rests on top of a piano. As time went on I took this self-identification to extremes beyond the world of *Peanuts*. I got a brown eighteenth-century wig from a costume supply store: it was close enough to the one in Mozart's portrait and I wore it while practicing at the piano. Later I took a music notebook and attempted to compose Mozartian minuets of my own; I wish I still had these good-faith forgeries. I gave up only when I realized that by my age, almost nine, the master was already writing symphonies. There was simply no way of catching up. The final variation on this overwrought theme was my translation of that popular card game Go Fish into Ask Mozart—with his bust on the floor in the midst of the cards to be drawn.

THURSDAY, FEBRUARY 7, 2002

That year a fresh gust of foreign culture blew into our lives in the person of a young au pair, Rosalinde, who had just arrived from Germany and came to live with us to take care of my brothers and me. She was in her early twenties, full of fun—and mischief. She used to take us north a dozen blocks to Yorkville, still then a neighborhood of German shops and restaurants and dwellings, though we seem always to have steered her into the all-American Lamston's five-and-ten-cents store, for toys for us and supplies for my pet parakeet, Jimmy. I think Rosie must have spent much of her salary on my most persuasive three-year-old brother, Johnny, whom she called Mr. Clean. I only wish she had taught me German instead of striving to perfect her English; for it was fun listening to her and my father speak German to each other. Alas, the only German I was taught—beyond *Guten Morgen, Guten Abend*, and *Wie geht's*—was a scatological curse, tame by today's standards, like Mozart's more colorful jokes in his letters to his cousin. Rosie's romantic entanglements with a jealous boyfriend named Boris resulted in my parents having to hire a private detective to protect her. There was a Hollywood denouement when Boris forced his way into our apartment to confront Rosie; my mother had to fend him off and ordered him out. Eventually it was all too much drama for this young mother of three, and a year later Rosie moved on, but we all loved her and missed her. We had several especially carefree weeks together when my parents took the *Queen Mary* to England for a long-awaited vacation and visit to my father's English authors and my mother's English cousins. We were never home alone, but we were home free.

By a strange coincidence our paths crossed again thirty years later, through a German publishing colleague, and we have kept in touch ever since. I had not known Rosie was Catholic—not that it would have meant much to me at that age anyway—but I discovered it only a year ago when my friend Father Andrew O'Connor was transferred to a suburban parish in a town I'd never heard of—New City—up the Hudson River. When I got Christmas cards from both him and Rosie I realized they lived in the same place—where Rosie raised her children, founded a day-care center, and now has a pair of beautiful grandchildren. It turned out that she was one of his parishioners. Father Andrew has just been transferred back to Manhattan, but not before this peerless artist-priest designed for the new church building a triumphal processional crucifix, which I commissioned in my father's memory—a private commemoration of those memorable, if incomprehensible, exchanges in German between my father and Father Andrew's parishioner. Once again, it seems, God had chosen to remain anonymous—until the next epiphany.

FRIDAY, FEBRUARY 8, 2002

Tonight we are at the Deerfield Inn for the weekend, visiting our son Christopher at Eaglebrook School's Winter Carnival. The television is carrying in vivid color and choreography the opening ceremony of the winter Olympics from Salt Lake City. But it takes me instead back forty-two years to my monochromatic, but no less vivid, images of the 1960 games in Squaw Valley, which I watched that winter from my sickbed on a black-and-white television rolled into my room while I convalesced from the flu. I have never since then followed the games with such attention. Not only was it a novel experience for that schoolboy home on sick leave, but it was charged by my mother with personal suspense and excitement since her skating friend and colleague Carol Heiss was the favorite to win the gold in ladies' figure skating. I watched with Mom each round of this competition—the school figures, the freestyle programs—with breathless intensity, almost as if it were my own mother out there. Heiss won—and all was well on earth, beginning in Squaw Valley.

But the joy of that vicarious experience on ice is telescoped into tragedy as I picture my mother a year later coming into my room, ashen, telling me that she had just heard the news that our U.S. skating team was killed in a plane crash en route to compete in the 1961 world championships. Carol Heiss was not on board, fortunately, for she had married Olympic champion Hayes Jenkins—they had been secretly engaged at Squaw Valley, unbeknownst to her coach—and she had decided to retire from competition after her gold medal. But our next-door neighbors at Seventy-ninth Street, a lovely older couple I knew simply as the Hartshornes, had perished with the team they avidly supported as patrons. Their kitchen door had faced ours, and my mother used to bring me over for impromptu visits with Mrs. Hartshorne. I had never seen a triplex, so I held them in neighborly awe. Strangely, two decades later I was to find myself on a plane to Sarasota, Florida, where I was flying to give a lecture on Rubens, sitting next to a young woman who in the course of conversation said she had grown up on Seventy-ninth Street: she was the Hartshornes' daughter. I was finally able to convey condolences over what had been my first memory of a human disaster that had struck so close to home. But no Olympics ever captured my imagination or attention as those pristine, fresh, and innocent images from 1960—before the crash, and our next president's assassination, and the following years of Vietnam. It was my mother's Olympics and it ended in triumph, pure and simple, in the graceful figure of Carol Heiss. That is the Grail I never sought again under those gold rings.

SATURDAY, FEBRUARY 9, 2002

That same year, the big Fisher radio-phonograph, to my unprepared delight, was moved into my bedroom once my father discovered stereo and bought his first Acoustic Research components for the living room. He began to buy new stereo LPs each week and was very religious about his classical listening—usually in the evening after dinner. He would later keep a diary of records he listened to, a practice he continued for decades. Meanwhile he bought for me a series of Vox records of composer biographies— Bach, Brahms, Tchaikovsky, Chopin, Schumann, and of course my beloved Mozart, among others. They provided an early course in music history, and I loved playing these narratives that interspersed samples of the composer's music while dramatically outlining his life and his genius. I listened to them over and over; the familiarity of each composer's story was as delightful as a child's favorite bedtime story. They brought to life the names that ap-

peared on my piano music, and in a simple but resonant way forged for me
a connection—historical, biographical, and even spiritual—between a piece
I practiced and the composer who wrote it. Music was never an abstract art:
the sounds themselves were always intimately rooted in the life and persona
of the composer; the notes, staffs, bars, rests, and dynamic markings offer
a diagram for a bridge between past and present as dazzling and elegant as
the Golden Gate—or, closer to home, the Verrazano. To play or to listen—
as driver or as passenger—was a way of crossing that bridge and entering
another world. It is a religious experience in the most literal sense of the
word. Its Latin root—*religare*—means to tie together. Music forges the ties
that bind us together, the living with the dead, mortals with the immortals.

TUESDAY, FEBRUARY 12, 2002

Yesterday I received an e-mail from a helpful man at the Vox Music Group
telling me that the *Man and His Music* series was still selling regularly—now
on cassettes and CDs—mainly to the home-schooling market. I have long
had my doubts about the wisdom of this movement, but I may have to revise my prejudices in view of its recognition of such a wonderful series of
music history. I ordered a dozen composers, most of whom I had studied
at home myself more than forty years ago. In music my schooling really began at home. But this fourth-grade year introduced me to one of the most
charismatic and gifted music masters in any school: Mr. Rotella. He taught
us music appreciation and music history, and he conducted the Glee Club,
which I joined that year, singing first soprano.

Our repertoire was varied and unusually sophisticated, all thanks to this
maestro who refused to compromise his standards. For the upcoming Christmas concert we sang sacred choruses by Bach, Handel, Mozart, Haydn, and
even Gregorian chant. Our texts were in French and Latin at times, in addition to our native tongue. In retrospect I realize that it was Paul Rotella who
first opened and led us through the door to this Narnia of ecclesiastical,
mainly Catholic, musical masterpieces. Years later I learned that our very

Protestant Episcopalian headmaster, Mr. Hubbell, once asked Paul if it was really necessary to perform so much Roman Catholic music for the Buckley parents. Paul replied that it was not his fault that that is where so many of the masterpieces are found. The headmaster reverted to his role of premier cheerleader at the concerts. So much from these early programs still resonates, especially at Christmastime: Bach's "Prepare thyself, Zion," from the *Christmas Oratorio*; Handel's "And the glory of the Lord" and "Hallelujah," from *Messiah*; Haydn's "The heavens are telling," from *The Creation*; Mozart's "Alleluia," from his *Exsultate, Jubilate*—I return to listen to them over and over and try to imagine the sensation of singing treble up to high C in those few years before a boy's voice finally breaks for good. As much as I was devoted to my piano, the greatest thrills came from those moments when the human voice becomes the supreme instrument, one that expresses emotions more profoundly than any man-made object, however intricate or technically dazzling.

That year I decided the time had come to make my first—it was to be my only—phonograph record as a pianist. My mother and I went to a recording studio recommended by Miss Pahl, where I recorded two pieces— a Mozart minuet and trio, and Schumann's "Knight Rupert" from his *Album for the Young*—one on each side of the 78 rpm lacquer disc. I was given a choice: I could record the pieces directly onto the record—the needle would be cutting the grooves while I played—or I could, for an additional fee, record them onto tape first, so that if there were a mistake the record would not be ruined. I chose the first option out of thrift—much to my amazement today. Without any nervousness or even awareness of that unforgiving process, I cut the two sides of the album. Or so I believed. When it was over, the engineer confessed that he had secretly recorded it onto tape in case I stumbled. I was amused by his doubts, but no less grateful when I had the finished product in my hands to take home. I kept that record for several years, then gave it to Nora, my mother's and my retired nanny, who kept it in the apartment she shared with her sister in Sunnyside, where I would later visit these spry nonagenarians during my college years. On one such visit I learned that the record had broken. I would now give anything to have it and hear it again with more critical, if charitable, ears. But I would give infinitely more to recover that long-lost sense of childhood confidence and poise, undaunted by the sharp needle cutting unalterable grooves in lacquer while I played on.

WEDNESDAY, FEBRUARY 13, 2002

Today is Ash Wednesday, the first in many years that finds me beyond the reach of a priest to impose ashes on my forehead. "Remember, dust thou art and to dust thou shalt return." I always found those solemn words of memento mori strangely consoling—I am not sure why. Perhaps because they reminded me that ultimately I would join those family members whom I had lost, and those I had never known, along with Mozart, Shakespeare, heroes and saints, in common ground. That the daily cares and setbacks and mindless worries of this life are fleeting, and that through the valley of ashes (to borrow Fitzgerald's inspired image from the landscape of *The Great Gatsby*) we would reach an eternity beyond paradise, with the Lord as guide and guarantor. But today, instead, I found myself on a plane to Anguilla, in search of a more temporal paradise, at least for the next five days. After September 11, I was sorely tempted to cancel this vacation that means leaving our two sons behind in school. But loyalty to our neighbor, friend, and travel agent Jock Goodrich in the end trumped the notion that we parents are indispensable to adolescent boys. And so began what soon seemed an odyssey into a pagan wilderness of tourists and resorts and stucco shacks punctuated by palm trees—the car to the plane to the cab to the ferry to another taxi to the hotel, seven hours of perpetual motion. The resort, Cap Juluca, looks like a piece of transplanted Morocco, or perhaps opera sets for Rossini's *L'Italiana in Algeri*. I fear I have found my own expensive wilderness to enter on this Ash Wednesday; at least it won't last forty days.

It was strange driving along this skinny island—its name means "eel"— without seeing any church steeples. Perhaps they fell victim to hurricanes past? It's a more consoling thought than the possibility that they were never built. I realize how accustomed I have become to architectural pillars of faith. I feel quite in exile without them. Walking back to our villa along the beach I tried to imagine that the domed, white stucco units could be those of the Holy Land two millennia ago. Did our Lord find shade beneath such palms in the wilderness outside Jerusalem? How barren was it? As I tried to decide how far to push this illusion, I caught sight of the setting sun—deep golden, bursting through a cluster of cumulus clouds on the horizon. With incredible radiance, like a medieval mandorla (minus the figure of Christ) turned on its side, streams of light emanated from the central cloud of mystery, while above, two dark shafts of shadow shot upward. It was the negative of the two horns of light beaming up from Moses' head after his encounter with Yahweh on Mount Sinai. At this very moment the opening lines of a poem by Gerard Manley Hopkins come back to rescue this day for me: "The world is charged with the grandeur of God. It will flame out, like shining from shook foil." There was a priest today after all, that poetic Jesuit, long returned to dust and awaited glory. There were no ashes today; instead, celestial fire.

THURSDAY, FEBRUARY 14, 2002

The peak experience of my fourth-grade year was the performance of the first movement of Mozart's C-Major Piano Sonata at a Buckley assembly. It was far longer than any of the children's pieces I had learned my first year and much more technically challenging. I had prepared for this moment for some time. The last thing I recall the day before taking to the stage was Miss Pahl rehearsing with me how to announce—and pronounce—its Köchel number. It was a nice footnote, but I am sure meant nothing to anyone in the audience save Mr. Rotella, who hardly needed to be informed. I can still feel the excitement of sitting down and then launching into this delicate chamber piece as though it were the final movement of a romantic piano concerto. I wanted this music to "flame out, like shining from shook foil." Perhaps it did: I felt fully satisfied with the result in any case, and the audience seemed approving, however far from Mozart's original intention it had surely been.

Yet strangely I felt a letdown. I couldn't get enthusiastic about moving onward to the next level. In hindsight, and in the view of my subsequent teacher, I had already gone further than my technical foundation could support. Ambition and impatience had outstripped preparation and basic training. By spring I announced that I did not want to continue anymore with my lessons. I was dropping the piano; or in the wiser interpretation of Miss Pahl, taking a vacation from it. I then compounded that negative act with another: I quit the Glee Club.

But I had not entirely abandoned music. I had just transferred my allegiance to a new instrument—the guitar. For me it was primarily an accompaniment to solo singing. And the new repertoire was to be folk songs. This was the dawn of the hootenanny era—the sounds of Peter, Paul, and Mary, and the Kingston Trio. I was hooked. My introduction to the guitar came from my teenage cousin Hildy, who along with her younger sister Mary had suddenly come to live with us for the winter and spring terms that year. Their mother, my aunt Dule (my father's only sister, Julia), had left with her husband and my two younger cousins for Florida, where she was convalescing from cancer. She was terminally ill, but no one said so then. All I knew is that one Sunday I came home from seeing the movie (decades later my absolute favorite) *Breakfast at Tiffany's* to find these two female cousins at our apartment, unpacking their suitcases.

Hildy and Mary quickly settled into our all-male corridor—a testament to my mother's adaptability and grace. Many years later I learned that her mother-in-law had not even consulted her about taking on these two boarders. But that was ever Granny's way: she simply took the lead and expected others to fall in line, like the horsemen galloping behind her as master of foxhounds.

FRIDAY, FEBRUARY 15, 2002

That summer my parents hired—for the first and only time—a college girl to live with us in Far Hills and take care of my brothers and me. Her name was Elaine, and she was from Skidmore College, a detail that introduced me, at age ten, to an early chapter of our family publishing history. My father was a trustee of Skidmore, as his father had been before him. Our family name was all about the campus, according to Elaine, since the college had been founded by my father's great-aunt Lucy Skidmore Scribner, who had married the eldest of the original Charles Scribner's sons, John Blair, and had been widowed in her twenties when her young husband had literally worked himself to death (at age thirty) running the publishing house after his father, Charles Scribner, died of typhoid fever in Switzerland in 1871 at the ripe age of fifty. The firm was then passed to John Blair's younger brother Charles, which launched a century-long succession of Charleses.

Lucy, in the meantime, returned to Saratoga, New York, and began a college for girls, originally focused on domestic skills like sewing and cooking, but soon broadened into a full liberal arts curriculum. A couple of years ago, when asked to write a recommendation to the now coed Skidmore for a classmate of our son Charlie's, I shamelessly exploited this family connection by enclosing with my letter a photo of Lucy's grave near my father's in our family plot at Woodlawn Cemetery. My batting average with such letters of recommendation for friends had been dismal—I was the epistolary strikeout king—so I felt the need for some novel ammunition. The photograph of the founder's grave, which I said—truthfully—I visited every year, hit the mark. Our young friend is now thriving there and rowing on the Skidmore crew.

Elaine earned a special place in my literary scrapbook as the one who announced to us playing on the back lawn one sunny July day that our most famous author, Ernest Hemingway, had died. He had shot himself. Two years later an entire nation would vividly recall where they were when they heard that JFK was shot. But for me, the news of Hemingway's death had already preempted that drama.

Later that Sunday evening, at dinnertime, my father wrote out longhand on a yellow legal pad his words of tribute to Hemingway for the press release. It is now in the Princeton University Library, where I saw it for the first time in 1999 during a special exhibition for the Hemingway Centennial. After that show, which I had sponsored as a memorial to my father and a prelude to our son Charlie's arrival at Princeton the next year, I kept the photographic enlargement and took it home. It hangs in the basement of our summerhouse, an artifact of my first memory of a death in the family, almost forty years earlier. Out of loyalty to Ernest's widow, Mary, who could not face the possibility of an intentional suicide, my father maintained for years her view that Hemingway's death had been accidental. Out of loyalty to my father and to that memory, I refuse to overturn that verdict, regardless of the weight of circumstantial evidence to the contrary.

I have never permitted the word "suicide" to appear in the author's biography in any of Hemingway's books that we publish. In the eyes of the Church, the mortal sinfulness of suicide is absolved if the perpetrator/victim was of unsound mind at the time of the act. Released too soon from a mental hospital, Hemingway was clearly out of his mind, ravaged by depression, when he took that loaded shotgun into the hallway of his Ketchum house early that Sunday morning. He was given a Catholic burial by a priest and he rests in hallowed ground. And to this day I consider the word "accident" closer to the spirit of truth than the heartless term "suicide." He left us many literary treasures, but no note of farewell. So who may read with any clarity, much less certainty, the final intentions of that troubled soul?

SATURDAY, FEBRUARY 16, 2002

The only book, besides a little booklet of daily Lenten meditations, I took with me on this trip was Father Andrew Greeley's prayer journal *My Love*. I could not have made a better choice for this spot, which has substituted daily reflections on the beach for daily Mass. This hiatus from my sacramental routine has been therapeutic, a more Protestant focus on words in lieu of ritual—in keeping perhaps with attempts to refocus my thoughts on my Protestant youth now dimmed with the passage of time. Besides, I have not been without a daily priest: Father Andy has filled that role admirably, as my private chaplain pro tem of Cap Juluca. The insights and often painful—if poetic—candor throughout his conversations with God have given me far more food for thought in these past few days than weeks of homilies might have offered.

Yet I was not prepared for the clouds of doubt and near despair that pass, however fleetingly, across the horizon of his faith, which I had always assumed to be as clear and sunny as the redemptive message he never fails to convey to the thousands upon thousands who read his novels and stories with an open mind and heart. I should have known better. The greatest saints always suffer the most. Perhaps they alone experience the darkest nights of the soul precisely because their souls alone are broad and deep enough to swallow up such darkness and transmute it into new light.

I am equally struck by how "marginal"—a term Greeley uses often—he feels he has been. Failure is another recurrent leitmotif of his reflections on his life and work. But did our Lord feel any more successful as he approached the end of his earthly ministry? The betrayal, arrest, and criminal's execution that awaited him must have made those forty days in the wilderness shine in retrospect. There he had defeated Satan at his own game; on the cross, he would ask why God had forsaken him. In the annals of the Roman Empire, even in the annals of that marginal outpost Palestine, he was a marginal man—a man marked by failure. No glowing obituaries, no official press reports, even of his Resurrection. The gospels were not to be written for another generation. Perhaps I may take the risk of sharing this response with Andy upon my return, and pray he will not be offended by my presumption. He spreads his capital faith and hope so prodigally that it seems unfair he be denied so small a dividend.

SUNDAY, FEBRUARY 17, 2002

Entering the small church of St. Gerard, I had an instantaneous sense of déjà vu, yet I could not tell why until I had been seated for a few minutes. I had never been inside an authentic Caribbean church before; its rustic and colorful mix of wood and rough-hewn stones was charming and called to mind an approving Latin phrase of my dad's: *sancta simplicitas*, holy simplicity. My only regret was that all the images of Christ and the Madonna—save for a modern freestanding crucifix beside the altar—were lily white, as pale as a recent tourist arrival. If ever there was a place that justified darkening these visages and bodies in the cause of a more inclusive iconography, it was here.

Looking to the right and left of my front, empty pew, I saw that the sides of this church were made of open, concrete latticework—a series of crosses within more elaborate patterns—and suddenly I realized why it had looked so familiar at first sight. It was the same porchlike concept that Ernest Flagg had designed for his sister's (my great-grandmother's) garden chapel of St. Mary of the Angels for my great-grandparents' home, the Gables, in Morristown, New Jersey. I have never seen the original, since it was deconsecrated and torn down after the place was sold following the death of my father's grandfather. His devout widow preferred to obliterate her brother's architectural gem rather than imagine it put to some profane use by the new owners. But I have photographs of it and have long placed myself within this chapel of stone and gracefully flared gabled roof—if only in the mind's eye. The stone altar and Renaissance statue of our Lady, along with the sanctuary lamp and other liturgical fittings, were given to a nearby Episcopal church, which still remains on my list of short pilgrimages to be taken. But in Anguilla, at last, I could feel what my family forebears—all dead now—felt as they worshiped in that chapel with a breeze blowing across the seats, nature's sacrament of the Holy Spirit, which blows "whither it will."

The convergence of Roman and Anglican memories within that sanctuary took me back again to my fourth-grade year, the year that weekly churchgoing (in the chapel of St. Bartholomew's) was followed by serious Sunday school classes upstairs. That year we had Mr. Orman, an earnest grandfatherly figure, who taught us next door to his wife, who would teach us the following year. He was anecdotal; she was no-nonsense. (He was a building superintendent; she, a schoolteacher.) The only topic I can recall from the first year was his asking if we knew the difference between the Pilgrims and the Puritans. We did not. He explained that one group wanted to break with established religion, the other to reform it, but I soon forgot which was which. He also sent us home to look up the longest word in our dictionaries, by way of enlightenment on this subject: "antidisestablishmentarianism." No wonder I eventually became a Roman.

In fact, one Sunday that year, after our class was over, I asked our new housekeeper, appropriately named Martha, to take my brother Blair and me over to St. Patrick's Cathedral, a block away, before going home, since I had heard a rumor that President Kennedy was there for Mass and I wanted finally to see him up close. (The best I had managed so far was to see him—from ten stories above street level—ride by our apartment house from time to time on his way to the Carlyle Hotel, two blocks north of us, where he stayed during his jaunts to New York.) We four now stood within a crowd of onlookers at the rear of the nave waiting for the final procession at the end of the service. I spent my time gazing in wonder at a wax effigy of a particularly austere, bespectacled pope in a white cassock under glass—was it Pius XII? (I must check with Monsignor Clark, the new rector.) What a strange, exotic religion, I thought. But obviously a very important one if it claimed our new president. Alas, he was not to be found among the group of African dignitaries that finally marched out behind the cardinal, priests, and acolytes. Our wait had been in vain and we headed for home. If Kennedy had been there after all, I now wonder whether I would have waited almost a decade before returning to that cathedral I now consider my midtown spiritual home.

MONDAY, FEBRUARY 18, 2002

Unbeknownst to me at the time, my father was undergoing the crucial spiritual crisis of his life, as he confided to me many years later. The cause was the diagnosis of his sister's terminal cancer, which she fought bravely and stoically. So bravely that it broke his heart. Here she was, under forty-three years old, with four children ranging from ages fourteen to three, and with only a few months to live. During one of her last hospital stays, her doctor left without comment a bottle of strong barbiturates on her bedside table for her to take home—presumably, my father assumed, as an unspoken act of compassion in the event that her pain became unbearable. My aunt, however, later told my father about the doctor's oversight in leaving such dangerous pills behind, "which could have caused a terrible accident if someone took them by mistake." She mentioned that she had pointed out this mistake to him. My father was never sure whether she had acted out of innocence or a wish to make a subtle point about how she would face her end, for she never spoke openly about her fate. Instead, she and my uncle took a trip to Europe that last summer of her life; she sent back a postcard from Paris to my grandmother, reporting that she had finally seen the Mona Lisa, and "she looked green."

During these final months, I had no idea that my aunt was so sick, and I recall nothing in my father's behavior that suggested anything was wrong in his life. It was no accident that he had written his Princeton senior thesis on neo-Stoicism in the Renaissance. But, in fact, the hopelessness of his sister's illness caused him to question every assumption he had held since childhood about the nature of God, the universe, and existence. This existential crisis rent his traditional Episcopalian Christian faith as irreparably as the veil of the temple at the moment of Jesus' death on the cross. He could and would continue to believe in Christ and Christianity as the highest embodiment of goodness, love, sacrifice, and compassion; but he could no longer reconcile the cosmos with the notion of a personal God. St. John's formulation that "God is love" caused him no problem, but this God held no sway over creation. In fact the very notion of creation had dissolved into existence per se.

The paradox for me is that my father's loss of faith—or better, loss of any *consolation* of faith—in no way diminished his service to the Church as a vestryman of St. Bartholomew's or his fostering of traditional faith among his children. He remained to his dying day a model Christian, in fact the rarest of Christians: one without a scintilla of self-righteousness. His only intolerance was toward intolerance. As he gently reprimanded me when I once suggested that it was more virtuous to accept belief rather than to reject it: why should belief be a moral matter at all, when all orthodox theologians going back to St. Paul himself have preached that faith is a divine gift, not something earned? I have yet to hear a convincing rebuttal to my father's simple disclaimer.

One autumn morning before I had risen to get ready for school, my mother came into my room and quietly announced, "Aunt Dule died last night." I was thunderstruck—the more so since I knew that my parents had gone to her apartment the night before for dinner. What I did not know was that she had already been given last rites at the request of her husband, an Anglo-Catholic priest and professor of theology at General Seminary in Chelsea, where they lived. Later that day, when I got home from school, I found my two middle cousins, Mary and Anda, at our apartment. Mary very quietly was sounding out the funeral march by Chopin on our piano. We spoke little of her mother's death that day. By evening, when my cousins had left for Chelsea, and my father was spending most of the time on the phone taking calls from friends an relatives, the one refrain I heard over and over was how "merciful" her death had been. Although I did not understand its meaning I repeated that Homeric formula whenever someone asked me about my aunt's death. It had a consoling ring to it.

I was not included at her funeral, nor were my brothers. Such events were "adults only," something I regretted. But I did later visit her grave in the little New Marlborough cemetery and read on her headstone the words my father had suggested: "I know that my Redeemer liveth." It was not until many decades later that I began to appreciate fully the poignancy of my father's choice of that simple affirmation of Job in the face of so much suffering and so much reason for despair. Just recently I received from Paul Rotella a tape of Elisabeth Schwarzkopf singing those words from Handel's *Messiah*, and every time I play it and lose myself in her soaring legato I think of my aunt, her headstone, and my father. "Though this body be destroyed, yet shall I see God." There is no answer to the problem of pain, to the riddle of evil and suffering. But Job said enough to lay the matter to rest until the last day, and Handel gave it definitive shape in sound. All that is needed is the voice of an angel.

TUESDAY, FEBRUARY 19, 2002

Amidst the pile of mail when we got home from Anguilla last night was a fat envelope from St. Patrick's Cathedral containing the music of the Lenten hymn plus various portions of the Mass I am to sing, beginning today, as a cathedral cantor. As soon as I had unpacked, I headed to the piano and began to practice these pieces, with so little time to spare, and prayed that they would settle into my vocal cords by the next morning. It was a moment of *déjà entendu,* for it took me back to my parents' living room halfway through the fall term of that fifth-grade year when I decided my quitting the Glee Club (along with piano lessons the previous spring) had been a big mistake and I wanted to return in time to sing in the Christmas concert. Mr. Rotella was most obliging; he gave me a sheaf of sheet music to take home and learn at the piano so that I could catch up in time for the next Friday afternoon rehearsal. I threw myself into the task with great gusto, for it represented an unofficial return to the piano as well, albeit as my own accompanist. I can still feel those words and notes of Bach's "Prepare thyself, Zion," Handel's "For the glory of the Lord," and the old French carol "Il est né le divin enfant," as I slowly worked them through, measure by measure. There was a private thrill in playing this game of catch-up alone at home. I never came to a rehearsal thereafter unprepared. And never again would I waver in my devotion to Mr. Rotella's Glee Club.

The St. Patrick's assignment was less demanding; the beautiful Lenten hymn "Forty Days and Forty Nights" was one I had sung since childhood; and the responses were for the most part familiar. Yet I found myself approaching everything as if new, no doubt because the prospect of facing a cathedral congregation as a vocalist was indeed dauntingly new. Reading or speaking was one thing; singing on key and sounding prepared, quite another. When I arrived a half hour early, there was no organist in sight—just some friendly guards and a helpful sacristan amongst the tourists and scattered worshipers mulling about. I was already a bundle of nerves. Then I caught a glimpse of the priest-celebrant ascending the steps from the crypt below the high altar. It was the new rector, Monsignor Clark. I was overjoyed to see this familiar face and to know a real pro would be at the controls during my first flight.

While waiting for the Mass to begin, we talked of my memory of that papal effigy under glass in the back of the nave, back when JFK was president and I a ten-year-old visitor for the first time (which was close to how I felt again today). He confirmed that it was indeed of the then recently deceased Pius XII, a gift to Cardinal Spellman by well-meaning Vatican officials. The wax dummy came with the late pope's own vestments and even his own spectacles. As a joke, someone had set it up at a desk in the chancery until unsuspecting secretaries began to faint at the startling sight

of Pius's posthumous return to New York! Thence it was moved to the rear
of the cathedral, where many of the pious prayed to Pius. Finally, after
Spellman's death, it mercifully vanished for good; the rector at the time
took the secret of its final resting place (one rumor held that he had melted
it down for candles) to his grave.

WEDNESDAY, FEBRUARY 20, 2002

This morning, walking from a doctor's appointment at New York Hospital
to the office, I resisted the habit of zigzagging toward Rock Center, and
instead found myself proceeding straight down York Avenue to gather some
more memories. I headed toward the Town Tennis Club, hoping I would
be granted a tour of a club I had not seen since 1965. The doorman was
most obliging, and I realized that I had no spatial recollection of the route
to the clubhouse, through an innocuous door in the apartment house lobby,
then down hallways lined with antique tennis racquets, down and up stairs;
I was almost at the boiler room before retracing my steps and arriving in
the familiar club room between the outdoor tennis courts and below the former ice rink. How little it seemed to have changed. The counter where we ate
our burgers and drank shakes between skating sessions had disappeared, but
the familiar courts and 1960s ambience were sufficient to turn back my
clock forty years. For the first time I understood the passion archaeologists
have for unearthing small fragments of a vessel that the mind and imagination together reconstruct into the flawless original. Not only the vessel but
the taste of its intoxicating wine is retrieved by mental alchemy. Climbing
the stairs to the roof, I walked around the paddle court and retraced the
route our skates cut over the years. The new additions seemed ephemeral,
impermanent, and as insubstantial as gossamer: they posed no threat to the
solidity of memory reengaged. Is this, I have often wondered sitting in
St. Vincent Ferrer, what a transplanted medieval monk would feel in that
building? Would the familiar elements—the Gothic space, the vaults, piers,
tracery, stained glass, liturgical fittings—overwhelm the new and strange:

the microphones, electric lights, modern pews, and occasional anachronisms of art? I like to think so. Is it the genetic impulse that allows us to see ourselves and our forebears in our children? Like the archaeologist—or jigsaw virtuoso—we focus on the pieces that fit the picture.

It was a fulfilling detour, and now I want to recover other such spaces. It's like returning to a long-forgotten piece of piano music. Once the notes are replayed, however tentatively after so many years, the fingers recapture the "muscle memory." The music has remained in the fingers all the time, just waiting to be released again. For the body, from eyes to limbs, it is the same. The physicist's construction of a space-time continuum suggests a new and personal expression. Not only in science fiction may a passage through space lead us back in time.

THURSDAY, FEBRUARY 21, 2002

Today the passage through space was far longer, and far more familiar: the early morning drive along the New Jersey Turnpike and Route I to Princeton. I have made that drive countless times over the past three decades, yet the journey always sends me back to the beginning—when I was an undergraduate, as my son Charlie is now. Before meeting him for lunch, I revisited the house, now empty, of my dissertation adviser and mentor, John Rupert Martin, to help his daughter go through his art library before the house is sold—a sad visit. I was there, last March, to see her mother for the last time, just a few days before her death and eight months after her husband's. Among the books I came across were a few of my own and my father's inscribed with gratitude to the professor who had changed the course of my career. There is something about a book that offers a tactile link between past and present. Will a digital library of the future serve the same sacramental role? It is hard to believe.

Lunch with Charlie at the Annex, which appears not to have changed even its place mats since the 1950s, was equally anachronistic and delightful. Much of lunch was spent on the subject of God, miracles, cosmology,

Catholicism, and C. S. Lewis—who has turned out to be no less persuasive to Charlie than he was to me at the same age, thirty years earlier. We both discovered him in a religion course at Princeton. I did not expect our brief meal to take such a turn—a very illuminating detour leading to a small epiphany. Just yesterday, I had been musing, rather wistfully, about how different Charlie's experience of Princeton so far has been from mine. Now I am not so sure: perhaps even at Princeton God draws straight with crooked lines.

SATURDAY, FEBRUARY 23, 2002

In the fall of 1961, I decided to end my self-imposed exile from the piano. My mother had the inspired idea to contact her childhood teacher, Isabelle Yalkovsky Byman, to see whether she might take me on as a second-generation student. It was perhaps the single most important decision of my education—in music and everything else. No one has had a greater impact on me than Isabelle Byman.

When, accompanied by my mother, I first met her in her walk-up apartment and music studio on East Fiftieth Street, just two blocks east of St. Bart's, my first reaction was of astonishment. Since my mother had begun to study with her at the same age, I expected to find an elderly, grandmotherly, mild-mannered teacher on the eve of retirement. Probably I subconsciously welcomed this assumption since my previous teacher had been young and energetic and, I thought, had pushed me too hard and fast.

I'll never forget that first lesson—a revelation, an epiphany of a new relationship with music. How could anyone so young and vital have taught my mother as a little girl? I wondered as I went home. In the hour that raced by like a freight train, she completely deconstructed my playing and assumptions: it was back to square one, to rebuild technique block by block—or in her favorite term, "piecemeal." Yet her idealism, her drive and dedication as a teacher immediately impressed me in a way that still eludes explanation. I was in the hands of someone who would never let me down.

On and off the keyboard Isabelle was an inspiration. In my eyes, over the next dozen years I studied under her, she elevated the idea of teacher to a level of enormous importance. Her resonant playing still resounds in my ear—she played with such strength that it was not hard to imagine her breaking a string—but it is her voice that strikes the most resonant chords: instructing, explaining, admonishing, reassuring—*piano* and *forte.* Through the sheer force of her personality and example, as much as by pedagogical method, she instilled a sense of discipline, self-criticism, and determination well beyond my natural inclination. She instilled the sense of joy that accompanied the effort. I am reminded of Henry Adams's remark that a teacher can never tell where his—or her—influence stops. "A teacher," Adams wrote, "affects eternity."

SUNDAY, FEBRUARY 24, 2002

My weekly lessons with my new teacher were on Friday afternoon, immediately following our Glee Club rehearsal at Buckley School: together they composed a musical prelude to each weekend. For the first year, at least, I was accompanied to Mrs. Byman's apartment either by my mother, who had tea with a friend in a town house across the street, or by our housekeeper, Martha, who sat immediately outside the music room and heard every note and word. Sometimes I found her proximity embarrassing since the lessons often had stormy moments. Isabelle's corrections were often sharp and emphatic; she had little patience for sloppiness and if she felt my preparation had been less than expected, her chastisement might sound brutal to an outsider. Once, after a particularly grueling lesson, which left me in silent tears, Martha offered a comment of consolation on the way home: "I couldn't believe how hard she was on you." While I appreciated her concern I knew in my heart that I had earned my grilling. However exacting Isabelle's standards might be, she was never less than fair. Constant and consistent, there was never any shade of ambiguity in her judgments.

A few months ago I met a former colleague of Isabelle's from the Manhattan School of Music. He had been suggested to me by a friend as a wonderful teacher (and distinguished author on piano pedagogy) with whom I might study at this late stage of my return to the keyboard. I liked him and thought that I might indeed try some lessons with him, until we got onto the subject of Isabelle Byman, and he said that he could not understand her approach to "teaching through fear." I knew what he was saying, but I also knew then that I could not take him up on his offer. Yes, I had feared disappointing her; I feared her temper—but always because it was never arbitrary; it was her honest and therapeutic response to my laziness or carelessness. If I were to take up another teacher at this stage of my life it would have to be someone who mirrored her perfectionism. (A year after Isabelle's death I found this very quality—of unyielding, solid brilliance— in the master classes of Elisabeth Schwarzkopf.) I felt I owed it to Isabelle's memory not to settle for less. So for now I practice on my own, with her picture on top of the piano, and I hear her voice as I read her boldly scrawled notations on the sheet music from those early days. A musical friend and occasional coach of mine, whom I consider both a genius and a saint, was horrified by these markings on my music. "I would never do that to a student," Mason said; but I am so grateful she did. They keep alive the unending dialogue between us each time I sit down to practice. Many of them reflect her early career as an opera singer, which was interrupted by the war, when she returned to the piano—her first instrument as a prodigy— for good. "Sing!" "Legato!" "More body on tone." These are just a few of the comments I now read again on the gavotte from Bach's Fifth French Suite, one of the pieces I learned that first year with Isabelle, to which I now return forty years later and—to my surprise and delight—not as a stranger.

MONDAY, FEBRUARY 25, 2002

This morning I got a call from my cousin Anda telling me that our cousin Jack Schieffelin had died after several brave years fighting cancer. On a happier note, it brought back memories of the most bizarre and extravagant

Christmas celebrations, with our Schieffelin cousins, that we have ever known, and surely will never repeat. Jack's grandmother, my great-aunt Louise, was my grandfather Scribner's only sister, and during the last years of her life our family Christmas gathering was held at her apartment at Eighty-ninth Street, which she shared with her only son—my godfather, George—and his wife, Cousin Louise (or Little Louise, as she was called).

Cousin Louise was an animal fanatic. She was always rescuing dogs and cats found along the road or at the pound and giving them a home. (My brothers and I referred to the Schieffelins' home as the Dog House.) But the payoff came each year at these raucous, noisy, wild Christmas lunches that even Dickens would have found hard to invent. Great-Aunt Louise supplied a sole grace note amidst a band of brass players following no score. Richard Strauss once cautioned conductors, "Never look at the trombones; you'll only encourage them." We needed no encouragement. At one point during lunch, my grandmother Scribner shouted, "Shut up everyone and listen to me!"

My father loved to recount stories of these Schieffelin parties past. As a child, he once saw his uncle George, well into his cups, leap to his feet when the maid came in to serve the flaming plum pudding, grab his water-glass, and shout "Fire!" as he doused the culinary pièce de résistance, to everyone's horror and delight. That spirit lived on another generation, though no longer fueled by alcohol. After lunch we went into the living room, where a giant tree was decorated not with sugarplums but Steiff animals from F.A.O. Schwarz, which we children were to divide up and take home. The packages around the tree had labels not only from "Cousin George and Louise" and their two sons, Jack and Dick, but also from "The Dogs," or "The Cats," or "The Maids." And no present was deemed too inappropriate. My own children were never to have the experience of such prodigal, eccentric relations as the Schieffelins, but they, too, may yet mold their memories into equally seductive shapes. In retrospect, the chaos of those gatherings is something I would never want to host; but I am grateful that my Schieffelin cousins were less prudent about Christmas. The recollection is feast enough.

TUESDAY, FEBRUARY 26, 2002

Today was my second Tuesday as a cantor at St. Pat's, and already I can tell that the nerve-wracking novelty will soon wear off. I actually found I could look up from the music and look at the congregation—a big step forward. It turns out the sexton, my stage manager before and during Mass, is part Presbyterian; and the organist playing today, a true veteran, is a Baptist; the associate organist, who conducted our cantor rehearsal in the music office off the choir loft, is a good Methodist from Tennessee. No wonder St. Patrick's runs so well, with such a cadre of solid Protestant souls supporting it. My hymn-singing Protestant youth serves me well in this new musical adventure. If I can encourage the congregation to join in song I may consider myself a success: if they end up drowning me out, the loser wins.

My new beginning with Mrs. Byman took what appeared to be a major medical setback only a few months after we had begun. I developed a painful infection in my left index finger, which resulted in my first overnight at Lenox Hill Hospital, a few blocks north on Park, for an early morning operation. I was relieved to be in the hospital, facing the prospect of general anesthesia and oblivion. When Dr. Andy, as we called him, had attempted to lance the problem in his office, I turned ashen and almost passed out before he thought better of it and recommended hospitalization. What I recall most about the operation was my opting for the gas mask over the shot; the surgeon seemed surprised, but I had no love of needles, however quicker that means of sedation might be. I was not disappointed. The sensation of counting out loud while I breathed in the gas was pleasantly intoxicating, and as I approached the last number I recall—eight—I saw myself drift away down a long dark tunnel. It was not at all frightening, and I have long since taken it as a prefiguration of our final journey beyond this life. Death lost its sting at an early age.

Once recovered, I had to face the prospect of piano lessons and practice without the use of my left hand for several weeks. Yet Isabelle was not fazed; she spent more time on ear training—recognizing notes and inter-vals—and written exercises, and getting a head start on a new piece, a taran-tella by Moszkowski, by learning the right hand as far as it would take me before the bandages came off the left.

For Isabelle, an obstacle was an opportunity. We forged ahead. It is only in recent years, as I approach the age she was then, that I have finally found fascination in exploring the new possibilities granted by these unexpected roadblocks in life. There are far worse fates than having to return "by an-other route." There may even be serendipity in these setbacks. Perhaps the Magi found it so.

WEDNESDAY, FEBRUARY 27, 2002

Last night I began the next volume of Father Greeley's prayer journals, *Let-ters to a Loving God,* which just arrived in the mail. I had called his Chicago office upon my return from Anguilla to leave a message with his assistant Roberta about how much his Christmas prayer journal meant to me on va-cation and how I regretted that it stopped two years ago. How long until the next installment? The answer was totally unexpected: the new book was just off press and would be in the mail to me that very day. Roberta should have a new administrative title: Father Andy's Angel. The new volume is thinner, and the challenge will be to savor it, read it slowly, day by day, and try to make it last through Lent. Mae West said that too much of a good thing is wonderful, but in this case I must ration my reading—to keep the wonderful as long as possible.

The sequential challenge of Lent, forty days of fast before the ultimate feast, runs counter to the present culture of instant gratification. Yet it taps into a deeper human need: the challenge of a course, a journey—a pilgrim's progress. It is the basic substance of myth and epic—from Hercules' labors to Tamino's trials in Mozart's *The Magic Flute.* From my first lessons with Is-abelle on through the years, she set me on a similar course of challenge and reward. It was free of danger—but not disappointment. Her formula was to award a gold star for each good lesson; at the end of a sequence of ten stars—ten weeks of gold—the student would receive a small plaster bust of a composer. These were the trophies of victory I sought to collect and line up on a shelf—and eventually on the piano when I finally got my own. No matter how many consecutive stars had been amassed, if a lesson was poor, it was back to the beginning. One had to get ten honor lessons *in a row.* To temper the bitter disappointment—and often tears—that would accompany a total setback after a long streak of stars (just imagine getting eight or nine only to lose them all), she offered a charitable indulgence: she would allow one probationary lesson, but only one. If the following week saw the student back to the highest standard, she would ignore the lapse of the week before. But woe to the student who had two poor lessons in a row—back to purgatory.

If this method sounds like a musical version of medieval merit theology, the only justification I can offer is that it worked miracles at the keyboard, and it was fun. Isabelle's approval was not easily earned, but it was given generously when merited. She never held back praise when the elusive goal had finally been achieved. As I look back on my experience, I doubt that many students would tolerate it today. In our age of grade inflation, gold stars are expected just for showing up. The current mantra is affirmation; criticism is relegated to the same ash heap of barbarisms as corporal punishment. Much as I lament this fact, I, too, have been corrupted by charity. I would be a pushover as a teacher (just as I have proved as a parent). I would want to give everyone a star all the time. But they would not shine as bright as Isabelle's.

THURSDAY, FEBRUARY 28, 2002

Yesterday I came quite unexpectedly upon that star of wonder—this time, through the German poet Heinrich Heine: *"einem goldenen Stern, der leuchtete lieblich und heiter"* ("a golden star that shone amiably and brightly")—followed by the Three Kings. I had drifted off to sleep the night before to an ethereal soprano singing a song by Richard Strauss that began, *"Träume, träume"* ("Dream, dream"), a sure formula for sleep. It was after midnight, and it worked, but not before I pondered the identity of the voice, sure that it must be that of Elisabeth Schwarzkopf. The next morning I went on the Internet and looked up the schedule of WQXR: yes, at 12:34 A.M. it was Schwarzkopf singing Strauss's "Wiegenlied," his cradle song. I sent her a fax to thank her for the song, and then found my CD of the recording and played it again, just to be sure I had not been dreaming. It was just as I had heard it before drifting off. But tucked away in the list of Strauss lieder was one I had not noticed before, though I must have heard it many times: "Die heiligen drei Königen aus Morgenland"—"The Holy Three Kings from the Orient." Its sacred, liturgical title, so unlike its companions and so atypical of Strauss's work, intrigued me. I played it and found it hauntingly evocative. The Three Holy Kings see the bright morning star and follow it, stopping young boys and girls in each town to ask the way to Bethlehem. They do not know; but the star leads the way and the Kings finally enter Joseph's house: "The bullock bellowed, the baby cried, and the Three Holy Kings sang." Strauss, who once said he could set a teaspoon to music, paints in vivid tones three distinct sounds—of ox, Christ Child, and Kings. And do they ever sing—in one long legato line soaring heavenward into the musical firmament, carried on the soft, sustained breath of Schwarzkopf. The program notes described this song as standing alone, as an Epiphany song. It was indeed an epiphany, and one that I was led to by the most fitting association: hearing his cradle song, after midnight.

Midday found me back at St. Patrick's, where after the noon Mass I ran into Father Fraser, who told me that he had discovered what had happened to the wax figure of Pope Pius XII. Evidently it had fallen into a "sad state," and was melted down to be recycled into votive candles. "You mean to say that the pope was burned on the altars of St. Pat's?" I teased him. "Yes," retorted, "but not in effigy." Touché! Actually, that practical solution had a symbolic elegance: the disintegrating effigy of a pontiff transfigured into flickering lights of prayers lit by the faithful, unaware of the source. I am sure that the devout, worldly pope would have enjoyed this irony. Lighting votive candles at St. Pat's will never be quite the same.

MONDAY, MARCH 4, 2002

The musical highpoint for me during the sixth-grade year—and arguably of any year thereafter—was Paul Rotella's production of Mozart's *Abduction from the Seraglio* as the first Glee Club operetta to be performed on the new stage. I was cast as Blonde, the English maid of Constanze and the beloved of Pedrillo, who together with Belmonte was determined to rescue us from the Turkish pasha's harem, where we had been taken prisoner. Mozart's singspiel, or comic opera with spoken dialogue, is pure Viennese whipped cream, with a bittersweet flavor that touches the heart as well as delights the senses.

I threw myself into learning the part; it had one glorious aria well suited to a boy soprano who could still reach high C without strain: "Oh, what rapture, what delight, burns within my heart so bright," it began (in our English translation). My father had bought me a copy of the vocal score, with piano accompaniment, of the entire opera so that I could practice and enjoy it in my room on the new piano. In those days boys played the female parts, a long-standing tradition with no more self-consciousness about gender switching than in Shakespeare's theater. It was all soon to vanish with the advent of the coeducational movement of the later sixties, but we were still innocents, and thus undertook for one last time this early Mozart gem, which was never to be staged again at Buckley.

The costumes were as splendid as the sets. Someone had fun ordering mine: Blonde was dressed as a harem belly dancer with multicolored silk skirt and separate sequined brassiere—filled with strategic padding—and a long platinum wig worthy of Marilyn. There were gasps from the audience when I came out onstage—before I ever had a chance to open my mouth. Years later I showed a snapshot of this ephemeral moment to Metropolitan Opera soprano Mary Costa, who exclaimed, "Why, it's me!"

The camaraderie of rehearsals, the excitement building toward the performances, two on the same day, the adrenaline-charged moment of singing and acting at the same time—it all left a profound mark on me, and to this day I have always admired and envied opera singers above all other artists and performers. They partake of that *Gesamtkunstwerk*, "total artwork" as Wagner called it, in a way no others do. Each time I go to rehearsals of this opera at the Met I inwardly recast the professionals with the boy amateurs and once again experience Mozart's magic in double time.

WEDNESDAY, MARCH 6, 2002

Sixth grade transfigured Sundays as well. After the children's service in the chapel of St. Bart's, we were now entrusted to a divinity student for more advanced religious instruction. What I recall, however, is a well-meaning but ineffective seminarian giving us assignments of memorization, beginning with useful things like the Apostles' and Nicene Creeds and the General Thanksgiving from the Book of Common Prayer, and then moving on to the more obscure Collects for the Day.

I don't think we were ever told precisely what a "collect" was: I probably assumed it was related to the collection, since that was a highpoint of the liturgy—the passing of the silver plates to collect coins and crisp green bills—and resulted in the heaps of cash being raised heavenward by the officiating priest at the altar while we all sang, "Praise God from whom all blessings flow." In hindsight, it seems a strange adaptation of the Catholic elevation of the Host in the Mass; perhaps less strange if one subscribes to Max Weber's thesis that Protestantism fostered the rise of capitalism. Our Lord may have overturned the tables of the money changers in the temple, but in his Protestant Episcopal Church the bankers had reclaimed a symbolic moment in the service of God. Wall Street was well represented in every pew.

MONDAY, MARCH 11, 2002

One June evening the following summer, my father had arrived home from the commuter train with a letter from the White House. He reasonably assumed it was for him until he read the envelope more closely; it was addressed to my six-year-old brother, John! Inside it read: "Dear John: The President received your letter and asked me to send you this note of reply. So many requests for items of various kinds are received that he simply cannot comply with them. The President nonetheless appreciates your friendly interest in writing and sends his best wishes to you." It was signed by Kennedy's secretary, Evelyn Lincoln.

I was able to solve the mystery: some weeks earlier John asked me to serve as *his* personal secretary—or scrivener—and take a letter of dictation to President Kennedy. He told the president how much he admired him and believed he was able to do amazing things and so he was writing to ask the president to send him a magic pencil, "the kind that when you draw a picture of a house you can open the door and enter it." My youngest brother was never short on imagination; though he never got that magic pencil from JFK he eventually became a professional artist and, perhaps not coincidentally, one who specializes in three-dimensional fantasies.

The White House letter ended up in my parents' scrapbook; it forged a link between that young president and the budding artist. But there was to be no magic pencil that could edit, much less rewrite, the tragedy of that Friday afternoon five months later in Dallas. I was seated at my desk in Buckley, awaiting dismissal from classes, when the shocking news came over the loudspeaker from the headmaster's office. Surrealism quickly supplanted shock, as in twilight disbelief we marched to Glee Club rehearsal—of which I have no memory. Then I took the bus downtown for my piano lesson with Mrs. Byman.

What I remember was the utter normality of the lesson. Music has a life of its own and it was not to fall casualty to a madman's bullet—or so that lesson appears in retrospect. We settled down to work at once, and I discovered then the therapeutic power of concentration and discipline in the service of music. There would soon be a time for reflection and sadness, but this was not it. With single-mindedness and determination Isabelle forged ahead with the task at hand—no minor matter in the eyes of a dedicated teacher who was not going to let her pupil be shortchanged. She would have taught during the Blitz of London or the bombing of Berlin: the composers—not the tragedians—would call the final tune.

As I write, the sixth-month anniversary of the September 11 tragedy draws to a close at midnight, and I am suddenly reminded of how strange my behavior on that day of terror must have seemed to my colleagues, my family, and even—though less so—to myself. Nothing was going to deter me from my original plan to pack up our son Christopher and drive him up to Eaglebrook School to begin the new academic year. Not the general emergency, or closed bridges, or flood of people in the streets, or Ritchie already in tears over our friends missing in the rubble of the Twin Towers. Nothing. My priority that day had been from the start to get him to school on time, and I was going to do it. I was on my own automatic pilot. Only when we were well along the highway did I turn on the car radio and listen to the reports of the disaster in progress. And, in an instant, November 22 came into focus and clarified everything. My response to tragedy had long been modeled by Isabelle Byman in that unforgettable lesson on a Friday afternoon when the world seemed to come to a halt—but not for her young student.

WEDNESDAY, MARCH 13, 2002

Fall is my favorite season of the year. It is not just the blazing colors and the brisk air between the dog days of August and the chill to come. No, it has more to do with the calendar, not the annual but the academic one: from our earliest school days, fall is the time of new beginnings—a new grade, a new class, a new teacher, a new chance. The Church is not far behind—just a couple of months—for its new liturgical year starts with Advent, with the four weeks of anticipation and preparation before the birth of Christ. It's ironic that just when nature prepares to shed its foliage in blazes of glory— a vibrant protest against the coming death or, at best, sleep of winter—children and Church alike prepare for something new and find common ground in the celebration of Christmas.

During my last two years of Buckley the fall also meant a series of weekend previews of the ultimate school to come: Princeton. I loved going down with my father or family friends to spend Saturday having lunch on the periphery of Palmer Stadium—usually at one of the eating clubs. I never counted myself a real football fan, and following the intricacies of the game took enormous concentration as I was constantly distracted by conversation and the various sideshows, both official and impromptu. But the marching band, the mascot Tiger, the parade—it all followed a magnificent ritual in orange and black. Alumni of all ages never failed to join in singing the Princeton classics from the nostalgic "Going Back to Nassau Hall" and "Old Nassau" to the fighting "Crash Through That Line of Blue." I had little notion of where I would be going after Buckley: for a while I wanted to break ranks with my peers (almost all of whom went on to boarding school in those days) and remain at a day school in New York in order to pursue my piano studies with Mrs. Byman, but down deep, along with my classmates, I also yearned for the independence of boarding school life. What never seemed in doubt was where it would all lead: to Princeton. I never saw a game at another college; the idea never occurred to me. Nassau Hall might as well have been a family church like St. Bartholomew's—even more so, for within the next six years I was to change my religion and my home church, but Princeton would provide the solid ground for both. That terrible autumn of our president's death marked the beginning of my love affair with a place where four namesakes had traveled the same paths for over a century, and where Kennedy had spent his first year of college before illness forced him to withdraw—and finish at Harvard.

THURSDAY, MARCH 14, 2002

My uncle Ned had gone from Harvard College to Harvard Law School—at the insistence of his father, for whom the law was the only profession worth pursuing. But having received his degree, he then crossed the country to follow his true vocation, into the ministry, graduated from divinity school in San Francisco, and was ordained a priest in the Episcopal Church. My first trip alone on an airplane was the shuttle to Boston, to spend the weekend with Uncle Ned and his wife, Aunt Cynthia, in the rectory of St. Elizabeth Church in Sudbury. I chose to sit in the business section at the rear of the shuttle, a kind of lounge with one large horseshoe banquette. I felt very grown-up as I ordered my complimentary beverage—a ginger ale.

At the time the church of which my uncle was rector was a tiny stone replica of a medieval monastery chapel befitting its original owner and architect, the famous Gothic revivalist Ralph Adams Cram (who designed the Princeton Chapel and whose partner designed both St. Bartholomew's and my present-day parish of St. Vincent Ferrer). A publishing colleague of my father's now owned Cram's house next door—Craig Wylie of Houghton Mifflin; the chapel had become a parish church. It was far too small for the growing congregation in this Bostonian suburb and Uncle Ned was overseeing the construction, on the other side of his rectory, of a large wood-and-glass A-frame church. It was the perfect ecumenical monument to 1960s suburban modernity, devoid of all the rich Anglo-Catholic heritage of Cram's architectural gem, whose rough-hewn stones, wrought iron, and stained glass had translated Gregorian chant into three dimensions.

I was then taking weekly classes at St. Bart's to prepare for my upcoming confirmation. Sunday school was as boring as ever but these classes redeemed religious study for me. There was real content, things to learn and discuss and a final test at the end to determine whether we were ready to approach the bishop of New York and receive from his hands the confirming touch of the Holy Spirit, the passage into adulthood in the faith. This was now something on a par with piano lessons—the real thing, and I loved it. Some of the fellow students were much older teenagers: the priest-instructor asked two very cool ones if they were "coming over from Rome." I did not understand the question (the answer was yes) but it sounded exotic and I learned that they had been raised Catholic. (My time would come later to redress that balance-sheet transfer of male teenagers from Rome to Canterbury.) The classes must have been late on Friday afternoon, for between my piano lesson and this catechism I once made a quick detour to Schirmer's music store a block from the church to buy an almost life-size bust of Mozart for my piano. Music and religion still remained intertwined: I had no problem with graven images—as long as they were of the divine Wolfgang.

The service of confirmation, in the main church, was magnificent; we proceeded in two files up the marble steps of the sanctuary to kneel before Bishop Donegan, who had once been my mother's childhood rector at St. James's and was now a confidant of the Queen Mother. He, too, was clearly the real thing. He gave me my own copy of the Episcopal prayer book; my grandmother Sunderland contributed a small gold cross and chain. But I was not to be there the next Sunday for the ritual First Communion. Instead, I was back with my uncle in Sudbury and received it from him in the more mysterious and evocative setting of Cram's chapel; there were only the two of us present. Looking back, I now realize how medieval and Catholic that First Communion was, the Book of Common Prayer notwithstanding. In some sublime fashion it may even have instilled in that prototeenager (still a few weeks away from my thirteenth birthday) a Catholic sense of sacrament, a visual, tactile reality conveyed through art, not language. Cram would have approved.

SUNDAY, MARCH 17, 2002

Today is St. Patrick's Day and I find myself far away from the Fifth Avenue parade. I am on another long, skinny island—not Manhattan. It is Jupiter Island, north of Palm Beach, where we spend the children's spring break visiting my father-in-law in Florida. Today at the noon Mass at St. Christopher's Church we sang as the recessional hymn "When Irish Eyes Are Smiling." That is surely one hymn I never would have found in the Episcopal hymnal of my youth. But somehow, amidst the sea of emerald sport shirts, slacks, and dresses it seemed fit for the feast. I enjoyed it all the more, joining in full voice as an adoptive son of Eire (by virtue of American Catholicism, not genes) as I imagined my father's bemused response to this recessional.

Yesterday's Mass ended on an upsetting note, as the pastor spoke of the recent sexual scandals among the clergy, which toppled the bishop of Palm Beach last week (I had naively assumed that the problem, like a virus, had been limited to Boston). That, too, made me wistful for the more wholesome church of my childhood, until an older and wiser priest today at Mass commented that he had no doubt that out of such tragedy would come a greater good. His simple words of reassurance at first seemed to add up to a plenary platitude; they sounded so obvious. Yet as my father used to say, the obvious is often too neglected these days. The old *"ex malo bonum"* doctrine—that good emerges from evil—has been at the core of our Christian faith for two millennia, ever since the Crucifixion and Resurrection. It is something to bear in mind as we approach Holy Week.

MONDAY, MARCH 18, 2002

In the spring of 1964 Michelangelo's great *Pietà* traveled from St. Peter's, Rome, to Flushing Meadows, New York—courtesy of the Vatican (and the successful lobbying of New York's archbishop, Cardinal Spellman). It was the highlight of the first World's Fair held in New York City since 1939. Alas, I never saw it; perhaps the lines were too long. My first view of Michelangelo would have to wait another seven years. But I did see virtually everything else at the fair, and it was the most exciting place I ever visited as a child—the more so since I had never been out of the country. Several acres of a park in Queens were transformed for the next year into another world, with the vast metal Unisphere at its center. That fountain sculpture is still visible from the car as I drive by on the Grand Central Parkway to and from Long Island, and it brings back a flood of memories. I have never been tempted to see another World's Fair; that one, like the 1960 Olympics, succeeded for a lifetime.

Looking back, I am grateful I missed Michelangelo's *Pietà* in Flushing; I probably would have found it as odd and alien as that wax effigy of the pope in St. Patrick's. As an art historian, almost four decades later, I am appalled that as sensitive a pope as Paul VI would have let our Tammany Hall cardinal con him into allowing such a risky loan: it could so easily have been damaged in transit or by some deranged spectator (as indeed it was a few years later back in Rome, before the protective glass went up). Perhaps the current cloud of terrorism hanging over the civilized world may have a silver lining: a reluctance to remove masterpieces of art from their proper setting, or context, in order to satisfy the lust for a commercial tour, box-office attraction, or curatorial coup. Such candor may bar me from a late career as museum curator, but the artists of these masterpieces deserve no less, as do generations to come.

THURSDAY, MARCH 21, 2002

A year after JFK's funeral, I attended my grandfather Sunderland's at St. James's Church, a few blocks from our home. It was my first exposure to a funeral in the flesh. I had not known him well. He had been a remote figure during my early years. His Pygmalionlike ambition vis-à-vis his only daughter—someone to be molded and possessed exclusively—had been foiled when she married my father. For a few years we had no contact at all with him or my grandmother, through no fault of hers. But after a series of debilitating strokes, my parents charitably renewed holiday visits at Thanksgiving, Christmas, and Easter.

He had been the law partner of John W. Davis, and as the nation's foremost expert in railroad law he later headed the firm of Davis, Polk. He had been enormously successful in a profession he regarded as a sacred calling.

To him there was nothing higher than the law. By the time I got to know him, already infirm and accompanied by a male nurse called Mac, he seemed benignly judicial. Whenever my brothers and I came to visit, he would pull out rolls of quarters, dimes, and nickels, hand them to us, and say: "Now, you three boys divide these up among yourselves." I took the quarters, Blair got the dimes, and we gave John the nickels.

Once Grandpa sent us all Yankee baseball uniforms, mitts, bats, and baseballs—then after a couple of months of backyard practice, he and Mac took us up to Yankee Stadium for a real game. Ever the cautious lawyer, he had arranged for us to sit under the net behind home plate, so as not to be at risk of being hit by a foul ball—much to the chagrin of Blair, who had brought along his mitt in hopes of catching one.

On another outing, he took us to Madison Square Garden for the Ice Follies. During one comic routine, a pair of skaters began some serious ice dancing, but soon started to make mistakes, trip each other up, and stumble. Things started going from bad to worse when suddenly a light fixture fell to the ice from the ceiling. The pair didn't seem to notice and were heading right for it. By this time my brothers and I had caught on to the joke—but not Grandpa, who was shocked. Mac shared his boss's alarm, which only added to our delight. When the skaters, as we foresaw, tripped over the fixture and went flying headlong in perfectly executed stage falls, Grandpa turned to us and intoned in his most somber baritone: "Someone will pay for this!" We had had already got his money's worth—and more.

Our last expedition, before his final illness, was to have been to a magic show at the Union Club. Alas, we arrived just as everyone was leaving. So he had Mac look up the movies in the day's newspaper; they settled upon "a nice mystery by Alfred Hitchcock." *Psycho* sounded harmless enough. So off we went to the Trans-Lux Theatre on Eighty-fifth and Madison. We did not stay long. After the infamous shower scene of Janet Leigh stabbed to death by Tony Perkins, my grandfather announced we were all leaving at once, whereupon six-year-old John started crying, "But I want to watch him mop up the blood!"

What I remember most about Grandpa's funeral was my mother in black: I had never seen her wear a black dress. She looked dazed. What I didn't know until many years later was that just before the service had begun, she had gone into the small room where the casket lay; not seeing it in the dark, she had stumbled into it, falling on top of the body. It would have unnerved a lesser mortal, but she always has had an extraordinary capacity to recover her equilibrium, on or off the ice.

I sat between her and my grandmother; somber as it was, that service marked the beginning of a new relationship. I hadn't lost a grandfather; I had gained a grandmother, someone I would come to know and love as an individual, not her husband's shadow, for the remaining ten years of her life.

FRIDAY, MARCH 22, 2002

This last year of Buckley I had been named music representative on the Student Council, the link between Paul Rotella and the student body. A generation later my son Charlie would be elected by his peers to the top post, Student Council president, and far outshine his proud father. But, truth be told, thirty years earlier I would not have traded places with him. Music was the center of my life, and that lower political rung on the ladder of student government was everything I aspired to.

As I look back on the various recitals of those last two years at Buckley, I realize how rich a musical treasure chest Isabelle Byman had packed for me in so short a space. Louis Auchincloss titled his memoir about his early years of literary apprenticeship *A Writer's Capital.* Isabelle gave me a pianist's capital, which has yielded dividends over four subsequent decades. The pieces I learned and never stopped playing gave those disjointed adolescent years a musical sostenuto. Even the first movement of Mendelssohn's virtuosic Piano Concerto in G Minor—something I had been assigned for technical training more than for ultimate performance—is a piece to which I still return to time and again, albeit vicariously through the recordings of Rudolf Serkin and Jean-Yves Thibaudet. Whenever I hear them I sense Isabelle demonstrating phrase upon phrase at my side; in slow motion my fingers try to work the chords and runs into muscles and bones and soul. The ultimate gift may not be so much the ability to perform as the chance to feel right down to the fingertips the performance of a master.

The same holds true for the last operetta we put on—Mozart's *Magic Flute*. I was cast as the comic harem keeper Monostatos—a Moor with a weighty turban and no chance of gaining the fair Pamina. My changing voice had meant graduating from Blonde to a swarthy eunuch—I guess it was a step forward. Jamie Murphy, our governor's new stepson, made a model bird-catcher Papageno. At one point, having forgotten to bring along his magic bells on stage, he reached out to conductor Rotella, who handed them to him just in time for his next line, delivered with gleeful irony: "Oh, what a fool am I!" It brought down the house. Every performance of that magic at the Met has evoked in me our Buckley abridged version; no subtitles required. Mozart operas have not been performed at Buckley in decades; to those who might argue that they are too ambitious for schoolboys, I would counter: such musical capital can never be too rich, nor amassed too soon. *Vita brevis, ars longa*—life is short, art is long. A life enriched by art, especially that holy art of music, can never be too long, or seem too short.

SUNDAY, MARCH 24, 2002

The profane—as well as temptation to profanity—overshadows the sacred procession of Holy Week. Hosannas yield to curses. There is much of which I would gladly, like poor Pilate, wash my hands. But as I sat in the Baroque splendor of St. Jean Baptiste this evening, holding a small sheaf of palms to be blessed, I looked at the rows of ornate, empty confessionals and recalled a sermon I had heard as a child at St. Bart's. The rector, Dr. Finlay, told a story of a young soldier who, on a bet with a friend, had gone into a confessional of a Catholic church to fake a lurid confession. The anonymous priest on the other side of the grille immediately sensed the charade and asked the false penitent to kneel before the crucifix outside and repeat aloud, "All this you did for me, and I couldn't care less." The young soldier obliged—it was all part of the bet—but at the end of his recitation he broke down and wept. He shared that story years later from a pulpit— as a priest. I remember few sermons from childhood; I am sure I am in good company. But that simple story remains as vivid as the day I heard it in that darkened church. The irony is that we had no crucifix at St. Bart's. The rector who told the tale was a staunch Anglo-Canadian, with little use for anything Catholic. He always preached the significance of "the empty cross" of Protestantism—the cross of triumph, not of tragedy. Yet, to his credit, he told the story of that latter-day centurion just as it happened, and he left at least one schoolboy with a lasting sense of the mystery and power of a chance encounter with the crucified Christ, if only in the mind's eye.

MONDAY, MARCH 25, 2002

Among the items of mail that arrived while we were away was a program of a current exhibition at the Art Museum of Princeton University, devoted to images of the Passion. The juxtaposition of these precious objects and artistic re-creations of our Lord's suffering and sacrifice with the all-too-real images, via CNN and other unvarnished media, of daily violence and blood in Jerusalem strangely called to mind a verse from the psalm chosen for the St. Paul's School anthem a century ago: "O pray for the peace of Jerusalem." It remains a prayer equally suited to the upcoming Passover and Passion of this Holy Week—to Jews, Christians, and Muslims alike.

Today, after Mass at St. Patrick's, I paused to look at the Victorian pietà in the ambulatory behind the high altar. It is beautifully carved in gleaming white marble—aspiring to the pathos and virtuosity of Michelangelo's prototype—and a favorite object of devotion for visitors to the cathedral; yet something about it has always troubled me. It is not quite convincing, except as an idealized image of a grieving mother holding her lifeless son. The problem is that he is seated on the ground, his head in her lap—a pose no corpse could sustain. The impressive torso and limbs, befitting that nineteenth-century era of muscular Christianity, requires a strong heart pumping blood throughout those full muscles. The veins are still visibly raised: he may slumber, but not in death. The sculptor was, it seems, all too faithful to his handsome studio model, not to the conceptual model of the dead Christ. Death had indeed lost its sting, but prematurely—even before they "laid him in a tomb." How often, I wondered, has the urge to idealize our Lord diluted the stark reality of his ultimate sacrifice.

Suddenly I was taken back to one of those many Sunday afternoons with my father at the movies. One that stood head and shoulders above all biblical films I ever saw was Pasolini's *The Gospel According to Saint Matthew.* I thought of that film today, as the Passion narrative this week was taken from that former tax collector turned evangelist. It was stark, minimal, haunting, and hypnotic: the Communist, agnostic director cast a Jesus who was utterly convincing. In the bleakness and aridness of the black-and-white setting Jesus conveyed a gaunt, frail physicality charged with spiritual magnetism. He was both real and Reality; the moment of his nailing to the cross was pure pain distilled by acceptance and love, unbearable to watch, but impossible to ignore. The grand Technicolor epics of Hollywood have never come close to capturing the faith conveyed by that self-proclaimed doubter/director. Only a Graham Greene could have put it into words. But the simple subtitles of Matthew's own text already said it all. I don't think I ever watched a movie with my father as unforgettable as this one. I should like someday to try it on my own sons—and pray it will stand the test of time.

TUESDAY, MARCH 26, 2002

I recall my short-lived role as an acolyte at St. Bart's during the fall of 1964, my last at Buckley. I had been thoroughly trained and rehearsed in all the details of assisting the priest during the service of Holy Communion, as we Episcopalians called the Mass. There were two of us, each with a velvet cushion on which to kneel beside the two large wooden candlesticks flanking the altar of the chapel. I was very nervous; but worse, I had worn my Sunday blue wool suit under the black cassock and white surplice, our acolyte uniform, on this unusually hot autumn day—before the advent of ecclesiastical air-conditioning. As the priest began reciting the canon, the long prayer leading up to the consecration and Communion, I felt myself involuntarily swaying back and forth, wishing that I might hold on to the candlestick to steady myself, but afraid that it would look unseemly—or, worse, that I might topple it. His voice gradually receded, as though echoing through a long tunnel; the altarpiece of the Epiphany began to cloud into shadow, and I felt light-headed and dizzy. The next thing I knew, the priest had stopped in the middle of his prayer, helped me to one of the seats along the side of the sanctuary, and told me to lean over with my head between my knees to bring back the circulation: he said I was as white as a sheet. He had come to the rescue just in time. I don't remember whether I stayed at that seat for the remainder of the service, or made a discreet exit with a parent. But I also don't recall ever serving again as an acolyte at St. Bart's; I must have reverted with relief to my earlier, behind-the-pews role of usher—close to the door and fresh air of Park Avenue. Standing or moving around suited me fine; but never again was I tempted to kneel in holy stillness in full view of a congregation. Perhaps that is why I like the new job of cantor at St. Patrick's so much—it is as mobile as musical. And why I have always had the greatest admiration for the statuesque guards at Buckingham Palace.

THURSDAY, MARCH 28, 2002

Today, Holy Thursday, the beginning of the ancient Triduum—or three days—culminating with Easter, found me back at St. Patrick's at noon. I wasn't sure whether I would be able to attend the traditional evening service of the Lord's Supper, so I played it safe. The cathedral was packed. I made my way to one of the front pews. The sanctuary looked different. It was the light. All the television floodlights were on, and the bronze gates with carved angels gleamed as never before: *luminous*—a hint of Easter before the darkness of Good Friday. The rector was no less enlightening; with clarity and economy, he distilled the essence of faith. The two focal points of Maundy Thursday (which commemorates the institution of the Eucharist at the Last Supper) are the meaning of our Lord's gift of himself in the sacrament of bread and wine two thousand years ago—a gift we receive at each Mass—and the mandate, illustrated by his washing of the disciples' feet, to serve each other likewise. Even more: to consider it a privilege to do so, and to accept the burdens of life and each other gracefully and gratefully. Never have I felt more in need of such a simple message. The very thought of a gift that could keep renewing itself for two millennia—for a start—is beyond words to express or even to conceive: it is the central mystery/miracle of the Eucharist, which is simply ancient Greek for "thanksgiving." Today, our Passover, is the first Thanksgiving, instituted by God himself on the eve of incomprehensible suffering. I have never seen bright spotlights in St. Patrick's, or any other church, that I have not wished to extinguish. Better the muted, natural light filtering through stained glass in a Gothic cathedral. But today for the first time they seemed right for the moment—like a burst of midday sunlight so bright as to banish all shadow. *Lux Umbra Dei*: it was a luminous epiphany; its afterglow endures.

FRIDAY, MARCH 29, 2002

"My God, my God, why have you abandoned me?" The words pour through loudspeakers as I turn on the radio, with an hour and a half left of Good Friday—half the time Jesus spent of the cross. They are playing Haydn's original orchestral version of his *Seven Last Words of Christ* on WQXR, each segment preceded by the recitation of text in Latin, English, and German. The timing is apt, for just a few hours ago on my way to pick up dinner, I was mulling over an invitation I received today from the new pastor and prior of St. Vincent's to speak on one of those seven last words at next year's Good Friday service. I had suggested that last lamentation of our Lord, a quotation of Psalm 22, as the text I have long wanted to study and perhaps write or speak about. That cry from the cross—*"Eli, Eli, lema sabachthani?"*—which some of the biblical bystanders mistake as a call for Elijah, and which two of the evangelists, Matthew and Mark, give as our

Lord's final words of his life, have always struck me as the most paradoxically consoling words ever spoken by the fully human Jesus. Consoling, because more than anything else in the Bible, they serve as testimony—under the most grueling torture—that God himself, in the flesh, experienced our darkest moments of doubt, loss, even abandonment. The problem of pain, the mystery of evil, is not answered from the cross; but it is fully shared. Even in despair we are not alone.

As I write these words, the source of the broadcast is announced: a recording of the recent performance at St. Patrick's Cathedral by the Vienna Philharmonic in memory of the victims of September 11. The director of the orchestra has just invited all the members of the congregation to light their memorial candles as they listen to the concluding piece, Mozart's "Ave verum corpus," conducted by Johannes Somary. At the end there is no applause, as requested, just pure silence to follow the most perfect music ever written.

This morning began at St. Patrick's with the first of the Good Friday memorials: the service of Tenebrae, with chants of psalms and readings interspersed with the extinguishing of seven candles on the high altar, one by one. The sanctuary that blazed with artificial light yesterday was now muted in the glow of candles and colored light through the stained clerestory windows above. It concluded with a piece I had never heard before, once again conducted by Somary: Allegri's "Miserere," a Baroque masterpiece composed for performance exclusively in the Sistine Chapel. This was the piece that the boy Mozart reputedly copied from memory after hearing it only once at the Vatican, and under the tightest security (no pens or paper were allowed in the chapel, to prevent any unauthorized transcription). After the service Maestro Somary told me the tale was probably apocryphal although he agreed that Mozart would have been fully capable of such a wonder. *"Se non è vero, è ben trovato,"* as the Romans love to say: if it's not true, it ought to be.

Midday found me at St. Vincent's: I wanted to do the Stations of the Cross, however quickly, before picking up Ritchie for the Seven Last Words. The church was dark and magnificent—the deep blues of the windows above, the shadows below. But I could find no prayer book with the ritual of the fourteen stations, here a series of oil paintings: Christ's trial, ascent up Calvary, bearing the cross, falling, being nailed and crucified, dying, and being taken down and buried in the tomb. I was forced to invent my own impromptu meditations and prayers before each scene, which I saw in a new way—a virtue born of necessity. One scene or station, in particular, struck me afresh: Jesus meeting the "daughters of Jerusalem." It was the women, the female followers of Jesus, who stood close by on Calvary with his mother and John. The other ten apostles, all male, were nowhere in sight. The women prepared him for burial. And they would be the first witnesses to the Resurrection—an extraordinary fact in a place and time when a woman's testimony carried no legal weight in court.

This scene found its sequel in the service itself: the short talks on the first five of the Seven Last Words were all given by women: they were so poignant, so eloquent, and utterly perfect as personal reflections on the Passion. The Church will survive its current crisis if women again take the lead. It is only a matter of time—perhaps a new pope, or a new council—when they shall finally receive their full voice, and full due. This, too, was an unexpected epiphany of Good Friday, along with the four-month-old son of one of the speakers, whose text had been Jesus' words to his mother. The baby reminded me of our first son, who will be joining us for Easter, just before his twenty-first birthday. I envied that young father who could *carry* his son to church—in a pouch.

SATURDAY, MARCH 30, 2002

I have never felt so grateful to the DMV, our state's Department of Motor Vehicles: its failure to send son Charlie's renewal for his driver's license in time for his twenty-first birthday has guaranteed his appearance at Easter, which is less than a minute away. The prospect of getting a new license on Monday morning here in Manhattan before his current one expires in a few weeks was sufficient to lure him away from Princeton for Easter lunch with his parents, uncles, and grandmother. He will arrive in the middle of the night, while all sensible folk, like the guards posted at the tomb, have finally fallen asleep.

Holy Saturday has always seemed to me to be a spiritual void, best filled with some useful activity. I usually feel I have missed something if I cannot at least step inside a church or chapel sometime during the day. But not to-day. The altars have been stripped, the sacrament removed from the taber-nacle, the door now opened to reveal its emptiness. It is a day of neither tragedy nor triumph, but of pause, repose, and waiting. This morning, how-ever, during a phone call to a retired Cuban schoolmaster, I learned that to-day was his late mother's feast day (more important in that culture than a birthday), and was called *Sábado de Gloria*, Saturday of Glory, because it her-alded Easter on the following morning. The Latins have a special gift for identifying the silver lining in every cloud—and celebrating it. But there is still too much of the Anglo-Saxon in me to celebrate prematurely. I have al-ways disliked those well-meant greetings of "Merry Christmas" in the midst of Advent, several days—often weeks—before the feast arrives.

SUNDAY, MARCH 31, 2002

The early morning hours before dawn were filled, or rather unfulfilled, with fitful sleep as I listened in vain for the sound of Charlie arriving. I finally got myself to sleep by replaying over and over in my mind Handel's "I know that my Redeemer liveth." By daylight I thought I would win another overanxious-parent award, until I called my office voice mail and heard his reassuring voice explaining that he had missed the last train out of Prince-ton and would not be able to get home in time for Easter. By then I could afford to become philosophical: I still had enjoyed the expectation of his return; he was safe; the homecoming was merely postponed until another day. Postponement does not negate the joy of anticipation; it prolongs it, punctuated by only passing disappointment.

The Easter service at St. Bart's was itself a homecoming: a mixture of the familiar and the new, it brought home to me in a very personal way the vital continuity of that church and of the broader tradition that stretches back over centuries of Easter mornings. Our seats were the same as those of my childhood, right below the pulpit. The traditional MacFarlane's

"Christ our Passover is sacrificed for us" was beautifully sung—now by a smaller but clearer choir than I remember from my youth, and at a much faster tempo, which evoked far more excitement and joy than I had ever heard before; it was like Tullio Serafin's early recording of the Verdi *Requiem*—thrilling. My eyes wandered over the same reliefs, inscriptions, marble columns, dome and apse mosaics as in years past; but they all seemed fresh, with still more to be revealed in the light of another Easter.

The rector's sermon in turn illuminated a new aspect of the gospel accounts of that first Easter, something I had never considered: the *ambiguity* of the descriptions of the Resurrection. Whatever it was, it was clearly not resuscitation. The risen Christ was a new reality experienced by the fearful, doubting disciples. A spiritual reality, *non novus sed nove*: our Lord appeared—and was recognized—in a new way.

My final stop before nightfall was to St. Jean Baptiste, for the evening Mass—this time alone. The contrast of this French Baroque interior with the Byzantine St. Bart's covered a millennium of architectural transformations, all in the service of an unchanging faith and sacrament of the risen Christ. The Communion anthem, a baritone solo in this choirless liturgy, provided the final Baroque footnote to the morning's sermon. It was from Handel's *Messiah*: "The trumpet shall sound . . . and we shall be changed." That was what happened on that first Easter when both Jesus and his disciples were forever changed; it is still our prayer two thousand years later: that we too shall be changed.

TUESDAY, APRIL 2, 2002

The summer after my graduation from Buckley, my father wanted to get me into the habit of reading worthwhile books for pleasure, not just as part of school assignments. His inspired incentive was a fifty-dollar reward upon completing his list of classics—not an insignificant sum in 1965, especially to a fourteen-year-old. Since I was spending the entire summer at home, I had plenty of time to read, so this was a welcome diversion and by no means a burden. The books, too, were a rich mixture of adventure and at-mosphere. I can still list them from memory: *King Solomon's Mines, The Mayor of Casterbridge, Silas Marner, The House of the Seven Gables, Ring of Bright Water, Of Mice and Men,* and *The Woman in White.* What strikes me in retrospect is that none of these was by a Scribner author. There was nothing chauvinistic about my father's choices. I suspect that, for the most part, he chose books from his collection of Modern Library editions that he had read as a young man himself. He wanted to share some of his early literary capital with me. I wish I could have done the same for my sons, but I never believed such a bribe would work in our era of video and Nintendo. Looking back now with clearer hindsight, I am convinced that the monetary reward was just a convenient excuse for me to do what I knew my father really wanted of me before going off to St. Paul's. It was a way of pleasing him and saving face at the same time. The fascinating thing is that I don't remember many de-tails of these books, but I do recall precisely where I was when I read each of them. They have become a part of the mental geography of that last summer before a new school. In a magical way the fictional places and peo-ple have become intertwined with the actual settings—in Far Hills and New Marlborough—of my youth. It is similar to the puzzling uncertainty of trying to determine whether a place or event in a dream was factual or just a vivid revision of a prior dream. The power of great literature, I am convinced, is its ability to fuse itself with actual experience so that one's memory, the mind's eye, makes no qualitative distinction between the two. The best books shape both memory and our view of the present—far into the future. They make it possible, in the words of Oscar Wilde, for nature to imitate art. We see the world through a prism of words.

SUNDAY, APRIL 7, 2002

"Ask not for whom the bell tolls . . ." For the next four years of my life at school, time was marked by the deep, resonant tolling of chapel bells. From the moment I arrived at St. Paul's School, I think I knew instinctively that

I would love it. Perhaps I had already made that decision before the fact. Perhaps my prejudice in favor of my new school—indeed new life—was strong enough to be self-fulfilling. That would be in character. It is difficult to understand in hindsight, much less explain, why we fall in love with a person or a place. Expectation and apprehension were at high pitch; those first days at the school must have sustained the first and relieved the second. St. Paul's did not let me down.

The one event of opening day that looms in memory, a ritual we repeated thirty years later with son Charlie, was standing in a line within the handsome gray rectory, directly opposite the towering redbrick chapel, waiting in turn to be introduced to the rector and his wife. They stood in front of French doors that opened onto the garden, our means of egress. I have never been invited to the White House, but I have always felt that I've had the virtual experience. For those of us at St. Paul's, "the rector" conjured up as much authority and awe as any U.S. president. I know that there are many who considered the Reverend Matthew Warren aloof and fearsome, but I was never one of them. For me, it was very simple: it was his school, he had invited me to come, and he remembered me (thanks, no doubt, to my father standing beside me). That was all I needed to know. Besides, he was a priest of the church, which in my mind already defined him as a benevolent father figure. As the sixties wore on, "paternalism" became the catchword for all that was wrong at the school. But I considered it a virtue. It all comes down to the *imago patris*, the image of the father. Mine was positive, and it was as easily transferred as a melody modulating into a new key.

MONDAY, APRIL 8, 2002

We "new boys," about a hundred of us (roughly divided between the third form, or ninth grade, and the "lower school," of first- and second-formers), gathered in the small Old Chapel, dating from the Civil War era, for a special introductory service conducted by the rector. That small cruciform building captured the cozy Anglo-Catholic spirituality of the school's first rector, Dr. Coit. It was a most benign, even seductive setting for our induction into a church school that featured required chapel services every morning and twice on Sunday: if you were a Roman Catholic you had three services to attend on Sunday, since Mass at the monastery down the road provided no dispensation from either of the two Episcopal liturgies at school. Catholics, in my estimation, were truly heroic churchgoers—though I had no idea what went on at their Mass, or why they alone were subjected to such redundancy of worship.

In the so-called New Chapel, erected during the age of the robber barons and reminiscent of English college chapels—that is to say, of cathedrals, at least in the eyes of a schoolboy—we were assigned permanent seats for the year in the long pews facing each other. The youngest boys sat in the front row and each year graduated to the next higher row behind them. The seats along the wall were assigned to the masters (as we called our teachers) according to seniority; the rector sat closest to the entrance and antechapel, just within the carved screen and facing the altar, which looked almost as far from the entrance as New Jersey from the Manhattan end of the Lincoln Tunnel. My seat was just below the pulpit and facing the lectern where students read the Bible verses for the day—a good location, especially since I had a good view of the choir and could at times feel the vibrations of the pipes in the organ loft when the organist pulled out the big stops. Those daily services always began with an organ prelude as we took our seats and ended with a rousing postlude to which we marched out in choreographed double files. In between we sang a hymn. For a music lover, it was a taste of heaven—between breakfast and the first class of the day.

THURSDAY, APRIL 11, 2002

"Where were you when the lights went out?" That was the question heard at home in New York for weeks and months afterwards. I was far from the action that brought the largest city in the Western world to a halt. I was in a soundproof practice room in the basement of Memorial Hall, seated at an upright piano, trying to squeeze in an hour of solid scales and fragments of repertoire before dinner. The lights flickered on and off, but I kept on playing, never suspecting that history was being made 250 miles away, aboveground. My daily trips to these Spartan practice rooms had already become part of the new rhythm of love at St. Paul's. My piano lessons had resumed the first week of school—with a new teacher, James Wood.

FRIDAY, APRIL 12, 2002

I am carrying around a recent letter from Jim Wood. Like all his letters, it is typewritten, long, filled with musical insights and anecdotes. What I recall most from those wonderfully refreshing weekly lessons with him are the conversations—as wide ranging as his talents and interests. Thirty-six years later, the conversation continues.

SATURDAY, APRIL 13, 2002

My renewed correspondence with Jim began three years ago while I was producing a CD of St. Paul's School chapel music classics from the 1950s through the mid-1980s. Half of the recording featured music from his tenure as head of the music department and school organist, including some splendid organ solos he performed and recorded in the decade following my graduation. From the time I started lessons with him in very different surroundings—the multipurpose "green room" behind the stage at Mem Hall—I thought that Jim should be running the music at the school. But I never then imagined that a future rector would have the same thought and act on it.

Back in 1965, and for several years after, Jim was commuting to the school from his home in Bristol, some forty-five minutes away, several days a week to play for a few minutes during the morning chapel services and then give private lessons in organ and piano to interested students. I always looked forward to his days at the organ, for he always enlivened that sleepy service with jewels from his vast repertoire. My favorite recessional was his rousing rendition of the second movement of Mendelssohn's second organ sonata—*allegro maestoso e vivace*: that combination of majesty and liveliness was intoxicating as we marched out, double file.

My weekly piano lessons with Jim were always a delightful change of pace from the rest of the academic schedule. They were totally without pressure—or grades—and combined the learning of new repertoire with a broadening of my musical horizons. Jim kept me connected with other parts of the musical world—from the Boston Symphony, to which he took students on occasion, to the Metropolitan Opera, to which he maintained a subscription—and kept me up to date on what was being performed. I still had never been there in person—in fact I never saw the interior of the old Met, which was to close later that year—but I kept in touch thanks to those Texaco broadcasts via my illegal transistor radio.

SUNDAY, APRIL 14, 2002

The organ recessional this evening at St. Jean Baptiste was one I don't ever recall hearing there before, but given the course of this book so far, I should have predicted it: the *allegro maestso e vivace* from Mendelssohn's second sonata. All I needed was an apparition of Maestro Wood in the organ loft to send me straight to Payne Whitney for a thorough psychiatric exam. I turned to Ritchie as we walked out of the church and asked if she thought it amazing that the organist should be playing the very recessional that just last night I had written was my favorite during those four years at St. Paul's. She tactfully agreed, but I sensed it was more out of spousal solidarity than surprise.

The gospel today, for long my favorite of all the Easter epiphanies, was the story of the supper at Emmaus. As I pointed to the stained glass window of that scene, still aglow thanks to daylight saving time, I whispered to Ritchie during the decidedly less colorful homily on the same subject that it had been the topic of my first major art history paper, exactly thirty years ago, a few weeks before turning twenty-one, as Charlie is about to do in the same place. That account of Jesus' revelation of himself "in the breaking of the bread" to his two unsuspecting disciples has always moved me more than any other miracle attributed to him. What struck me more than ever tonight was the fragile thread of human hospitality from which that amazing, life-changing epiphany hung—suspended in time. Luke makes it clear, but with no apparent emphasis, that the resurrected Jesus who had joined the two downcast disciples during their walk from Jerusalem to Emmaus on Easter evening had given every sign of intending to continue along the road after the two men had reached their destination, that little village whose name would otherwise have been forgotten for the last two millennia. Instead of saying a polite good-bye, or "Maybe we'll meet again," or any other such friendly word of farewell, they invited the stranger to join them for dinner. For no special reason. If they sensed their fellow traveler was special, it was a subconscious glimmer. But their spontaneous gesture of friendliness resulted in sharing with the risen Christ himself the first Mass celebrated after its institution in the Last Supper: the meal in which he reveals himself in the breaking of bread, then and now.

At the back of the church I spotted the new colorful poster for this year's Cardinal's Appeal: it features—without any identification of either subject or artist—Rembrandt's sublime *Supper at Emmaus* in the Louvre. I wonder whether anyone in the cardinal's office realized the delicious irony in the choice of that illustration. They passed up dozens of masterpieces of this very scene by Catholic artists—Bellini, Caravaggio, Rubens, Vermeer, among others—in favor of the greatest Protestant painter of all time. But then, the Jewish-born Mendelssohn was also a Protestant. Thus the spirit of ecumenism, so sorely needed in this time of sadness and strife within the Church, may yet cast its spell. And how better to reveal itself than in such small epiphanies of sight and sound? No trumpets blared at Emmaus.

MONDAY, APRIL 15, 2002

Today my uncle Ned called and left the message that the preacher in Charlottesville, Virginia, yesterday gave a sermon on the supper of Emmaus, and he remembered that I had once written a paper on the subject and wanted me to send him a copy to give the priest. I am beginning to get used to the rhythm of these coincidences. My father used to quote the French essayist Montaigne in describing an author's consubstantial relationship with his work: "I have no more made my books than my books have made me." I wonder whether, in a twist on his meaning, this journal is shaping my daily life more than reflecting it. Father Andrew Greeley believes that the computer is an effective medium for prayer; in one of his novels he creates a character that converses with an angel through cyberspace. I am growing less inclined to dismiss such possibilities as charming metaphors or poetic conceits. I don't expect to converse with angels, but the interaction between words and the Word seems endlessly mysterious. Perhaps epiphanies are, in fact, more a matter of connections than revelations. Or rather, the perception of connections, of relationships, or identities once the veil of distortion or confusion has been lifted, if only for an instant. How else to explain the failure of the disciples to recognize the risen Christ on the road to Emmaus, or Mary Magdalene's earlier mistaking him for the gardener outside the empty tomb—until he addressed her by name? There is no suggestion that our Lord was disguised or that he changed in appearance; the changes seem instead to take place internally, within the disciples themselves; in these instances epiphany is in the eye of the beholder. It is as though a kaleidoscope becomes a telescope; the beauty of fragmented confusion is given the instant clarity of a Van Eyck landscape of luminous wonder. But how to keep the mind's eye or ear attuned to them—that is the daunting thought. We may bear more responsibility for revelation than we would like to imagine. Not every wise man saw the star; nor, presumably, did every shepherd hear the same celestial chorus over the hills of Bethlehem.

WEDNESDAY, APRIL 24, 2002

Madalyn Murray—the name meant nothing to me at the time. Her claim to fame was that she spearheaded the fight all the way to the Supreme Court that outlawed prayer in public schools and precipitated a fundamentalist literalism in the definition of the wall of separation between Church and state under the First Amendment. It was bizarre enough to read about her fight ensconced in my room at St. Paul's, but what struck me even more than her philosophical crusade against any vestige of religious belief in public life was her strident hatred of the very notion of God. The greatest saints had from time immemorial been plagued by doubts and barren stretches of disbelief—right back to the doubting Thomas. But here was someone consumed—or so she presented herself in the interview—with passionate hatred for a God who did not even exist. I was deeply disturbed—and yet impressed—by the idea that nonexistence could nourish such malice. For the first time in my life, I felt that strident atheism was more than something to be pitied; it could be a powerful destructive force. In an unwitting way, she strengthened my faith in a God whose very existence could fuel such determination to prove the opposite.

Meanwhile, my father had given me a more nourishing reading list for my off-hours; he called it his seventy-five-dollar list (a fifty percent increase over the summer before). Some of the books I remember reading that first year in my third-floor room after homework was done were Conrad's *Lord Jim*, Dumas's *The Count of Monte Cristo*, Collins's *The Moonstone*, and short stories by Chekhov. The last inspired me to try my hand at writing a story of my own to submit to the school literary magazine, the *Horae Scholasticae*, edited by Max Perkins's grandson. It was, not surprisingly, ersatz Chekhov—about a desperately lonely and homesick boy in a prep school in St. Petersburg. Upon its publication, my housemaster summoned me to his apartment and said he was very worried about me—until I reassured him that my story reflected only my recent reading, not my life. It's something I try to remember whenever I find myself slipping into what scholars dub the biographical fallacy of inter-preting an artist's work. Art rarely mirrors its creator's life: some of Mozart's brightest movements were written during his bleakest days. I was a very happy third-former when I wrote the saddest story of my life. In the opening words of the school anthem, now playing on my son's CD in the background, "I was glad when they said unto me, 'We will go into the house of the Lord.' " That is precisely what we did each day, and how I felt about it.

FRIDAY, APRIL 26, 2002

I opened Jim Wood's most recent letter this morning to find another jour-ney—Emmaus revisited. It seems my letter to him about Emmaus arrived two days after he and his wife, Connie, had attended a midweek Eucharist at their Florida parish, St. Paul's by the Sea (is it possible?). Their favorite priest preached on the Emmaus story, which he considered "the essence of the appearances of Christ after the Resurrection and thus for him the essence of the importance of the breaking of the bread." Now how's that for another coincidence? Jim asks. Apropos of my comment on the poster of Rembrandt's *Emmaus* at the back of St. Patrick's, Jim added the follow-ing aperçu: "It all reinforces my basic sense that we all travel the same road to the same destination, albeit taking different routes along the way. And in God's eyes it makes no difference—but we do seem to have problems, we in our finite way, of letting those small and unimportant differences make the separations so huge. Now in my later years I find more and more that the differences matter less and less. Maybe others will join us too?"

That comment struck a memory I have of walking along Lexington Av-enue a dozen years ago with Scribner's longtime publicity director Susan Richman. As we passed the Lutheran St. Peter's Church at Citicorp and then, a block later, the historic Central Synagogue, she told me of the me-morial service in 1965 she had attended at another East Side synagogue for Scribner author Martin Buber, the great Jewish theologian, philosopher, and mystic. She recalled that another of our religious authors, the equally illustrious Lutheran theologian Paul Tillich (who was our patron philosopher at St. Paul's in my day), had given a eulogy that explained their friendship across a seeming theological divide: Tillich said we all are approaching the same God—only by different routes.

Memory is elusive; I wanted to be sure that I had not transposed the eulogist and the deceased. So I turned to our books to see which one, Buber or Tillich, had died in 1965. No help: they both did. Then, with the aid of the Internet, I learned that memory had for once not played me false. Buber died in June—four months before Tillich's death, in October. And then, just as I was about to shut off the computer to go to St. Patrick's for Mass, I heard the chime of a new e-mail hitting my in-box. It was an announcement that Danish rights have just been sold to Tillich's *The Eternal Now*. Perhaps his title is the closest we may come to solving the riddle of time. It appears, in any case, the perfect phrase to embrace both the journey to Emmaus and our elder son's rite of passage today, Charlie's twenty-first birthday.

SUNDAY, APRIL 28, 2002

The climax of the winter term was the school's one-act-play competition. For our house entry Nick Bruce, son of our ambassador to Great Britain, composed a dark tragedy called *The Room*. It was about an eccentric—indeed insane—millionaire widower living in a small town who keeps his only son locked up in a room to protect him from the evils of the outside world. When his son begins to chafe and finally rebel against his captivity, the father orders his butler to kill the boy with a knife to prevent his corruption by evil. The butler cannot bring himself to do it and flees to the townspeople, who return as a lynching mob, confront the father, kill him, and free the boy. When the liberated lad surveys the horror around him he turns back to his room and shuts the door.

I was cast as Mr. Pelson, the insanely protective father. Was it typecasting? Or did that role, instead, inspire my approach to child rearing? During these later years of raising teenagers I have had uncanny sympathy for Pelson's overprotective instincts; and I did receive the first Overanxious Parent Award ever given by St. Paul's, the year Charlie graduated.

I made one key change to the script: I added a line after giving my shocked butler the knife to stab my son. In an aside to the audience, I confessed that I knew, of course, he would never be able to bring himself to complete the horrid deed, but that the aborted attempt would itself be enough to scare my son into changing his mind about wanting to leave the room. The very idea of a father killing his son, even as a sacrifice to the perceived lesser evils, was anathema. I could play a crazed eccentric, but never such a monster. It is why today I cannot abide even the most magnificent painting of Abraham about to sacrifice Isaac; the biblical story is no easier to bear. I prefer to think that "our father in faith" simply misunderstood God's wishes—and was corrected by divine intervention before he performed that most inhuman of all sacrifices.

THURSDAY, MAY 2, 2002

This morning I stopped by the small church of St. John the Martyr to catch the seven-thirty Mass. I was a few minutes late, and so as I entered I heard the priest reading the gospel. The first words were most apt for the journey today: "The disciple is not greater than the teacher." Whenever I return to St. Paul's, it is never first as a trustee, past (or future) parent, or even alumnus; I reenter those grounds as a student. The arrival always engenders the residual rush of excitement and anticipation I felt upon returning there from each vacation as a student. This time, the five-hour drive alone was accompanied by some of the most sublime music imaginable. I had thrown into the duffel bag several CDs. Bach cantatas and a lieder recital by Dame Elisabeth carried me to Elysium along the parkways for the first half of the trip, and then a 1952 recording of *Die Zauberflöte* conducted by Karajan brought Mozart's incomparable magic to the long stretch of interstate highways in the pelting rain for the second half. I arrived at the school gates before the opera's end, but after Tamino's successful conclusion of his ordeal by fire and water. The final chords will have to await my trip to the gas station tomorrow, and I have saved *Der Rosenkavalier* for the trip home on Saturday in time for Ritchie's birthday.

SATURDAY, MAY 4, 2002

For the spring play of my first year at St. Paul's the director, Mr. Greaves, enlisted me as piano player during the lengthy set changes between acts. I brought along my sheet music of a Bach prelude, a Haydn sonata, Chopin waltzes, and Rimsky-Korsakov's *The Flight of the Bumblebee* to rehearsals and timed the selections to fit the scenery changes. The stage manager was the nephew of New York's new mayor and a sixth-form supervisor in my house—George Lindsay. The play was Graham Greene's *The Potting Shed*. I had no idea who the author was, and of course I had never heard of the play. It would take me another four years to discover Greene as the modern novelist most influential on my religious life. But in hindsight that play, which I watched with utter fascination throughout rehearsals and the two performances, marked the beginning of a new journey of faith, one that would ultimately lead to Rome—as it had for Greene himself.

The play at first seemed to be a mystery. The protagonist, played brilliantly by André Bishop, was a middle-aged Englishman who returns home for the funeral of his father, a famous rationalist philosopher who preached and practiced a pure atheism. The son cannot fathom why he was treated as an outcast ever since childhood. The answer lies in something that happened to him in the potting shed, but he has blocked out any memory of it. His family, led by his aloof mother, stonewall his effort to discover the truth.

SUNDAY, MAY 5, 2002

After my intermezzo of Bach and Chopin, the son finds the solution to the mystery in the person of his uncle, an equally estranged black sheep of the family, who is a Catholic priest. He is also that quintessential Greene figure of ecclesiastical paradox—the "whiskey priest" who believes he has lost his faith yet continues to go through the motions of piety out of habit and charity to his flock. The alcoholic English and agnostic priest was played by none other than James Greaves himself. My housemates and I quietly joked about him typecasting himself in the role, since our housemaster was famous for his constant glass of scotch or gin never farther than arm's length in the evenings, and his breath always had a pleasant aroma of alcohol mingled with Benson and Hedges cigarettes. Yet little did we suspect how close we were to the mark; that would not be revealed to me for another two years, and in a scene no less dramatic than his stage encounter with André Bishop. I don't think any one moment onstage has remained more vivid than that one. I can still see James Greaves nervously fidgeting with his cigarette and drink, dressed in a stark black cassock, while André earnestly probes for the answer to the mystery of the potting shed. The electricity between these two actors—a generation apart—was as charged as though Gielgud and Guinness had taken over our student stage. They both lived their parts so thoroughly that the veil of fiction, as of theater, opened to reveal a sacred moment, an epiphany of two wounded souls finding a final consummation in an unexpected reunion.

Uncle and nephew had been very close, years ago, much to the father's consternation that his son was attracted to the beliefs and rituals of the Christian faith that he, the atheist philosopher, had spent a lifetime of scholarship proving fraudulent. Eventually the struggle between father and uncle had been too much for the sensitive boy, and in an act of desperation he went off to the potting shed and hanged himself. It was his uncle, the priest, who cut him down and found him lifeless—beyond the reach of last rites. So he knelt and prayed a desperate bargain with God. But what had he to give in exchange for his nephew's life? Finally, the words came forth: "Take away what I love most. Take away my faith, but let him live." And then the boy stirred and began to breathe. He hadn't been dead after all. Or so it seemed. But at the end of this powerful confrontation between uncle and nephew, between present and past, it is clear to us—and soon to the pitiful, faithless priest—that God accepted the offer and kept both sides of the bargain. He gave the boy back his life; he took away the priest's faith. At the end of the visit, the nephew leaves, his mystery solved; and he leaves his uncle praying for the first time since that last desperate prayer in the potting shed.

In the third act, with the family gathered at the father's house, a final revelation explains why the boy's failed suicide attempt and the timely save by his uncle caused their double banishment from the family. It is now the mother's turn to part the curtain: her late husband was a self-confessed sham. All his life he had demanded proof of the existence of God. He had believed the proof offered in the potting shed that day, however hard he had tried to resist it. As it threatened to undo his whole life's work, he had suppressed it and banished all reminders of it, including his own son. His atheism had been shattered by a God he forbade to enter his home again. He had maintained his fortress, against an enemy who had already conquered him, to the day he died. Epiphanies are not universally welcomed. The light that glows and warms the hearts of some may be the light that scorches and burns to ash the very certainties that sustain others.

I must go out and buy a copy of this play and read it again. Everything depends upon a production I saw thirty-six years ago as I sat waiting for my cue to go to the grand piano and keep the audience from getting restless while they awaited the next act. I must test my recollections of meaning against the playwright's original text. Perhaps I should also cross Lincoln Center Plaza and speak at length and at last about this play to André Bishop, who in his incomparable performance gave me my first taste of a miracle on the stage of St. Paul's. The closest I have come to experiencing that taste in the years since is in the slim wafer of bread repeatedly offered by a priest who may, or may not, think that God answers his prayers.

MONDAY, MAY 6, 2002

I had no luck finding a copy of the play, but I did track down the star. We had a good talk before he ran to give a lecture. But under the rubric of divine coincidences, I learned that while André was a sixth-former about to play the part, he wrote to Sir John Gielgud, my all-time favorite actor, who, unbeknownst to me, had played the part during the London premiere. He told André that the only good scene Greene had written for that part was the act-two confrontation between nephew and uncle. My memory had not played me false after all. Andre said he would call me in a few days and set up a lunch date. It is one I truly look forward to; I have waited only thirty-six years.

FRIDAY, MAY 10, 2002

I have never paid much attention to recording events. I rarely bring along a camera, or tape recorder, or, in more recent years, camcorder. I enjoy my few artifacts of the past all the more because of their rarity. I came upon one of them recently, while combing through a desk drawer in our country house: the only journal I ever kept. It covers only a month and a day—from July 15 to August 16 of 1966—but it chronicles my first trip abroad and offers a chance to retrace those memorable and impressionable steps with a precision I can not replicate for any other period of my life. As a condition of taking this trip my uncle required me to keep this journal (unlike his fifteen-year-old nephew, he was aware of the literary precedents); my father evidently concurred, for the small leatherette book has his name embossed on the cover. I never missed a day. But I am as grateful for its brevity as for its completeness. Its bare outline of people and places leaves plenty of room for the landscape of memory—a lush, atmospheric topography that remains undimmed through the intervening decades. The mystery of such memories, from this late vantage point, is that unlike photographs, they do not fade with time or exposure. That trip is as vivid and immediate as if I took it last summer—or right now, as I write of it. The mind must have special places for such moments, niches of memory that shelter, preserve, and frame them; in other words, reserve them as if a sacrament.

SUNDAY, MAY 12, 2002

My view of buildings and grounds, I realize, was already being shaped by that first visit abroad. It was medieval in its hierarchical assumption of beauty: so long as the church was the crown jewel, the rest—the houses, businesses, gardens, even palaces—however mundane or prosaic in themselves, would shine by reflected glory. I find support for this outrageous claim in those famous photos of the bombed-out City of London, with only the untouched dome of St. Paul's Cathedral looming as hope triumphant amidst the smoldering rubble where earlier there had been streets of beloved and bustling buildings. That rubble of centuries-old houses of business, by the time we arrived in 1966, had been for the most part replaced by glass-and-steel office buildings. No matter: the beauty and the soul of the City were still preserved by Sir Christopher Wren's cathedral. I am reminded of what changes and what does not by an anecdote that Greaves told me to illustrate the shifting meanings of words down the centuries. At the conclusion of Wren's royal tour of the newly finished cathedral the king said that he found it "awful, amusing, and artificial"—and he meant all three as high compliments: it was full of awe, inspired by the Muses, and wrought with great artistry. The shades of those compliments have shifted 180 degrees, but no matter how many shifts in taste and style over those past three hundred years, that cathedral's claim to those kingly compliments is beyond revision. Time and prejudice can no more level it than could the Luftwaffe's tons of explosives. Both have missed the mark, I like to think, by providential design.

MONDAY, MAY 13, 2002

With the beginning of the workweek, London sightseeing began in earnest. I returned to the City with Uncle Ned and saw at last the magnificent interior of St. Paul's Cathedral; then lunch at the famous Cheshire Cheese, followed by a visit to the Old Curiosity Shoppe, immortalized by Dickens, and an old bookshop. I discovered a new form of transportation: the Underground—a far cry from the creaky and tawdry subways of New York. It took me to Bond Street. The shops were endlessly fascinating and picturesque: it was as though I had entered a movie set only to discover it was real all along. The next morning I went off to Pall Mall to stand in the rain and watch the procession of the king of Jordan's state visit to Buckingham Palace. When the royal carriage finally passed by—we had an excellent view—I noticed that the queen's dainty umbrella succeeded in protecting her at the expense of her royal visitor: the stoic King Hussein got a double dose of English weather that day. A dozen years later he would wed my Princeton classmate and pal Lisa Halaby, today the widowed Queen Noor of Jordan.

TUESDAY, MAY 14, 2002

In Cambridge the touring of colleges began in earnest, camera in hand: Peterhouse, St. Catherine's, Selwyn (where Uncle Ned had studied), King's, Clare, Trinity (where my Pease cousins went), and St. John's. The next day added Emmanuel, Christ's, Sidney Sussex, Jesus, and Magdalene colleges to the list. After lunch, with the great Reformation historian Owen Chadwick, master of Selwyn, whose books I would one day study at Princeton, we drove out to the first manor house I'd ever seen—Sawston Hall. Along the tour, I was shown a "priest's hole," but since I knew nothing about the dangers of being Catholic in Elizabethan England, much less why priests had to be hidden in makeshift cupboards within stairwells, it just seemed another English eccentricity, an ecclesiastical hide-and-seek.

Back in our hotel, my uncle was engrossed in a huge scholarly book, *Contraception*, by the American Catholic jurist John Noonan, which he was reviewing for a journal of canon law. Again, I had no idea why that subject should be given such a weighty book or why it would be a matter of religious concern. If only the reigning pope had been equally disinterested, the Church might have been spared the tempest he unleashed two years later with his encyclical *Humanae vitae*, in which he rejected the thoughtful conclusions of his own panel of experts. Little did I know how timely my uncle's reading of Noonan's book was that summer—or how ironic, in the tranquillity of those Anglican quads and cloisters. Rome was as remote as the priest holes.

WEDNESDAY, MAY 15, 2002

Today was interwoven with art and epiphanies. I was hoping to get together with Father Andrew O'Connor for dinner, but he will be out of town, celebrating the sixth anniversary of his priesthood; so, instead, we met at Rockefeller Center for morning coffee before he ventured farther south to pick up some art supplies for his latest sacred creation. He explained it to me in great detail, but he is such a poet at heart that I must await the unveiling to grasp it. For now, I'll have to settle for glimpses through a glass darkly. He sees and draws connections that elude us mortals. First we went to the Met Museum Store, where I wanted to purchase a Renaissance candleholder for Ritchie. It turned out to be a wine holder but still held the large candle perfectly. When I mentioned this convenience to Andrew he spun it into a discourse on the liturgical links between wine and candle. The common referent is our Lord—both Vine and Light. Andrew lost me when he got to Joyce's "epiphanies," but someday with his help I'll catch up to that train of thought. Meanwhile I must rely on the more prosaic epiphanies around me.

There are no images of suffering to match the pain of those around us who face desolation daily: My godmother Patsy, who keeps a lonely vigil so soon after her husband's death while her only son is dying of melanoma at the age of forty-four. Our neighbors who are coming to dinner tomorrow, whose beautiful twenty-three-year-old daughter perished in the inferno of the World Trade Center. Our friends whose only son, age twenty-two, was killed in a car crash soon afterward. The twenty-five-year-old woman I heard about from my doctor this afternoon: she and her parents must face the mortal diagnosis of melanoma with scorching clarity.

It was time for confession: I had not been since Easter. I had almost gone at St. Patrick's, but an usher, mistaking me for a tourist, told me to sit down as I ambled indecisively back and forth outside the confessional. Another time. Later, after the doctor's, I stopped by St. Jean Baptiste, but the light went out over the booth as I tried to decide if that was to be the place of absolution. A half mile farther, I stepped inside St. Vincent's, where the new organ pipes still lay over the pews. After a long discussion with the organist and the new pastor, I had found my confessor standing right before me. (Not the organist.) He gave me the most illuminating penance in my thirty-one years of that sacrament: to read and ponder St. Matthew's account of the first Epiphany—the journey and visit of the Magi to the Christ Child.

As I reread this familiar story, I realized how much of it I'd never considered before. There was no explaining why these Wise Men thought a "new king of the Jews" was someone worth following a star to see, much less worship. Their goal, as they explain to the paranoid Herod, is to "worship" the child. But how do they fulfill it? By giving gifts. Is that the main point of this magnificent ceremony that so impressed young Lord Sebastian in Waugh's *Brideshead Revisited*—that true worship ends in giving? And also, that true wisdom—for they were indeed Wise Men—ends in returning home by another route? Perhaps that is the point of this unexpected penance tonight. Penance as pilgrimage—the willingness to come home to the Lord himself "by another route."

On my regular route home, I encountered the grief-stricken mother of our young friend killed in the car crash. He was the perfect son in every way, the role model of his generation, and his mother desperately seeks a reason to explain the tragedy of her loss. C. S. Lewis's classic book *The Problem of Pain*, my sole recommendation, had been of no help. Music, she said, was better—though it offered no answer to her question. Indeed the question appears unanswerable this side of paradise.

Is it possible that the problem ultimately lies not with the elusive answers but in the questions we ask? Perhaps we ask the wrong question in seeking to assuage unbearable grief. Perhaps the question is not "why?" but "where?"—or better, "to whom?" That is, to whom (or, more impersonal, where) do suffering and death point? For those two markers are surely passed by us all, without exception, along our earthly journey. And if, as faith may prompt us, the answer is God, then all other questions become circumstantial—matters of timing. Of course, it makes the loss of a loved one no less painful, for it is the unbearable separation itself that hurts and never fully heals—however temporal or temporary that separation may appear in the prism of eternity. That pain, the open wound of grief, is the price of love. But if we believe that our beloved—and we are all beloved by God—has returned, by whatever untimely and perplexing route, home to the God of love, who paid that very price of pain on the cross, then we cannot reasonably grieve for any but ourselves—the temporary survivors. Those whom we desperately miss have already arrived before us at the manger. Our road is longer and lonelier than even that of the Magi, but it leads to the same place—in God's time. The question is what to do along the way.

THURSDAY, MAY 16, 2002

Oxford was a letdown after Cambridge, or so it seems in memory. The opening lines of that sad poem I had to memorize in Buckley capture the relative mood after sunny, bucolic Cambridge, with the series of bridges along the Backs, the river Cam with the punting boats, the lazy aura of end-less summer: "I saw the spires of Oxford as I was passing by, the gray spires of Oxford against a pearl-gray sky." The tour of Christ College with the chaplain and a view of Oxford from atop a cupola somewhat brightened my dim view of this university town, but it would take another fifteen years and the opening episodes of *Brideshead Revisited* to revise that view and infuse it with the romance and beauty I reserved for Cambridge—and, across the Atlantic, Princeton.

After lunch at a professor's house, we took off for Woodcott, my Pease cousins' country place in Hampshire. The village of Upper Woodcott comprised this house, once a vicarage, parts of which date back to the Middle Ages, and a small stone church, separated from the house by a tiny grave-yard and a fenced-in paddock for my cousins' horses. We arrived in time for tea, followed by a short horseback ride and then tennis on a homemade grass court beside the garden. I had never seen grass so manicured except on greens of golf courses: there are, after all, some advantages to English weather. Those first days at Woodcott were but a foretaste of the happiest summer days I can recall spending anywhere.

SATURDAY, MAY 18, 2002

My first tour of Europe—from Amsterdam to Brussels and Paris—was a long weekend whirlwind. Yet I would have gladly traded it for an extra five days in the English countryside. We flew to Amsterdam and went to "a museum with Rembrandts" (surely the Rijksmuseum) before meeting a cousin for lunch in some modern tower restaurant and touring the canals on a barge. Then we boarded a train for Brussels—the first time I'd ever eaten dinner on a train—and arrived in Brussels in time to walk about and see the main square aglow with lights. The next morning we drove across the border to France, where at Thumeries we stayed at the country estate of the mother of the great film director Louis Malle. His brother François had been at Harvard with Uncle Ned.

My most vivid memory was a story Mme. Malle told about the beautiful Degas painting on the dining room wall. As an elaborate amusement for a visiting American friend, who had an equally dominating mother, her sons François and Bernard had secretly taken it down and replaced it in its frame with an exact copy. Then, at dinner one night, François suddenly jumped up from the table and complained that something looked wrong with the picture; it had been damaged, it was ruined—and with that, he took his table knife and began to slash it in disgust. His mother nearly fainted with horror until the pristine original was brought back into the room. It seemed perfectly reasonable to me that such a household of high imagination if not high jinks had produced one of France's greatest filmmakers. Years later my uncle told me that the scene was reproduced in Louis's film *Murmur of the Heart*.

SUNDAY, MAY 19, 2002

Back in England, and in my new Arcadia, called Woodcott, cousin Jonathan's grandmother Lady Portman arrived for the weekend and promptly took the two of us off to the Newbury Races, my first trip to the track. Jonathan was already a veteran and knew every horse and jockey and trainer, and he was uncanny in his ability to predict the outcomes. He had no interest in placing bets himself but was happy to tutor me in doing something sensible. And in fact, I won the last race; or rather, Petite Marmite won it, as Jonathan had predicted. Between races I enjoyed my new discovery of English hard cider at the bar, where at the age of fifteen I was served whatever I wanted. How much my glowing memories of this first day at the races owe to Woodpecker cider only God knows.

That evening, cousin Sandy came down from London for the weekend. He was amazing in his ability, at six foot seven, to navigate through doorways built for inhabitants no more than five feet tall, five hundred years earlier. He played the role of paterfamilias in the most wry and understated way that defined coolness as the highest compliment a teenager could bestow in the sixties—on either side of the Atlantic. On Saturday, we returned to Newbury Races; this time, I had my younger cousin Christopher as my charge. Together we did quite well with our bets and forged the beginning of a bond that, twenty years later, would prompt me to name our second son after him. He is now the master of Woodcott, and his youngest daughter, Carola Rosemary, is my goddaughter. Whenever I think of that cherished honor I hear Gore Vidal's witty rejoinder "Always a godfather, never a god." Gore may be right; but this goddaughter is an angel, and her home was my foretaste of heaven.

THURSDAY, MAY 23, 2002

Today, the last day I can claim to be fifty, I motored down to Princeton as both pilgrim and tourist—to revisit memories of my sojourn there and, on a more practical plane, to pick up Charlie's belongings at the end of his second undergraduate year. I always love crossing Lake Carnegie on arrival, and I parked at the University Press, in the visitor space behind the Scribner Building, where my great-grandfather, grandfather, father, and finally I had attended meetings for most of the past century. From there I walked over to my old club, Ivy, and visited the library I had newly refurbished in memory of my grandfather; only the books looked tattered with time. Then on to the music building, where I found an old Mason & Hamlin piano dating from my student years and earlier, in one of the underground practice rooms. It served for a brief rendition of "Bist du bei mir," which I had been practicing in the car all the way along the Jersey Turnpike, and enough of my Haydn sonata to remind me how much more I need to put into it again, measure by measure.

Then on to the art museum, to see the exhibition of the Van Dyck *Ecce Homo.* The large Picasso statue out front is about to be removed and relocated after three decades to give way to the library expansion—no loss. I only wish the new museum director had not rearranged the museum so that we have to pass through the antiseptic (at best), toxic (at worst) display of contemporary art before encountering the treasures of centuries past. But it was good to see my Bernini crucifix again before the masterpieces of Van Dyck. I was amazed to find that the Van Dyck etching I had found in London and given to the museum to go with its *Mocking of Christ* was the frontispiece of the catalog; like any good tourist, I could not resist purchasing this souvenir of my years as a student there. The security guard turned out to be Catholic and very knowledgeable about the art he protected, and as a young soldier stationed in Europe had met the pope—and written a book about Rome. On my way out, I looked about, and then touched the bronze of the Bernini crucifix that had once been mine, as though a holy statue still in St. Peter's, where such tangible acts of adoration are allowed. If caught, I was prepared to claim a proprietary right to touch that one object—still sacred and liturgical in my eyes. I had told the guard of how, before I had donated it to the museum, I had brought it over to the chapel one Good Friday for the veneration of the cross, where hundreds of us kissed the bronze figure reverently, in mute procession.

I proceeded to the library, where there was an exhibition on Woodrow Wilson, which I glimpsed briefly before heading below to find a copy of Greene's *The Potting Shed* to check out and bring home. I stopped first in the Scribner Room to pay homage to the family portraits I had left there a few years ago when refurbishing it as a memorial to my father. There I found E. M. Forster's story "The Celestial Omnibus," first read to me by Greaves at St. Paul's. It was his favorite allegory—a magnificently Baroque fantasy—about the truth of poetry. I had forgotten that the first driver of that omnibus was Sir Thomas Browne; I never knew that I had first encountered him there, long before I discovered him as author of my favorite maxim, "Light is the shadow of God."

In the chapel, a few minutes later, just in time for the noon Mass, I saw that maxim illustrated by the most radiant stained glass windows I have ever seen—thanks to the recent multimillion-dollar renovation of Cram's neo-Gothic chapel. *Non novum sed nove*: I had never seen those windows in such a light—or rather, such light transmuted through glass. I lingered after Mass in the Marquand Transept, talking to the chaplain, Father Tom, long enough for my son Charlie to appear.

Memorial Day has taken me back to the script of *The Potting Shed*, to reread that powerful conclusion of the meeting thirty years later between the alcoholic priest and the nephew he loved and allegedly raised from the dead though prayer. In his cups and bereft of any vestige of faith, at first he reverts to the official Callifer line of denial when asked if it were possible that his nephew was dead when he found him, not merely in a coma. But how could that be? "If you were dead," he insists with impeccable logic, "it would have been a miracle, and if it were a miracle God would exist. That hideous picture there"—the Sacred Heart of Jesus on his wall—"would have a meaning. But if God existed, why should he take away his faith from me? I served him well. I go on serving him. The saints have dark nights, but not for thirty years. They have moments when they remember what it felt like to believe." Surprised that his nephew thinks he could be of any use to anyone at this point, the priest presently adds, in a non sequitur, "It was an awful moment finding you dead in that way."

"Dead?"

"I mean you seemed to me dead," the priest equivocates.

"What did you do?"

"I'd have given my life to you—but what could I do? I could only pray. I supposed I offered something in return—something I valued—not spirits then. I really thought I loved God in those days. I said, 'Let him live, God. I love him, let him live. I will give you anything if you let him live.' But what had I got to give him? I was a poor man. I said, 'Take away what I love most. Take . . . take . . .' "

His nephew interjects: "Take away my faith, but let him live."

"Did you hear me?"

"Yes. You were speaking a long way off and I came towards you through a cave of darkness. I didn't want to come. I struggled not to come. But something pushed me to you."

"Something?"

"Or somebody."

The priest begins to weep, adding, "I even forgot what I said to Him, until you came."

"Do you really believe . . . ?"

"He answered my prayer, didn't he? Look around you. Look at this room. It makes sense, doesn't it? You must forgive me. I'm tired and a little drunk. I haven't thought about that day for thirty years. Will you see me to my room? It's dark on the landing." Then, pausing to look up at the hideous picture, he concludes, "I thought I had lost Him forever."

In the final act, an act Greene himself found dramatically unsatisfactory—something I have never understood, based on my repeated experience in the audience—James confronts his ex-wife, whom he now wishes to woo again and marry, as someone he loves for the first time and sees anew—*non nova sed nove*, as it were—as "someone who will never die forever." When Sarah protests that she doesn't belong to his new world of God and prayer, James retorts that he doesn't want to pray, he doesn't want God, he doesn't love God. "But He's there—it's no good pretending. He is in my lungs like air."

To his mother, he admits that a miracle in the family is a bad case. When she asks him for proof, he simply replies that seeing his uncle's room was proof enough. "I've seen my uncle. I don't need any other proof of God than the lack of Him there. I've seen the mark of His footsteps going away."

"It's a cruel God you believe in."

"Perhaps He had no choice."

"A God who can't choose?" His mother is incredulous.

James answers in what must surely be one of the most succinct formulations of Greene's credo: "God is conditional, isn't He? If He's all-powerful, He can't weaken. If He knows everything, He can't forget. If He's love, He can't hate. Perhaps if someone asks with enough love, He has to give."

"People are asking all the time."

"Are they? It needs a lot of belief. And a lot of love."

"But your uncle doesn't believe."

"Oh yes, he does. I left him praying."

Looking back, I have no doubt that these scenes did more to launch my spiritual quest for miracles, certainty, and unqualified claims to truth than any course or chapel service I attended in the next four years of schooling.

Greene, at his Catholic christening decades earlier, said he chose St. Thomas "the Doubter" as his patron saint. But then, this was the very doubter who exclaimed on seeing the risen Lord—even without touching the wounds as he had insisted on doing—"My Lord and my God," the very words we utter each time we receive his sacramental body at Communion. The depths of faith rarely run deeper than in Greene's most insistent doubters—above all, himself.

SUNDAY, JUNE 2, 2002

Today, the Feast of Corpus Christi, I learned in Father Mario's homily at St. Jean Baptiste that some of the California redwoods date back as far as King David—three thousand years. These ancient, miraculously durable trees, it appears, do not have unusually deep roots to withstand millennia of wind and hostile weather. Their roots, in fact, are surprisingly shallow; what sets them apart from others is their closeness, which in turn has resulted in their roots being intertwined and reinforced like a tightly woven fabric. They stand as a symbol of the power of interdependence, of community—indeed, of the Church, or body of Christ, composed of so many millions of bodies and souls, yet one.

I also relearned today something I had long forgotten, despite those years of ancient Greek at St. Paul's: that our word *poem* derives from the Greek "to make." If creation is one vast poem, then our divine maker is, literally, a poet first and last, alpha and omega. This epiphany, as the stained glass windows glowed in twilight reflected by the windows of surrounding apartment houses, is cast in a simple, one-word translation: to see the universe as a vast epic (or lyrical) poem. God the poet requires no great leap of imagination or sublimation of science—only an equation between word and creation. "In the beginning was the Word."

We celebrate that literal link on this special feast day: by equating bread with body (and wine with blood) our Lord established at the Last Supper an eternal Eucharistic banquet that ties past, present, and end-time—the *eschaton*—more durably than even those enmeshed roots of the redwoods. This simple meal, made endlessly holy through the renewal of Christ's sacrifice, is the sustenance that has sustained the Christian community through centuries of war, divisions, suffering, sin, and scandals. I was glad that on this particular feast I happened to be at a parish tended by the Blessed Sacrament Fathers; I had been running late, and it was a couple of minutes closer than St. Vincent Ferrer. Another moment of serendipity.

This Sunday is the much-needed response to the malaise I have shared with so many others as our Church stumbles through its most recent scandal of abuse and betrayal. The sin of silence can be deafening; it reverberates for a long time. We still witness the effects of Pope Pius's silence in the face of the intentional extermination of God's Chosen People, our spiritual ancestors in faith. But the ever hopeful, ever renewing words of consecration, "This is my body, this is my blood," are sufficient to answer even the most poignant of lamentations and reproaches. I only wish that the feast were still called by its Latin name, Corpus Christi. That harmonious pairing of words better captures the poetry of the miracle than its English translation. Perhaps my father was right to insist that I stick with Latin a while longer; at this far distance the reward is less the (much diminished) ability to read it than the pleasure of hearing it. That, too, may be a matter of poetry—perhaps even of music.

MONDAY, JUNE 3, 2002

During a rare weekend away from school, Uncle Ned took me to a movie in Boston that moved me in a way no other film has ever done; it was to change my religious identity within three years of its winning the Academy Award in 1967 for best picture—*A Man for All Seasons.* I had known nothing about the history of Henry VIII's battle of will with the pope, a conflict that led to his break from Roman authority and his establishing the Anglican Church (with himself as supreme head). The price was the life of Sir Thomas More, Henry's chief minister, the lord chancellor of England, who went to the scaffold rather than compromise his religious conviction that Christ's investiture of St. Peter and his successors as head of the Church and his vicar on earth superseded the boundless ambitions of a talented king on the path to tyranny.

Paul Scofield's rendering of More was intoxicating; he made Robert Bolt's prose sound positively Shakespearean in its richness and resonance. As soon as I got back to St. Paul's, I checked out the play from the library and later bought a copy in town. I set to reciting (in private) the best of More's speeches. My favorite was the one to his son-in-law, Roper, which begins, "God made angels to show him splendor, as he made animals for their innocence and plants for their simplicity. But Man he made to serve him in the tangle of his mind." More's wit and legal dexterity—all underscored by his uncompromising faith—created the perfect historical model to capture the imagination of an adolescent during the unfolding of the Vietnam tragedy that cast our own President Johnson as a railing Henry, determined to have his own way, come what may. The showdown between More and his accusers in the final trial scene was better than anything I recalled from a childhood of watching Perry Mason.

More is convicted of treason and sentenced to death upon the perjury of his former protégé Richard Rich, who has been rewarded with a gold chain of office. When More asks what it signifies, and is told it goes with his recent appointment as the king's official in charge of Wales, he replies with the most understated irony I have ever heard uttered on film: "Why, Richard, it profiteth a man nothing to give his soul for the whole world . . . but for Wales . . ." He tells this latter-day Judas that he is sorrier for Rich's perjury than for his own peril. Finally, facing his beheading with equanimity and unflinching faith, he tells the executioner not to be afraid of his office: "You send me to God." When the turncoat Archbishop Cranmer, who has sided with Henry, counters (as much in envy as in doubt), "You are very sure of that, Sir Thomas?" More replies, "He will not refuse one who is so blithe to go to him." The ax falls as the screen goes black.

As soon as I got back to New York on my next vacation I watched the movie again, the first of several viewings. When people ask me today what turned me Catholic, I reply that it was seeing *A Man for All Seasons* as a fourth-former at St. Paul's—and in the company of my Anglican-priest uncle.

WEDNESDAY, JUNE 5, 2002

Earlier that winter, in chapel, we all had to rehearse the congregational singing of something new and anathema to me—a so-called folk Mass, a rock version of traditional pieces like the Kyrie, Gloria, Credo, Sanctus, and Agnus Dei—all in English (no problem), and all set to accompaniment by electric guitars, synthesizer, and percussion (big problem). I considered it a profane assault on the church music I loved so dearly. The pagans had invaded Rome—or in this case, Canterbury—a second time. I wrote a scathing op-ed piece for our student newspaper on this descent into musical purgatory, contrasting it to the Masses of my beloved Mozart. I did eventually purchase the record that was made of it, and listening to it years later, I was puzzled by my initial horror. It was quite tame, harmonic and musically pleasant as compared with the real hackwork then invading the churches of our Roman brethren in the wake of Vatican II. But that discovery lay three years away, post Woodstock. I remember one of the clergy pointing out to me that Mozart's church music had been considered too profane by some of the ecclesiastical authorities of his day; I did not buy that argument. Mozart had genius on his side—along with angels of the heavenly choir. I may have had a soft spot for Victorian schmaltz, but not for second-rate rock—at least in church. Yet I sang along, and somewhere my voice is recorded on that LP as part of the "folk," a term I abhorred—until I later became a Roman Catholic. Now it seems a nostalgic term of endearment. Yet I still prefer Mozart.

FRIDAY, JUNE 7, 2002

The one quality of Agatha Christie's mysteries that makes them so satisfying—indeed addictive—to me is the neat resolution at the end of each of them, the final summing up and tying up of loose ends and scattered clues, like the final bars of a Mozart symphony, a return to the tonic chord. I don't like loose ends, or nagging questions, or doubts of recollection. My earliest "What happened that?" question still resounds in my ear. Each small piece that falls into place, each small confirmation or correction of memory, is a small epiphany.

But today the best discovery came at the end of the afternoon. I had been distracted during the last of the midday Masses at St. Patrick's. The Feast of the Sacred Heart of Jesus does not resonate: it sounds like an ecclesiastical version of a Hallmark card holiday to be illustrated with corresponding sentimentality—a Victorian Jesus. The earlier discovery that one of Chris's blazers brought back from school was not his, but had been borrowed from a classmate for the commencement ceremony last week and then forgotten, took me north to the FedEx office on Eighty-sixth Street; once uptown, I decided to walk a bit farther and stop into the Church of St. Thomas More, my first adoptive Catholic parish in New York, and the church where both our sons were later baptized. More to the point, it was the church that honored the "Man for All Seasons."

I expected the church to be empty, but there was a scattering of worshipers keeping watch during the Exposition of the Sacrament. I had forgotten that it was the first Friday of the month. As I knelt in what had been our family pew, with its small plaque inscribed to honor my father, I gazed at the gleaming gold monstrance containing the simple white Host. On each side was a candelabrum. One of the lights had gone out and I was briefly tempted to go up and relight it, until discretion won out. (My fellow worshipers would surely not have appreciated the distraction.) My first thought was how alien this Tridentine devotion is to me, a post–Vatican II Catholic and, before that, a confirmed Episcopalian. To me, the sacrament is embedded in the Eucharist—the Mass, or service of Holy Communion. This adoration of the abstracted Host is still a devotion to be mastered. But as I looked around for some aid in meditation, I caught sight of the glowing window of the Adoration of the Magi—a multihued Epiphany—and, below it, the stark wooden crucifix on the wall. And I thought: This is the central miracle of creation, after all—that the same historical Jesus in the manger two thousand years ago, executed on that cross three decades later, is here today, present in this simple white wafer of bleached wheat. This is the miracle of transubstantiation—well beyond and above, and yet deeper than, all the other cosmological wonders in the heavens. Then, distracted by the gleaming metal pipes of the new organ at the left, I wondered: Is this miracle any more incredible or mysterious than the transubstantiation of air, of wind, through those pipes into the heavenly music of Bach or Mozart or indeed the Handel "Hornpipe" I heard earlier today at St. Patrick's? Is the existence of such ethereal music, produced and carried by nothing more than the air we breathe, any less miraculous than the presence of Christ, in both divinity and humanity, in the substance of bread, the food that sustains us? Once again I hear the words of Strauss's librettist Hugo von Hofmannsthal: *"Musik ist eine heilige Kunst."* Yes, music is a holy art—also a mystery and a sacrament.

SUNDAY, JUNE 9, 2002

I am profoundly uncomfortable—or maybe just inept—inventing people, places, and events. I'd rather interpret the real ones—or the inspired inventions of others. I suppose that some are born to compose and others to play from the score: I surely am among the latter. I never played the piano by ear, nor improvised; but I loved to take the notes on the page and make them my own. The same instinct applied to literature and drama. By the end of that fourth-form year, it was clear who was my Mozart of the spoken word: Shakespeare.

Greaves had decided to stage Shakespeare's *Richard II* as the next fall play. He was himself to play my uncle, John of Gaunt, duke of Lancaster; my other uncle, the duke of York, was to be the other great Shakespearean on the faculty, George Tracy of the Classics Department. But to my ears— opened by Gielgud's recording—I had been given the richest role in all of Shakespeare, or at least the most lyrical and overtly theatrical, to the point of exquisite self-indulgence. Richard's soliloquies were like great tenor arias—the closest I'd ever come to singing on the stage of Mem Hall. As for the usurper of my crown and the future King Henry IV? That role was played forcefully by bass-baritone William Rogers, today the president of the Trust for Public Land!

MONDAY, JUNE 10, 2002

When I returned home for summer vacation, I had not only a royal part to learn before rehearsals started in September, but a new horse to get to know—and ride—before leaving for England to spend a month with Jonathan and his family at Woodcott. Jonathan is today one of the leading racehorse trainers in France—an extraordinary achievement for an Englishman in that chauvinistic land. Last night, quite by chance, I turned on C-SPAN and saw the ceremonies surrounding the Queen's Jubilee. It reminded me of that year, fifteen (not fifty) years into her reign, back in the summer of 1967, when I felt she was as much my queen.

Before I left for England my father wrote a letter to his author C. P. Snow asking whether his "English son" might come and pay a visit to him and Lady Snow in London. By the time I arrived at Woodcott, Snow's reply was waiting for me; my cousins were as amused as I was puzzled by the fact that under his signature, a very neat "Snow," his typist had added (in parentheses and all uppercase letters) "LORD SNOW." He was obviously very pleased with his life peerage, bestowed by the queen at the behest of his fellow Labor politician, Prime Minister Harold Wilson. I did, in fact, go in and visit the Snows at their house on Cromwell Road, where I met their son, Philip, who was then a student at that most un-Laborite Eton, along with my cousin Jonathan. Philip was so skilled in the classics I was struggling to master that I felt like a latter-day Tom Sawyer coming from the colonies for tea. But to my surprise I discovered among my father's office papers, shortly after he died, a letter from Snow about that visit. It was most complimentary, though with a bemused observation by the novelist that had he not known my father he would have assumed I was simply another English boy. It wasn't really an act, at least not a conscious one; I think that during that perfect summer in Woodcott I simply became what I wanted to be.

TUESDAY, JUNE 11, 2002

I settled into the blue guest room, opposite Jonathan's room, for my month's stay at Woodcott—except when weekend guests took it over and I went camping in the nursery. The first book I pulled from the shelf to read was an illustrated account of the trial and beheading of my royal namesake, Charles. I was utterly fascinated and equally horrified by this incredible account of the overthrow of a king by his own subjects. My incredulity must have been ideal preparation for learning the role of his predecessor in such tragedy, King Richard II—the last Plantagenet and last king of England with a credible claim to rule by divine right. All his successors derived their thrones from a lineage traced back to his usurping cousin, Henry Bolingbroke.

Meanwhile the London *Times* reported more immediate tragedies—the race riots engulfing America that summer and the endlessly escalating war in Vietnam. Yet both seemed civilizations away from the farmhouse in Woodcott, as remote as the civil war between the Roundheads and Cavaliers three centuries earlier. There life continued seamlessly from the summer before: weekend races at Newbury and Goodwood with Jonathan and Lady Portman. My cousin had already grown so expert in rating the horses and jockeys that, following his predictions, I almost won the Tote Jackpot one day at Newbury—a huge purse that went to the bettors that correctly picked, before the first bell, all six winners that day. I was batting a thousand right up to the last race—which I lost. The suspense was excruciatingly wonderful; it was all so improbable that the final loss carried no real sting; it couldn't dispel the thrills of winning the five previous races. But after that I have never been lured by the prospect of gambling on any event, except as a token of camaraderie.

Nine-year-old Christopher, meanwhile, successfully ignored the horses in favor of the flourishing lettuces, carrots, and beans of his kitchen garden. He distinguished himself as a natural green thumb at a local garden show, beaming with pride as he returned with his version of horse-show ribbons. During a sibling debate as to what was the most dangerous of the family sports—tennis, riding, cricket—I argued on Christopher's behalf that his gardening was in fact the most lethal: you could lose your balance picking his huge heads of lettuce and fall into the nearby bramble of stinging nettles. After watching a test match at Lord's, I was convinced that whatever the relative dangers, cricket was surely the most boring of English pastimes. But its slow-motion dignity redeemed the lack of action—a tableau vivant of landscape with perfectly starched figures.

WEDNESDAY, JUNE 12, 2002

Before coming over to England that summer, I had concocted a fantasy future beyond St. Paul's: I would apply to Eton for a postgraduate year, and from there proceed to Cambridge for my university years, to be followed by the Royal Academy of Dramatic Arts leading ultimately, I hoped, to the Royal Shakespeare Company. This English dream was no doubt reinforced on rainy days at Woodcott by my continued reading of assorted Agatha Christie mysteries and an obscure novel by Somerset Maugham called *Theatre*. But before I had even arrived, my plan was already undermined by deepening roots in Far Hills, a result of our new cottage and my new horse, Mischief. Foxhunting became the central event of my weekly schedule as I got ready for the return to St. Paul's. Mischief had only one problem, true to his name: he was wont to kick horses and riders who got too close. I soon had to sport a red ribbon on his tail to warn others to keep a safe distance. Among my companions in the field was our former first lady, who often took Caroline and John along on their ponies. I had the great privilege of speaking to her only once in my lifetime, as we waited in line to take a jump: "I hope my horse didn't kick at you." Thank God, it didn't.

A family friend named Frank Markoe lived in the large Tudor house about a mile up Holland Road from us; it had once belonged to my mother's uncle Thorn Kissel. His daughters had gone to Europe that summer with their English au pair and their neighbor Holly Pyne; before coming home they had bought out most of Carnaby Street in London in order to transform the downstairs, stripped of furniture, into a sixties disco for a big local bash before we all returned to our boarding schools. The rock band was a group from Buckley days called the Four Fifths, led by my cousin Alfred Vanderbilt. Virtually every teenager in Far Hills was there. But I have another reason to look back nostalgically on that party and to hang framed pictures of it on our wall today: a dozen years later the older of the two swinging sisters became my sister-in-law; the younger, my wife.

THURSDAY, JUNE 13, 2002

I saw a photograph of a young Alfred Vanderbilt today, not as a rock musician but as Gilbert and Sullivan's "modern major general" in Paul Rotella's scrabooks of operettas produced during his years at Buckley. For most of today I have been researching and writing a memorial article on Paul for the next newsletter. Nothing illumines or reveals a person more than stories preserved and shared. Two reveal important facets of his sparkling personality that still shines beyond the horizon—the one, his candor; the other, his childlike wonder.

At Parents Day in 1953, Paul met the actress Rosalind Russell, who had a son at the school and was currently starring in the hit Broadway musical *Wonderful Town*, to rave reviews. When Paul complimented her on her success, she replied with charming false modesty, "Well, you know, Mr. Rotella, I can't sing a note." Before he could catch himself, he chimed in, "Yes, I know." Too late. Every teacher got a free ticket to the show—save one.

Paul never had a credit card—or a driver's license. But on one trip out west, riding along the interstate through the desert outside Tehachapi, California, he offered to relieve the driver. It was a straight road, no other cars in sight, so why not? But as the speedometer hit eighty-five, a police car appeared in the rearview mirror. No problem. The two men deftly changed places in the front seat while the car gradually slowed down—like crossing hands in a Chopin étude—unfortunately in full view of the officer, who ordered Paul (now once again in the passenger seat) into his patrol car. "You don't have a *license?*" the officer asked incredulously. "I'm going to have to give you a citation." Paul replied that he was honored: he thought he was being given an award.

Paul's posthumous message—received last week, more than a month following his death—has added a final flourish to his recessional: "While seemingly macabre, even though it is a natural occurrence and conclusion, this occasion is a 'first' for me. I have met my Maker (hopefully on most forgiving terms) after a happy terrestrial sojourn. Much of that happiness emanated from your friendship, wrought with vivid, warm and very comforting memories. For that I am most grateful to you. And so . . . *Arrivederci!*"

SATURDAY, JUNE 15, 2002

My favorite final movement in all music is the rondo allegro of Beethoven's Fifth Piano Concerto, the *Emperor.* The first time I heard it live in concert was also the most memorable performance I have ever attended. I can still place myself in the seat, close to the stage, enough to the left to have a perfect view of Van Cliburn's hands and the keyboard they dominated. It was one of those open-air concerts at Tanglewood in the 1960s. The excitement of this pyrotechnical performance was doubly indelible, for the applause after the conclusion of that triumphant movement was so deafening and sustained that, after innumerable bows, Van returned to his seat and the conductor took up the baton once again, and the entire movement was repeated as an encore.

I have never witnessed such an encore, with full orchestra, and it lost nothing in the repetition. From that day forth, I have never tired of hearing the *Emperor* Concerto, and no recording of it—not even Rubenstein's—has displaced Cliburn's as my touchstone of perfection. The work seemed to have been written for him. Perhaps it was: in God's eyes, or ears, what difference does a century or so make? It's one of those instances, profoundly subjective yet objectively defensible, when one performer takes ownership of a musical masterpiece (or operatic role) for a lifetime. For me, Van owns Beethoven's *Emperor*, just as Elisabeth Schwarzkopf owns Strauss's Marschallin; or Mary Costa, Puccini's Musetta; or Flicka von Stade, Mozart's Cherubino. They become the frame of reference, what Shakespeare calls "the constant image in the eye of the beloved." Others may come along and borrow these roles for an evening—or even a career—but their ownership remains secure.

THURSDAY, JUNE 20, 2002

A call from London yesterday reawakened the Mitty within: it was the producer of the BBC/Bravo documentary on my undercover Rubens adventure of a decade ago. She wanted to know whether I would be available to fly to Miami in July to film my role in the undercover operation. The answer was a resounding affirmative. Walter Mitty is always available for a film crew.

The call brought back memories of a one-act play with a title too true to be good: *The Morning After.* Surely the reason that schoolboy play looms so menacingly in memory is its immediate juxtaposition with triumph and tragedy in the spring of 1968. In March, just before our spring vacation, we took it to Durham, New Hampshire, where we won the statewide one-act play competition. All four of us in the cast were elected by the judges to the All New Hampshire Cast, which gave us a nice boost to the New England Competition held in Providence, Rhode Island, the following month. Greaves drove us down in a school station wagon for the weekend competition. We students camped out at the home of a local high school boy who was also competing in the event. I remember the pizza supper, the large theater at Providence College, and the packed showers after all the performances—but nothing of a rehearsal or even the performance itself, which won us the highest rating. Perhaps the trauma of the return trip—"the day after"—has cast the pall of amnesia over most of that lost weekend.

We had seen very little of our director, Greaves, that weekend; we assumed he was mingling and, later, celebrating with the other faculty from all over New England. He seemed very detached at the farewell luncheon. We soon discovered why, when one of us happened to open the glove compartment in the car before leaving and discovered a flask of whiskey. But it was only after taking off for New Hampshire that we realized how bad our situation really was. I was in the rear of the station wagon as it swerved in and out of its lane at eighty miles an hour. It was terrifying. After a few vain entreaties to slow down, we finally managed to get Greaves to stop at a service station for a break. Then three of us mutinied and refused to go farther. Only the youngest, who played the Boy, obeyed his order to get back in the car and return to school. The rest of us called a parent and arranged to be picked up and taken back to St. Paul's.

We had done the right thing but I was sick at the thought of the consequences. I returned to Drury house for the night; the next morning I heard from one of the cast that Greaves had said to him that we probably had cost him his job. He was scheduled to see the rector later that day; in desperation, I, too, made an appointment to talk with the absolute ruler of our little realm.

FRIDAY, JUNE 21, 2002

Here, with only a couple of minutes left in the longest day of the year, a midsummer's eve, I am at a loss to describe that moment of light that pierced the gloom welling up inside me, spilling into silent tears, as I faced the rector in his office and sought to intercede on behalf of my mentor, teacher, and friend. I felt certain, as I am sure Greaves did, that the price to be paid for his drinking—indeed for endangering the lives of the students in his charge—was dismissal from the school. Students were expelled for far less. But I was wrong. I heard no words of justice or punishment—only those of grace. Mr. Warren spoke of getting help for Greaves; he explained that he was arranging for him to go to a rehab facility for as long as needed, probably a matter of weeks, perhaps months. But he would return to the school as soon as he was well again. I don't remember his words, but I do recall facing not the rector so often described as aloof and forbidding by his critics, but a pastor, priest, and man of God. From that moment on, my gratitude and loyalty to him would never waver. He embodied the words of the school prayer recited at the end of each Sunday evensong: "Grant, O Lord, that in all the joys of life, we may never forget to be kind. Help us to be unselfish in friendship, thoughtful of those less happy than ourselves, and eager to bear the burdens of others, through Jesus Christ our Savior. Amen." Let that be this midsummer night's prayer.

SUNDAY, JUNE 23, 2002

Monsignor Frontiero, assistant to Archbishop Martino, the papal envoy to the United Nations, said the Sunday afternoon Mass today at St. Jean Baptiste. His homily dwelt on the central paradox of our Christian faith: that our new life begins with a death, whether death itself or, more often, the many smaller deaths we experience in the course of our lives. That spring day when I helped James Greaves pack up his small Austin-Healey for his journey south to a rehab (then called a "sanitarium") and waved a final good-bye, I felt as though my best friend had died. I walked to evening meal in the daze of deep mourning. We were reading *A Separate Peace* in English class that term; like Gene, I felt responsible for the course of events that led to my grief—the despair of a Judas over the betrayal of a friend. But a couple of weeks later, I received a letter from James, which opened with the absolution I so badly needed: "The whole dreary business of the Sunday before last has had one very positive and valuable result (as well as several also very valuable side-effects): it has helped to point out and underscore my *real* friends and has shown to me a depth of friendship on which I could never before have counted with such confidence." Receiving these healing words, I was already finding new life and joy in the most unlikely of roles.

Before the debacle of *The Morning After*, Greaves had cast me as Madame

Desmortes in the spring play—Jean Anouilh's *Ring Round the Moon*, as adapted and translated for the English stage by Christopher Fry. My character's name meant literally "of the dead," but this spirited, wheelchair-bound, ancient grande dame was the ultimate escape back into a life—of comedy, romance, and transcendent role-playing. The old gal was out of this world, and that is where she took me.

Since I never had to walk anywhere or even move about the stage, except for some abrupt wheeling around, I was free to focus entirely on the instruments of voice and eyes to convey that "most characterful of characters," as the reviewer (the future Senator John Kerry's younger brother) described her. I drew her affectionately from both my grandmothers—with an added dash of Dame Margaret Rutherford's Miss Marple. Before leaving, Greaves had explained why he wanted a boy in the part: as women age, their voices deepen, they sound more masculine, and so an adolescent boy would be far more convincing than a girl. That insight liberated me to model my natural voice, not some falsetto caricature of it. The play is pure romantic comedy—my favorite genre. And Madame becomes, in the end, the *dea ex machina* who sets all the romantic entanglements aright—the unlikely, but effective, voice of love and reason. It was as profoundly healing as it was fun.

TUESDAY, JUNE 25, 2002

Today was a day of unexpected epiphanies, small pieces of mosaic falling into colorful patterns—with the hint of a contour. It started with a trip to the twenty-second floor of Rock Center, to exchange my mother's air ticket for another. As I took the new one from the young travel agent, I thought of his predecessor, Joan Clifford, who had died a year ago, soon after Ritchie and I had returned from Venice and Paris for my fiftieth birthday; it was the last trip she lived to plan for our family. A couple of hours later, I was beside the altar of St. Patrick's for my weekly stint as cantor and feeling drowsy when not called upon to sing, when suddenly my nodding head jolted up as the priest prayed for the repose of the soul of Joan Clifford, in whose memory the Mass was being offered. It was the first time I had ever known the honoree being invoked at the high altar—and here I had been just standing in her office. Once again, What are the odds? I ask myself. I left the cathedral by a secret door in the apse and took a new route, as I wanted to stop by the parish office and find out who had arranged that Mass for Joan. But I was detained almost an hour, in the garden by the statue of St. Francis, as a jovial man thanked me for the singing. He seemed—and was, after a sort—a casually dressed tourist from out of town. But as we started talking about the cathedral, the music, the new rector, and on along the links of a chain of associations, I learned he was in fact a priest from Delaware, Father McMahon. The vast Catholic world suddenly seemed no broader than two or at most three degrees of separation. Amidst the gloom of politics, cover-ups, envy, and ambition in the higher echelons (if no more than in other institutions entrusted to us humans), he reminded me of two central truths about our Church. The first was the writer Flannery O'Connor's saying that the Catholic Church was "here comes everybody." The second was his father's simple insight that it is the place we go "to find the sacrament."

Yesterday I had been walking nostalgically around the vast, almost empty, yet resonant church of my youth, St. Bart's. Alone with my memories, I felt the tug to return, to call it home again. Yet something was missing there: the architectural beauty, the evocative spaces that called forth a parade of images from the past, the philosophically appealing openness were not enough to reclaim me as more than a grateful revisitor. Later that afternoon, I went to Mass at St. Vincent's. I found there what binds me to that more ancient rite (however uncomfortable those bonds may feel at times like these): the "here comes everybody" to share that precious sacrament, preserved after the Mass was over and we had dispersed, behind the flickering votive lamp of the tabernacle. The words from Brahms's *Requiem* filled the void: "How lovely is thy dwelling place, O Lord of Hosts."

THURSDAY, JUNE 27, 2002

It was a Requiem—and a Kennedy—that brought me back a second time to St. Patrick's Cathedral. I was at St. Paul's when the terrible news came of RFK's assassination. But thanks to the magic of airwaves, I was able to join the thousand mourners and dignitaries packed in St. Patrick's for the Requiem Mass for our assassinated senator a few days later. I followed the Mass, for the first time, with no sense of any real distance from the familiar Episcopal service, owing to the introduction of the English vernacular after Vatican II. The service itself was of only passing interest as my eyes were fixated on the people who played their heartbreaking parts in this all-too-real drama: the Kennedy men who carried the coffin, Ethel and her children all in a row, the matriarch Rose, and the next in line to carry the torch, Ted, whose eulogy touched the heart with the simple eloquence of a grieving brother. Their overwhelming stoicism was too much to bear.

This was the moment I first equated the superhuman equanimity and courage and generosity of the grieving Kennedys with their Roman Catholic faith. Like Sir Thomas More, they never seemed to waver from their sense of duty—or of divine purpose, even if shrouded in the darkest of mysteries. However flawed (like the rest of us) they might appear while enjoying the best of times, they offered to their country an unflinching example of how to live in the face of the most violent and senseless death. I am sure in hindsight that my later curiosity about that older and wider (if not necessarily wiser) communion of Catholic Christians, of which my Anglo-American church was an elegant offshoot, was inextricably bound up with the experience of that televised funeral, just two blocks north of my family's bookstore and publishing offices—in the very center of the town I called home. But it was a piece of music that consummated the Requiem and that, in my ears, has been forever bound up in that moment: a Protestant hymn, completely American, and yet with universality that defines the word "catholic" in its broadest sense: "The Battle Hymn of the Republic."

I have sung it, mostly in church, countless times since that June day of 1968; yet each time it takes me back to that cathedral as the casket of the might-have-been ruler of a restored Camelot was slowly carried out. The last time I sang it at a funeral was for our good friend and "Christian knight in armor," as the eulogist so aptly described him, David Alger, who was killed on September 11 in the World Trade Center. There the familiar hymn telescoped that tragedy into the Kennedy assassination and the terrible Civil War that first elicited those soaring vocal lines. There was, of course, no casket at David's service: instead, doubly choked up, I saw for an instant, in the mind's eye, a casket carried from St. Patrick's once again. Hard as I may try, I can never finish the hymn in full voice. And I never enter St. Patrick's without hearing its silent echoes in the vaults.

TUESDAY, JULY 2, 2002

Today comedy supplanted memories of tragedy as I finally found a script of *Ring Round the Moon.* I had forgotten how many delicious lines Madame Desmortes is given. She even gets to indulge in a little theological lecturing to her long-suffering and homely companion Capulet, telling her, "A dull life in this world is a splendid recommendation for the life to come." When Capulet protests weakly, Madame continues: "You will be hobnobbing with the Blessed while I'm roasting over a slow fire for two or three thousand years. Well, perhaps it won't seem so long."

Capulet: "God's mercy is infinite, Madam."

Desmortes: "Certainly, but He must abide by what He says, you know, otherwise the Just like you, who have staked everything on it, are going to feel very badly let down. Suppose a rumor started circulating among the Sheep that the Goats were going to be pardoned as well? They'd use such bad language that they'd get themselves damned on the spot. Don't you think it would be rather comic?"

Capulet: "Oh, you can't really think that, Madam?"

Desmortes: "Why not? I can think anything I like, it's all I have left to do."

I can still hear my grandmother Scribner speaking through my alter ego as I reread these lines by the poolside and chuckled aloud—but not so loud as to disturb the prostrate bodies awaiting their massages.

WEDNESDAY, JULY 3, 2002

I look back on my final, sixth-form year at St. Paul's as the culmination of academic interests, a serendipitous synthesis of courses and extracurricular passions—which is, I suppose, what a senior year is supposed to be all about. It was not my happiest year of life; in many ways it was fraught with the turmoil, frustrations, and heartbreak of those riotous times of Vietnam and student protests. But it was one of those turning points in life when alpha and omega fuse into one, a consummation of past and future in a present that seems to slip away just as it is savored all too briefly and inadequately. If there is one year I could revisit, that would be it. Dawn and dusk together: innocence and the death of innocence. Also the beginning of a religious search—a quest for the sacred.

THURSDAY, JULY 4, 2002

For my fourth and last year of Greek, we plowed through Plato's *Dialogues* and on to Sophocles' *Oedipus the King.* But the Greek that meant the most to me that year was of a far commoner variety—the koine Greek of the New Testament manuscripts. And we read it not in a classics course but in what was then called "sacred studies," my final requirement for graduation. No other requirement ever made a deeper impression, or left a more lasting sense of gratitude.

This course, the successor to the Old Testament course of my first year, covered the New Testament, Christian theology, and a history of the early Church. The teacher was a young Episcopal priest, Howard White, from West Virginia. He brought a Southern, conservative, and no-nonsense sensibility to the New England liberalism that prevailed among his fellow clergy. I admired his independence, his nonconformity, and his rock-solid faith. He taught the Christian faith in all its essentials, without a flicker of apology. He was politically incorrect—decades before the term had been coined—but C. S. Lewis would have found in him a kindred soul, and so did I.

I remember reading on a bus to Boston a red paperback on the four first Christian heresies: Arianism, Apollonianism, Nestorianism, and Donatism. I now have only a faint grasp of how each one veered from orthodoxy in its peculiar subtleties, but what remains is the conviction that these matters really mattered. The Nicene Creed was not just a nice poem, but a testament to several battles fought and won over words and their meaning, over several centuries as the new faith was put to severe tests—as much for understanding as for survival.

At the same time, I am sitting at my desk on the third floor of Brewster and finding a more modern revelation in a sermon by the German theologian Paul Tillich—"Born in a Grave." I enjoyed the fact that I was again studying one of my father's gray Scribner Library paperbacks and that this theologian—like Paton, Churchill, Fitzgerald, Wharton, and Hemingway (from previous courses)—was a family author. But it was not just chauvinism that caught my attention; his voice was as compelling as his formulations were difficult. Tillich was worth the struggle; he raised matters of faith and belief to a cosmic plane, something far beyond Sunday school, something worthy of adults. On the other hand, Bishop Robinson's polemical book *Honest to God*, a radical demythologizing of the New Testament—from the Nativity through the miracles and even the Resurrection—was more than I could stomach. I saw it as the creed of a crusading agnostic—surely an unfair reading of the English bishop's intent, although many years later he expressed regret that he had written the book. While hardly a fundamentalist or literalist, I sought more certainty than the new breed of contemporary Anglican theologians were prepared to offer. Howdy White had a very simple way of dealing with such doubting anti-Thomists. On the blackboard he wrote: " 'God is dead'—*Nietzsche*"; then immediately under it, " 'Nietzsche is dead'—*God*." I was reassured.

SATURDAY, JULY 6, 2002

Reading in class the gospel of Mark in Greek and translating it into English provided a perspective on those sacred scenes similar to the wonder of peering into the past through the lighted viewer. It was the literary and linguistic equivalent of the Stereo Realist, as that viewer is labeled. Like those colorful three-dimensional scenes so clear and tangible that the eye lingers on each detail as in a Van Eyck altarpiece, the translation was only the portal to a closer analysis of each phrase, and often each word. We were introduced to that exalted term "exegesis"—a digging out of meaning, the mining of biblical gold. Finally I had my spiritual reward for four years of struggle with that intractable ancient language.

One fifty-minute class rose to the level of epiphany. Our visiting teacher, from the Classics Department, Dave Barry, was illustrating a great subtlety in the Greek text early on in Mark's gospel, when he describes Jesus' baptism by John—something that English was not quite supple enough to duplicate, or so it seemed at first sight. We have an active and a passive voice, that's all—*You hit me* and *I am hit*. But the Greeks had a third, a middle, voice for their verbs, something that may convey a passive experience in which the subject initiates the act and receives the effect of it.

The King James Bible says that the people of Judea and Jerusalem "were all baptized" by John in the river Jordan. But it was not simply a passive act. They had taken the initiative and "went out to him" to subject themselves to John in this act of repentance. So Mark cast the verb in the middle voice, combining active and passive. With a flash of insight Mr. Barry suggested that we might translate *ebaptizonto* "got baptized"—they got themselves baptized by John in the river Jordan. A bit colloquial, "got" or "get" is a blunt Old Norse word that sounded somewhat crude, but it worked. It did the job. It precisely conveyed the nuance of the Greek middle voice and St. Mark's intention in describing the significance of the event.

I suppose that the reason this episode in translating a single word looms so large in memory is that in a very simple way it encapsulates my St. Paul's experience. I can no longer remember the Greek vocabulary I labored so long to learn with the aid of small flash cards, and I am at a loss to conjugate that middle voice today. But that Greek subtlety captures the essence of those years of study at St. Paul's. The learning experience, to use a popular term among teachers, was both active and passive as we *got ourselves educated* (middle voice). It was, as it should be, collaborative and communal. It dissolved the grid of the daily schedule, blending together the curricular and extracurricular and transcending the course of four academic years and the bounds of the idyllic grounds, true to the school's motto from St. Jerome: "Let us learn those things on earth the knowledge of which continues in heaven." Constructing a course, much less a curriculum, around such a motto is an impossible task for mortal teachers and students in a mere lifetime. Yet it sets a goal that rewards both effort and journey—if only we have the heart to follow the Wise Men along their new route home.

MONDAY, JULY 8, 2002

As the fall term drew to a close, my focus shifted from the stage to the chapel—for two intertwined reasons: first, it represented the heart of St. Paul's School's identity, and second, it was coming under increasing attack as a relic of the past and a burden to students who wanted total freedom of choices in all their endeavors. Almost two years before becoming a Catholic, I was earning my stripes as a Counter-Reformationist. I loved the traditional Anglican liturgy as much as I loathed attempts to update it and make it "relevant"—the catchword of that moment. Four hundred years earlier I probably would have volunteered to join the Roman Inquisition. On a higher plane, I recall reading the opening of John's gospel during a Christmas service of lessons and carols and feeling that it was surely the most beautiful and poetic distillation of theology in all scripture. At the same time, my father had accepted on my behalf an invitation by the rector of St. Bart's in New York to read the Incarnation narrative from

Matthew's gospel at a similar—and much larger—service there after I got home for the holidays. So just when my career onstage ended, a new one—as a reader and speaker—was beginning. And it began in church, the place I most enjoyed.

When I returned to school after Christmas, I brought with me my grandfather's full-length raccoon coat from the 1920s. For my yearbook photo I posed in that coat, wrapped in a Princeton scarf, and pretended to converse (with rhetorical gestures of debate) with the statue of St. Paul on the chapel lawn, then covered with several feet of snow.

My strictness about rules and rubrics led me into one lamentable lapse, worthy of the worst Pharisee, that has pained me to this day. During one Sunday Communion service, a week or so before my brother Blair's confirmation by the bishop of New Hampshire, I spotted Blair going up to the altar to receive the sacrament. He was just following the herd, oblivious to the official rule on the issue that only after confirmation may one receive the Host and chalice. After the service, I stopped him and scolded him for his mistake, suggesting that he was not taking his instruction seriously. My intervention was shameful, totally lacking in charity, the very thing our Lord preached against. It is a moment I never forgot, and to this day I have always chosen to err on the side of inclusion and encouragement when it comes to participation in the sacraments. Who are we to discourage, much less reproach, an internal invitation that may indeed come from the Lord himself? Perhaps that is not in keeping with the strictest Catholic regulations, but I'll take the risk for the day of judgment. The one time I invoked the rules with my own brother I felt deeply un-Christian. Counter-Revolutionaries can be as cruel as their adversaries; after that false start I was determined to be a benign one.

TUESDAY, JULY 9, 2002

I was soon given a chance to redeem myself with a younger student, a classmate of my brother's, Mark Hollingsworth, who lived a floor below me in

Brewster and was one of the boys in my charge as a house supervisor. Right after his confirmation, he asked me if I would get up early and accompany him to his First Communion, before breakfast in the little chantry chapel, which housed the magnificent Great War memorial sculpture by Daniel Chester French of a young adolescent soldier (naked but for a strategically placed loop of leather belt, by order of the trustees) with broken sword, swooning in death and supported by an angel. Long before I studied Baroque sculpture, particularly the masterpieces of Bernini, I had been entranced by this neo-Baroque vision of sensual pathos, if not piety. The chantry, with its copy of a Renaissance altarpiece, was and remains a little jewel beside that long tunnel of a collegiate chapel, and the Communion service fitted its intimacy, with just Mark and me seated together while the priest said the Mass. For most of the past decade, Mark, an Episcopal priest, has been running the diocese of Massachusetts as the archdeacon for the bishop. He soon will have a miter and crosier of his own, I have no doubt; someday I want him to repeat the early morning service—perhaps just the two of us—only this time it will have an Anglo-Roman ecumenical twist.

WEDNESDAY, JULY 10, 2002

Today, a surprising number of pieces of this mosaic of memory fell into place. First a letter arrived by fax from the archivist, Barbara Perkel, at the Boston Symphony Orchestra; she enclosed two press clippings of Van Cliburn's concert at Tanglewood on August 14, 1965, with a note that she hoped "the reviews will put your mind to rest about the encore!" They did indeed: after mentioning that the crowd was record-breaking, the reviewer of the *Holyoke Transcript-Telegram* noted that the ovation after the *Emperor* Concerto, with Leinsdorf conducting, "was such that the usual rules were broken and the third movement was repeated as an encore." So my memory was confirmed; I had forgotten only the apt timing of this concert. It was just before I was to go off to St. Paul's for the first time. As I wrote to Van today, his *Emperor* gave me the best send-off of a lifetime.

SUNDAY, JULY 14, 2002

T. S. Eliot notwithstanding, April 1969 was anything but cruel. That last spring at St. Paul's was the happiest and most productive of all my schooling. I got the letter from Princeton confirming that I would be moving south for the next four years—but not at once. That same month, the rector asked me to serve, along with two other graduating classmates, on a six-week Summer Study Committee on Religion at the school. The twelve of us—three clergy, three lay teachers, three graduates, and three prospective sixth-formers—were to live on campus and study all aspects of religion at St. Paul's, particularly the role of formal worship and sacred studies, and then write a report of recommendations. As a result, I had not only my first paying job to look forward to, but also an extension of my life at the school I was so loath to leave.

I don't recall whether the two independent study projects I chose to pursue for those final weeks of school were specifically chosen with this summer project in mind, but they certainly dovetailed: the first was a study of Paul Tillich with Howdy White. It was a very informal tutorial—just the two of us. Most of the time, we sat and watched a series of films of interviews with the great theologian. The complexity and opaqueness of Tillich's thought seemed to fit the times to a T. The films were supplemented with readings in his *Systematic Theology* and several evenings of discussion as I sought to have them translated into a layman's language. For that, I would have to wait for my age to double: eighteen years later I was to commission and publish an anthology entitled *The Essential Tillich*, which brought me into contact with the great man's daughter and a friend and scholar, Forrest Church (son of the late Senator Frank Church), who served as editor and made sense of it all for me and countless readers.

The second project was a tutorial in the history of St. Paul's School. Pete Flynn and I (fellow oarsmen and future classmates at Princeton) enlisted Señor José Ordóñez to take us through a century and more of our beloved school. Together we tackled both original materials in the school archives and published histories of the school. Our faculty guide was the school's future archivist and the resident counterrevolutionary on the faculty (his family having suffered through the recent revolution in his native Cuba, he had no taste for even minor campus imitations).

In our sixth-form show the week before, I had played the part of our rector giving a sermon. The text was taken from Genesis—and more immediately from the comic English recording *Beyond the Fringe*: "My brother Esau is an hairy man, but I am a smooth man." It was a silly yet affectionate encore on a familiar stage I thought I had left for good.

TUESDAY, JULY 16, 2002

For the few days leading up to my graduation, my housemaster and mentor James Greaves had vanished; no one in our dorm had seen him. The mystery was solved only on my last day, a few minutes before the graduation commenced behind the chapel on a shaded lawn beside the lower school pond. He had been taken to the infirmary several days earlier. Returning home highly intoxicated from a wedding reception for a fellow drama coach, he had placed his head in the gas oven with the intent to end his life—only to find that he could not follow through. Instead, he called a friend to take him to the infirmary to recover from alcohol poisoning and depression. It was there that I paid him a brief, awkward, and muted emotional farewell just minutes before joining the line of graduates outside awaiting the opening measures of "Salve Mater," the signal that we were to proceed to our seats for the commencement exercises, that joyous concatenation of prizes, diplomas, and applause. The poignancy of our parting was mitigated only by the thought that I would soon be returning to the school for the summer study program and would have another chance to talk to him under less clouded circumstances. Little did I know.

The day after graduation, Greaves climbed to the catwalk several stories above the stage in Mem Hall and either fell or jumped—it was never quite clear. But he survived: a chair broke his fall, along with several ribs, and punctured his lung. By the time I returned to the school a couple of weeks later, I heard he was recuperating in the hospital at Dartmouth. As soon as the opening symposium on religion was concluded, I got into my Dodge Dart and drove up to Hanover to visit him, accompanied by a younger member of the English Department, Steve Ball, who was teaching at the summer school and soon became a good friend—and thirty years later my son Charlie's most supportive and inspiring humanities teacher.

The first visit was unexpectedly awkward as we encountered the vice rector sitting in his hospital room, engaged in a monologue of forced joviality to mask the real purpose of his visit: the rector had sent him to tell Greaves that he could not return to the school after these two alcoholic suicide attempts (if that is in fact what they really were). It seemed a cruel and ironic revision of Greaves's role of the alcoholic priest in *The Potting Shed* almost four years earlier. Some days later I drove north to Hanover again—alone this time, listening to the least memorable tunes of 1969 on the radio the whole trip up: Neil Diamond still evokes that tearful solitary drive. This time I visited James alone, but he was heavily sedated, his normal English reserve muted. But I was glad I went. In ways that an eighteen-year-old can not convey I think he must have known how much he meant, and how much I mourned his immanent departure. I had Princeton to look forward to; what had James? Before the rector left for his summer holiday, I visited him in his office to see whether there might still be another reprieve. No, there could not be—and I understood why. I don't think I ever offered a word of protest, just gratitude that Matt Warren had done the most he could, and far more than any other head of school would ever have dared under the circumstances. The safety and welfare of the children in his charge had to come first: if only our Catholic cardinals and bishops had followed his example in the years to come.

THURSDAY, JULY 18, 2002

Past and present keep stepping on each other's toes, as I try to inch along through the summer of '69. Yesterday I ran into a publishing colleague from fifteen years ago, Terry Mulry, on Fifth Avenue. He had introduced me to Forrest Church as the ideal editor for our Tillich anthology; Terry then became Church's research assistant. How many more important footnotes shall I encounter on foot? I continue to believe that God has a serious sense of humor—and corrective perspective. Last night I finally got through to Van Cliburn, who had left a phone message to thank me for sending him the review of his *Emperor.* He confirmed for me that it was indeed the only time he had played the third movement as an encore. The amazing thing about his voice is that it sounds two decades younger than his age. Is music the ultimate elixir of youth? I must drink more of it.

Today the director of the BBC/Bravo documentary came into the office and interviewed me for over two hours about my *Miami Vice* escapade in trapping a gang selling a stolen Rubens eleven years ago. The timing was uncanny, for I had not yet recovered from the news this past week that Rubens had claimed the gold—for now at least—in commanding the highest price at auction for an old master painting. His *Massacre of the Innocents* sold at Christie's for $76 million. It turned out that the buyer is our son Charlie's ultimate boss this summer—Lord Thompson, whose company owns Charles Scribner's Sons reference publishing, where Charlie is apprenticing again as a summer intern. I must confess that of all the Rubens paintings to set that record, it would not have been my choice. The slaughter of innocent babies, no matter how biblically faithful the rendition or sensual the contours and colors, leaves me chilled with disgust: it's too much like the evening news, as it surely was in Rubens's day as well (minus the cameras). Perhaps I have misunderstood its message: perhaps he intended it as a protest, like Picasso's *Guernica,* driving home the full horror of war and man's inhumanity. At the time he painted it, a truce was being sought in the long war between the two Netherlands, north and south—a war that Rubens later spent his diplomatic energies to end once and for all. He failed in his lifetime, but not for want of effort or for portraying in paint the passion that prompted his deepest yearning for peace. Perhaps if I revisit this painting in that light it may strike me more sympathetically than it did on the page of the *New York Times.*

Meanwhile I got to relive for those two and a half hours my favorite Walter Mitty adventure, a fantasy played out amidst the pastel hues of the Art Deco hotels along Collins Avenue in Miami, where I shall fly next month for the filming. I especially look forward to the reunion with those brave and often brilliant special agents of U.S. Customs, who orchestrated the successful capture and conviction of the criminals. Toward the end of our conversation, I realized how much of my present sanguinity I owe to them. I never once worried about going about daily life after September 11, and today I had a small epiphany that suggested the reason. My work with that group of special agents lasted only a few days, but long enough to convince me that once they set their sights on a problem, they could solve it. The present priority transcends a hot Rubens painting; they will bring that same expertise to homeland security.

FRIDAY, JULY 19, 2002

Before returning through the portal of memory to that bucolic campus of St. Paul's for my first and only summer there, I stumbled this afternoon upon a vision of paradise on a familiar corner outside the priory of St. Vincent Ferrer. A man in work clothes was hosing down a flower bed in front of the white statue of our Lady. I had noticed the array of flowers each day as I passed by. They seemed incrementally more varied and colorful. I assumed that was simply a fact of nature with the waxing of the season, but today they appeared positively ablaze in color and variety, and I called out to the man, "So that's the secret to this garden—the hose!" Then, spotting some familiar flowers from my own garden, whose proper names have remained annoyingly anonymous to me, I began to ask him to identify the various species and tried my best to memorize them. My grandfather Scribner had a more practical solution to my problem decades ago. My grandmother was an avid gardener, but he—like me—didn't know a daisy from a daffodil. Whenever a guest asked him the name of a flower, he would reply in his best imitation of ecclesiastical Latin, "Oh, that's a *pax vobiscum.*" I love the correct Latin names: somehow *Rudbeckia hirta* sounds better than "black-eyed Susan."

After quizzing my new acquaintance more than I would have tolerated in his place, I moved on to the church. But I was still early, and something

nagged at me to return and ask him more about his garden. I couldn't figure out whether he was a Dominican friar or an employee, and I felt I
should ask his name and congratulate him on his work: this small garden,
complete with bumblebees, birds, and two flourishing apple trees near the
Madonna—the New Eve celebrated by medieval theologians. It turned out
that both my guesses were wrong: Lyle is a neighborly volunteer. Originally
from the countryside and now living only a gardenless block or two away,
he has created and tended this little Eden as though it were his own. He
told me he works in publishing—directly across the street from my own
office. We exchanged business cards and I returned for Mass with the conviction that epiphanies and coincidences are but two faces of the same god;
like Janus, one looks forward, the other backward, fusing future and past
perfect. I entered the Gothic church, already darkening with an approaching thunderstorm, with a profound sense of awe that such a small plot of
cultivation, a pocket park, could evoke so brilliantly the glory of creation.

After Mass I finally realized why the scene had seemed so appropriate
beside our church and the statue of Mary. Renaissance paintings suddenly
came into focus as I recalled that the first appearance of the risen Christ (in
John's gospel) was in a garden outside his empty tomb, where Mary Magdalene saw him, spoke to him, and mistook him for the gardener. (Some
artists actually show him wearing a hat and holding a hoe.) So the risen
Christ infuses the image of the gardener with something still more miraculous than even the rebirth of perennials in years to come. There is nothing like them for miles along Lexington, all the way south to Gramercy
Park. In a final footnote, the priest informed me that Monday will be the
Feast of Mary Magdalene. Another coincidence wherein God chooses to
remain as anonymous as that gardener on Easter Morning?

SATURDAY, JULY 20, 2002

Up at St. Paul's in the summer of '69, our all-male group of twelve met
each morning in an upstairs room of the School House—my old Greek

classroom. Two topics given to me to research in the library stick in my mind, for both served as introductions of sorts to that exotic Roman Catholicism that always hovered outside the gates: the first was ecumenism, a theme of the Second Vatican Council; the second, parochial schools. I can only guess that some of that long-forgotten research must have lodged within my imagination, seedlings of a new faith—or at least an older Church—that would sprout a year later.

On another occasion, during one of our morning meetings, the Reverend Mr. Welles passed around a photograph of an ornate liturgical object—it looked like a sunburst cast in precious metal—and asked whether any of us could name it. No one could. He said it was called a "monstrance." That medieval shrine for the Eucharistic Host seemed as alien then as it would soon become familiar—especially after I began to specialize in the art and liturgy of the Counter-Reformation at Princeton. But each time I see it now, more than thirty years later, whether on the sacrament altar at St. Patrick's or in a Baroque painting, I am transported back to that classroom where it first appeared as an object of bizarre curiosity. If truth be told, there is still a part of me, call it Protestant purity, that wonders even during those moments of adoration of the exposed sacrament whether such an ornate, triumphalist object of human handiwork is at odds with the stark simplicity of our Lord's identification of himself with a broken piece of bread: "This is my body." Sometimes a solitary candle may appear more brilliant than a crystal chandelier. In any case, I do not feel deprived by having had a monstrance-free induction into the sublimity of the sacrament. St. Bart's and St. Paul's served me well in preparing for modern Catholicism, post–Vatican II.

SUNDAY, JULY 21, 2002

When the time came at the end of our study to write our report, I found myself a minority of one on the issue of required daily chapel services at St. Paul's. The other eleven had concluded that all expressions of worship must henceforth be voluntary. I alone clung to the belief that to abandon the all-school services would forever alter the character of St. Paul's as a Church school. Once secularized, it could never regain its former identity. I had loved those gatherings too much to forsake them for political correctness. My colleagues were more than tolerant; they graciously included my minority report at the end of the document, without a word of reproach. Perhaps in the light of their overwhelming, near-unanimous majority, they felt bemused by my lone voice of traditionalism. As I reread today what I wrote then, I wonder whether it was already a foregone conclusion that I would someday seek out the solidity of the rock of Peter, in the wake of Episcopalian experimentation. What I best remember about the dissenting document is that I copied it late one night on the Xerox machine outside the rector's office. He was away at his beach house, but he was very much in my mind as the one reader I sought to persuade—and I did. Chapel is still required at St. Paul's.

WEDNESDAY, JULY 24, 2002

I have been sitting almost an hour facing this screen, reluctant to return to my freshman year at Princeton. In the background plays a CD of lieder: Schwarzkopf spins a legato line that contrasts so painfully with my memories of that year, a year of discontinuities and discord. I wish I could rush through it. And yet I know I must not: so much of the discord and disappointment, I am sure, prompted my search for a new harmony and a new resolution that soon led to the Catholic faith. This is, admittedly, premature speculation at this point, but it seems reasonable enough that I dare not ignore the awkwardness of revisiting so much I might prefer to leave in oblivion.

First, I dropped my piano lessons; or rather, I never got around to taking them up again. My father had given me his earlier AR stereo system for my single room, and the phonograph became my musical focus. Most of what I listened to was choral and organ music—a substitute for all those missed chapel services at St. Paul's? Then, despite attending a splendid performance of *A Man for All Seasons* at Theatre Intime, I made no effort at all to get involved in the theatrical life of the university. I heard that it was run by a small group of backstage bohemians. Not for me: I wanted the Royal Shakespeare Company, or at least the Ivy League equivalent. Crew was also turning out to be a disappointment: since half of the freshmen oarsmen had never rowed before, the afternoon practices felt like returning to the fifth crews of my third-form year. It never dawned on me that by spring everyone would be up to speed—in fact, so much so that the boat I soon abandoned went on to sweep all the races at the Worcester Regatta. But I was no longer on it. As soon as I heard that we would be driving to Florida to practice for a week of the upcoming Christmas vacation, I opted out: I preferred to attend the white-tie debutante balls in New York. Not a priority to be proud of—and yet it turned out to be a fortuitous choice, for there I met a girl who would lead me to her family and ultimately to their Catholic faith.

But before Thanksgiving even came into view, the campus was beset with its first political upheaval—the Vietnam Moratorium. I wanted no part of it: I had not come to Princeton to march (or even sit) in protests. My hall mates in our motel-like, postwar dorm represented the full range of radicals—from benign to belligerent—and did not appreciate my aloofness; they equated my father's being a university trustee with all the sins of the Nixon administration. I returned to my room one afternoon to find pinned to my door the opening paragraph from Fitzgerald's story "The Rich Boy." It begins with that notorious observation "The very rich are different from you and me."

By Fitzgerald's lights I would hardly have been considered "very rich"—I was closer to Nick Carraway than to Tom Buchanan, but no matter: I was politically incorrect. Yet I was intrigued by this literary rebuke; after the sting had worn off, I went to the library and found the story and read it. I loved it—and I loved Fitzgerald. I was hooked. So onward I proceeded to the University Store and bought a copy of our paperback of his first novel, *This Side of Paradise*, his youthful ode to Princeton. It was my first of several epiphanies that year that pointed the way to Rome.

THURSDAY, JULY 25, 2002

University officials have long bemoaned Fitzgerald's satirical depiction of their school as a country club in *This Side of Paradise* (if they could ban any book, this would be the one). They ignore the redeeming poetry, the sacramental effect of that early, flawed novel on the majestic campus. For me, the book infused the green quads and Gothic spires with a spirit, with a soul, with new life. Fitzgerald transfigured Princeton. I now saw it not as a stranger but through the wondering eyes of freshman Amory Blaine:

> *Princeton of the daytime filtered slowly into his consciousness—West and Reunion, redolent of the sixties, Seventy-nine Hall, brick-red and arrogant, Upper and Lower Pyne, aristocratic Elizabethan ladies not quite content to live among shop-keepers, and topping all, climbing with clear blue aspiration, the great dreaming spires of Holder and Cleveland towers. From the first he loved Princeton—its lazy beauty, its half-grasped significance, the wild moonlight revel of the rushes.*

For me, Princeton had not been love at first sight—at least not that first term as a student; but thanks to Fitzgerald it was love at first reading, and it proved that Oscar Wilde had been right: art doesn't imitate life; life imitates art. The arts—whether visual, musical, or literary—have the power to transform our very surroundings as well as ourselves. They alter our perception, our emotional responses, our lasting memory of time and place. At their best, they serve a redemptive role. If my view of Princeton in the late sixties was profoundly altered through the turning of pages—as of a kaleidoscope two generations old—it was a benign fantasy. Amory was everything I was not: a Midwestern Catholic boy, raised by a charmingly eccentric single mother, with an overripe innocence. Yet he was also exotic, a seductive protagonist: I wanted to trade places—and eras—with him. On one level of the imagination I soon succeeded by making his Princeton mine.

Another character came into my life along with Amory—the worldly and magnetic Catholic priest who mentors and befriends Amory: Monsignor Darcy. He had been a convert to the faith, an intellectual, a man of culture, and of romantic yearnings for older worlds:

> Monsignor was forty-four then, and bustling—a trifle too stout for symmetry, with hair the color of spun gold, and a brilliant, enveloping personality. When he came into a room clad in his full purple regalia from thatch to toe, he resembled a Turner sunset, and attracted both admiration and attention. . . . He was intensely ritualistic, startlingly dramatic, loved the idea of God enough to be a celibate, and rather liked his neighbor. Children adored him because he was like a child; youth reveled in his company because he was still a youth, and couldn't be shocked. In the proper land and century he might have been a Richelieu—at present he was a very moral, very religious (if not particularly pious) clergyman, making a great mystery about pulling rusty wires, and appreciating life to the fullest, if not entirely enjoying it. He and Amory took to each other at first sight.

I have spent the past thirty years looking for Monsignor Darcy. Of course, he doesn't exist; he never did. But the search has brought me into close friendships with priests, and the Amory Blaine in me never stops seeking for some guidance and insight—at times, a complete renovation; at times, a fine-tuning of the spirit, like so many piano strings stretched tight to the breaking point within a wooden body awaiting resonance.

Last night I had dinner with Charlie Weiser, the first Catholic chaplain I was to meet at Princeton and who would outlast me there by another decade. We have now known each other for thirty-two years. Tonight I had dinner with a young priest I have known a tenth as long—Andrew O'Connor, who is an artist in human relations as much as in mixed media. He is wonderful company; his kaleidoscope never stops turning.

FRIDAY, JULY 26, 2002

At the office I silently bemoan the fact that I cannot find a copy of *This Side of Paradise*. Then, after a most welcome call from my favorite Princeton English teacher, Tom Roche, about a Fitzgerald matter (he is a now trustee of the literary estate), an editorial colleague comes to the door just as I am about to leave early for the weekend and asks whether I can locate a few of the more obscure Fitzgerald titles to be converted into electronic books. Reluctantly I go upstairs to the paperback department on a treasure hunt; the books are nowhere to be found. Finally, as an afterthought, a secretary mentions a box of old books about to be sent to our storage warehouse across the Hudson. I open it and find not only the titles I was seeking (in nice original Scribner editions bound with nostalgic memories of first reading at Princeton), but also, as an added dividend, four editions of *This Side of Paradise* spanning the three decades following my freshman year—the first (published in 1970) illustrating on its cover a debonair Amory standing before the bronze tigers outside Nassau Hall. Add another check to my lengthening list of providential coincidences. I have long since ceased to wonder at the timing of these moments of serendipity, but I remain grateful to Whom It May Concern—as Unitarians address God, according to Schuyler Chapin.

I am delayed in getting to five-thirty Mass at St. Vincent's; then, in total distraction, I lose my briefcase—only to find it. My annoyance and delays suddenly dissolve into a comic conclusion as I approach that resplendent garden at the corner of the Dominican priory and bump into my son Charlie, who is rushing homeward from the more scholarly branch of Scribner books. I cannot resist pointing out the glorious garden to this former expedition director of the Millville Geographic Society, claiming with Baroque exaggeration that it's the loveliest urban garden south of St. Paul's. He diplomatically assents, seems most impressed that the two apple trees really bear fruit, and then proceeds northward to his e-mails while I disappear inside the church for the next half an hour. The sanctuary is aglow in the summer light of late afternoon, and as I take my seat I whisper to myself, and maybe to God: "I am so glad to be here. . . . How lovely is thy dwelling place." It is the feast of Joachim and Anna, the parents of the Virgin Mary. The Church in her wisdom long ago chose these two nonbiblical figures, whose very names are rooted only in popular legend, in order to accentuate the family ties of Jesus—and by extension his ties with the rest of humanity. It is about the human side of parenthood. My chance encounter by the apple tree a minute earlier was all the preparation, or hint of an explanation, I needed. But now I wonder: Was that encounter really by chance? Perhaps the answer lies somewhere within the fruit of the tree.

SATURDAY, JULY 27, 2002

As my first Christmas vacation from Princeton approached, science and religion clashed on two fronts. In physics class, we explored the conflict between Galileo and the Roman Church over the new, heliocentric models of the universe. For my European history paper, I had chosen to write about a book on this subject (it must have been recommended by my father), *The Crime of Galileo*, by the historian of science Giorgio de Santillana. The science was far more comprehensible than the ecclesiastical skirmishes in the Vatican between the Jesuits and the Dominicans that caused most of Galileo's troubles: the pope, Urban VIII, after all, had been the astronomer's friend and patron. In the end, Galileo's punishment for political incorrectness was no worse than Alan Paton's, three centuries and a hemisphere away: house arrest.

A more immediate conflict between science and religion sprung from a clash in my schedule: I was looking forward to my first candlelight service of Advent lessons and carols in the University Chapel, only to find that our physics exam began at the same hour. This time, Galileo's champions won.

As I walked back to my dorm in the dark, I wondered whether I had made the right choice—but of course I had no choice. The only similar service I would attend that year was at St. Bart's, where again I had been asked to read the beginning of Matthew's gospel. But it wasn't the same: following the Christmas Day celebration, and candleless, it lacked those essential Advent features of anticipation and the light shining in darkness.

SUNDAY, JULY 28, 2002

This morning I spoke with my godmother, Aunt Patsy. In March her husband, my father's Princeton classmate Uncle Lin, died of cancer. Now, only four months later, her only son and youngest child, Garrison, is himself in the last stages of cancer. For the past four years he has fought with courage and persistence a heroic battle against melanoma, defying all expectations for endurance. But the end is in sight, a matter of weeks at most. This is the first unbearable coincidence of this journal to date: just as I am about to meet this happy and devoted family of five children in my recollection of 1970, I realize that the next time I see them all together will be at Garrison's funeral in Darien, the very town where my mother and I are planning in four days to revisit our summer rental of 1955.

The Miller home in Locust Valley became my second home during that freshman year. No idealized 1950s television series—including my favorites *Leave It to Beaver*, *Father Knows Best*, and *The Donna Reed Show*—came close to capturing the warmth and attraction of that family. They were the American counterparts of our Pease cousins, and in the months to come I spent as much time with them as possible. Now in their greatest test of suffering, I can only pray that the Lord will sustain them—and show me some way to lighten their burden. Perhaps retracing my steps in these pages to their home may give me a hint of the way, perhaps once more returning home by another route.

MONDAY, JULY 29, 2002

Even before I attended my first Catholic Mass, or had any idea of inquiring into the Roman faith, I introduced two Catholic images into my cell-
like room in Princeton: the first was a poster of an early Netherlandish
Annunciation in the Met Museum. A late-Gothic Virgin, attenuated and elegant, kneels in a bright Netherlandish interior rendered in crystalline precision while an androgynous teen-angel Gabriel, robed in vestments of an
acolyte, announces the good news. Soon thereafter I bought a small, highly
stylized crucifix in bronze, mounted on a simple wooden base. Freestanding, it was no more than a foot high, the corpus as lithe and abstracted as
a Giacometti. It had pathos without flesh-and-blood gruesomeness, as
though a melodic line in Fauré's *Requiem* had been transposed into physical
form—an ideal compromise between the empty Protestant cross, the symbol of sacrifice, and a Catholic crucifix of corporal passion. No doubt it
reflected my own transitional state at the time. I have kept it all these years
with a special nostalgia for the first of my graven images. Having lost its
base, it now hangs—tentatively—in son Christopher's room. I should like
to restore it to its original equilibrium.

By this time I had become a regular at the Sunday night Episcopal services in the Marquand Transept of the University Chapel. That small side
chapel perfectly suited our intimate congregation. I don't think we were ever
more than a dozen or two late-weekend arrivals at the manger. After the Eucharist, a small group of us went on to the chaplain's house for refreshments
and conversation until midnight, at which time I walked back across the
empty tennis courts to my room.

Father Snow was an excellent preacher and pastor. It was from him that
I learned that according to Karl Barth, although Bach was the court composer in heaven, the angels listened to Mozart every afternoon. He also offered an intriguing introduction to a story by John Updike called "Giving
Blood," which described a bickering married couple going to donate blood

on a Friday (Good Friday?). As the husband looks over to the table where
his wife lies, hooked up to the IV, and watches her blood flow out through
the transparent tube, he experiences an unexpected pang of empathy and
compassion. Father Snow explained that no story better captured the meaning of our Lord's atonement on Calvary, and that he had mentioned it to
Updike's wife, who urged him to share his reaction with the author, who
happened to be an avid student of the theologian Karl Barth. I don't know
whether he did, but twenty-five years later I wrote to Updike about it, hoping to include it in an anthology of great Christian stories. Updike politely
feigned ignorance of any sacred dimension to his tale. To this day, I don't
know whether he was being coy. Perhaps he had simply composed more
than he realized: the sacramental imagination need not be self-conscious,
even in a virtuoso.

By the time Lent approached, we were treated to an agape meal at the
Snows', an informal counterpart, around the dining room table, to the Anglican ritual at the altar. Whenever possible, I also tried to attend the one
weekday afternoon Eucharist at the chapel, but it was sadly private. Often
I was the only one there beside the priest, which made me regret those times
I had to be elsewhere. Beyond St. Paul's, the Episcopal Church seemed to
have shrunk to a small island of faith: down deep, I was already yearning to
be "a part of the main," as the poet Donne put it.

WEDNESDAY, JULY 31, 2002

The gray winter of 1970 offered the first intimate interplay between visual
arts and literature, which was eventually to become my intellectual and spiritual passion. My father supplied the crucial link.

Seated at my old desk in my room in New York, where I had done my
homework for so many years, I was laboring over a short English paper an-
alyzing a poem. Most of the volume of contemporary verse left me perplexed, but I had found one poem that sounded suitably antique: "In Santa
Maria del Popolo," by Thom Gunn, who was then poet in residence at

Princeton. Little did I suspect he was better known for verses such as "The Un-Seated Motorcyclist Envisioning His Approaching Death," since this poem was about a painting in a Renaissance church in Rome—*The Conversion of Paul*, by Caravaggio, an artist I had never heard of. It seemed a perfect opportunity to use some of the exegetical tools I had honed at that saint's school the year before. Halfway through my labors, my father entered the room carrying an art book. "I thought you might like to see the painting the poem is about," he explained with unassailable reason.

Gunn intended to convey his essential agnosticism in his descriptions of the few old ladies scattered throughout the church trying to clutch some consolation in their clasped hands, in contrast to the painter's broad, expansive gestures. But I would have none of it. I was determined to give a Christian exegesis to both painting and poem, giving every doubt the benefit of faith (in the tradition of Tillich). Even a line such as "No Ananias croons a mystery yet, casting out pain in the name of sin," I took at face value. That was, after all, what had happened to the converted Paul at the moment his temporary blindness was cured. The final image of the poet—a faithful insight into the ambiguously raised arms of the saint-in-progress at the moment of conversion—resonates to this day every time I visit this masterpiece, my favorite painting of all time: "The large gesture of solitary man, resisting by embracing nothingness."

The prostrate figure, a male counterpart to Bernini's *St. Teresa in Ecstasy*, conveyed the sensual duality of fending off the supreme Lover who ultimately must be embraced in order to fill the void of existence, both internal and universal. Even though the teacher bemusedly questioned my unvarnished Christian gloss on the poet's words, I felt secure in what I had done and wanted to do in the future: pursue sacramental readings of text and image. Without my grasping the implications, this brief assignment sparked a Catholic imagination waiting to be liberated. It would take more than a year for me to set foot in that Roman church and see the painting in the flesh; but I could wait. I had already been transported there through the magic of the poet's art and my father's timely intervention. I only wish now I had had the chance to meet the poet; but perhaps I was spared. Years later a beloved publishing colleague told me that if I ever especially admired an author, the best thing to do was avoid meeting him.

THURSDAY, AUGUST 1, 2002

After nine o'clock Mass I got the car to drive my mother and myself up to Darien for our day trip. We arrived at the driveway right on time. I found myself crawling down the long home stretch at a snail's pace to savor the final moments of our approach—it had taken only forty-seven years. Cici Lefferts was standing outside the garage as we pulled up, and after introductions and greetings I pulled out my Stereo Realist viewer to show her some 3-D slides, beginning with my brother and myself in a small garden of perennials. Moving back and forth from stereo viewer to current view was a surreal experience of almost tangible three-dimensionality with identical rocks and background. Only the figures from time past disappeared and reappeared in succession. I felt so frustratingly close to bringing them back for good, if only for an instant: trying to rationalize the elusive vision made me think of Mary Magdalene on that Easter morning seeing her risen Lord unexpectedly in a garden, near a rock.

I turned and saw an angular rock protruding from the ground beside a tall tree. The rock, Cici explained, was called the "chair rock" since it was just the right size and shape for a child to sit in. Once again I tried to find my father's spot from which illusion and reality might fall into alignment. As I flipped back and forth between those forty-seven years, amazed at how quickly I disappeared and reappeared, I had my epiphany of the obvious: unlike us—or trees or bushes or flowers—rocks don't change: they are the constant touchstone of time. No wonder our Lord founded his Church on a rock called Peter.

FRIDAY, AUGUST 2, 2002

Combing through our basement shelves in Locust Valley, I found a slim volume from Malcolm Diamond's tour de force course on religious thought in 1970: *The Ontological Argument—From St. Anselm to the Contemporary Philosophers.* The eleventh-century saint from Canterbury defined God as "that than which nothing greater can be conceived" and went on to prove as a matter of logic that his existence was therefore necessary by definition. The book goes on to trace the objections and responses back and forth down the centuries like some cosmic philosophical tennis championship. I remember trying hard to follow the finer points, but my eyes glazed over as I read the small type. This classic, logical, rationalistic proof of God's existence seems so cold and bloodless, so alien to the experience of faith—and of its other face, doubt—as recorded in both testaments, Old and New.

Malcolm Diamond's lectures, on the other hand, breathed life into the driest of propositions. He was dynamic, passionate, and funny. At the end of one class, a fellow student mumbled: "He's the Billy Graham of agnosticism." But that was wittier than fair. While this liberal Buber scholar clearly had no personal stake in traditional (much less conservative) Christian belief, I never felt he was an apostle of unbelief. He made the very act of religious exploration seem worthwhile and exciting. Sometimes he was so good that, like the poet Gunn, his wry agnosticism could provoke faith. One lecture struck me like that flash of light that turned Saul into Paul en route to Damascus: Diamond's sardonic and deadpan account of how the Catholic Church goes about investigating claims of miracles—the full range of Vatican thoroughness, scrutiny, scientific procedure, and bureaucratic ritual.

If Diamond intended to satirize the pope's methods of ratifying (or rejecting) purported miracles, the effect on me was quite the opposite: there were serious people who thought miracles a serious matter—*The Potting Shed* revisited. I knew nothing of popes and prelates; I had never seen the Vatican except in pictures. But the basic premise was literally a *Romantic* revelation: that a loving God might occasionally turn the world upside down, upset assumptions, heal the sick, even raise the dead to new life. I had finally found a theme that engaged me emotionally and intellectually. So I went out and bought a copy of C. S. Lewis's book *Miracles*. Lewis transformed my outlook on Christianity as profoundly as Fitzgerald had on the campus around me.

When it came time to write my paper, there was no contest between the believing Lewis and the doubting Hume. As Lewis pointed out, the difficulty of belief lay not in the details but in the overarching question of whether there is God. To concede even the possibility of a *yes* is to open the door to a world of possibilities—of miracles great and small. I found the clarity and elegance of that Oxford don utterly irresistible: no wonder he is revered (and claimed) by Catholics and evangelicals alike. He made Rome seem a short step from Canterbury. I started taking my Episcopal faith even more seriously. To ritual was added substance—and even abstinence: I gave up alcohol for Lent.

SUNDAY, AUGUST 4, 2002

Tonight, as I turned on the radio, the opening measures of Berlioz's *Harold in Italy* instantly transported me back to the Woolworth Music Building, where Professor J. Merrill Knapp took us on a magical tour of classical and Romantic music through winter and spring of my freshman year. It must have been my father who prompted me to sign up for the course; he had often said how much lasting joy he had taken home from a music survey during his own undergraduate years. So many of my favorite pieces were first introduced—and brilliantly explained—by Knapp: Berlioz's *Harold* was joined by Liszt's *Don Juan*, Strauss's *Don Quixote*, and Brahms's *Variations on a Theme by Haydn*, among other treasures. Knapp was one of those professors of the old school who combined expertise (in his case, the operas of Handel) with infectious enthusiasm. Had I not found the study of music theory and harmony—during a brief try at St. Paul's—so daunting and dry, I would have happily declared myself a music major. But I knew it would have to remain an avocation.

Before his course concluded with Mahler and Stravinsky (one composer too many, in my more tonal view), Knapp gave us a foretaste of what would later become one of my favorite operas: Verdi's *Otello*. I'll never forget taking the record of act four (Desdemona's murder and Otello's self-execution) to the basement listening room of Woolworth, putting on the headphones, and experiencing what can only be called an aural epiphany. Desdemona's hauntingly plaintive "Ave Maria" conjured up the Virgin Mary with more presence and power than any prayer or painting in memory. My Episcopalian training had not included even a passing Hail Mary. But Verdi more than compensated. I was intoxicated by the beauty and the simple faith evoked by music and words so perfectly matched—a pair of velvet gloves. I played it over and over, until her voice lingered long after I had left the building for my room.

In another of those blessed coincidences, at the very time I was discovering Verdi's "Ave Maria," I was hearing on the car radio a new and instantly popular Beatles song, "Let It Be." I don't care whether pop scholars now claim that Paul McCartney was writing about his own mother (named Mary) or, more profanely, marijuana. In my mind those words heard in times of trouble when "Mother Mary comes to me, speaking words of wisdom," are forever paired with Desdemona's prayer. Mother Mary is the mother of us all. At the end of one class, Professor Knapp came up to me and said he had heard something about a current pop song involving the Virgin Mary; he asked if I knew of any such song. Without a moment's hesitation I said yes, and gave him the reference, the only time in my life I have posed as an expert in pop culture. How very odd that in my case a profoundly Catholic response to the image of Mary was first awakened by two composers—the anticlerical Verdi and the agnostic (or at least unorthodox) Beatle—who had little use for organized religion. But then, God has ever drawn straight with crooked lines—even musical lines.

MONDAY, AUGUST 5, 2002

In February of 1970 I headed east to the Millers' home in Long Island for the first of many weekends there. On Sunday I dutifully went off to the local Episcopal church (with driving directions from the lone Episcopalian in the household, Aunt Patsy), while the rest of the family went to Mass. I returned to a lunch with several Bloody Marys, after learning for the first time—thanks to Roman Catholic expertise on such fine technicalities—that Sundays were not part of Lent, so that my giving up drinking for Lent did not include the Lord's Days! Somehow it all seemed too true to be good, but I took the loophole.

On my next weekend there, curiosity—or perhaps camaraderie—got the better of me, and I trundled off with Uncle Lin and the children to Catholic Mass at St. Paul the Apostle Church. The church building itself was an architectural epiphany—of poor taste: one of those supercontemporary structures that sprung up throughout suburbia in the wake of Vatican II, something between a theater in the round and a supermarket. Above the altar hovered a huge golden crucifix that seemed at least twice life-size, as if to rival Prometheus at Rock Center. Even the English translation of the service (virtually identical in content to the Episcopal version) was overly prosaic, as though any poetic cadence might be displeasing to the Almighty and distracting to the congregation. The guitar-led folk music was consistent with everything else in sight. And yet, despite the cultural shock to my system, I left that Mass profoundly impressed by its simple conviction. The people there clearly did not come because of the beauty of the architecture, or music, or liturgy—but simply because they *believed.*

Somehow the Mass itself trumped everything else. Or so it appeared in my eyes, and I am sure that was the beginning of my quiet seduction into a church that, on the surface at least, was so lacking in familiar elements of aesthetic attraction (at least in the suburbs). I think on another level I wanted what my Miller cousins had: the authentic reality, not a historical offshoot or derivative or imitation, however elegant. But this is all speculation long after the fact: at the time I still considered myself a confirmed Episcopalian, and when I left with my parents for spring vacation on St. Simons Island, Georgia, I made plans to fly back to New York early so that I would not miss the Good Friday and Easter services at St. Bartholomew's.

TUESDAY, AUGUST 6, 2002

Today I sang a new hymn at St. Pat's—" 'Tis good, Lord, to be here." It was specially chosen for the Feast of the Transfiguration today, a feast that reminded me at once of the apse mosaic in my childhood church of St. Bart's, a block away. In his homily, the monsignor explained that Jesus, after that brief epiphany of white radiance to his apostles Peter, James, and John, had to continue to Jerusalem to fulfill his destiny of redemption through his crucifixion, death, and resurrection. I felt suddenly perplexed by these traditional words of preaching the gospel: was Jesus indeed condemned to such a destiny from the start—or was he simply subject to all the possibilities of free will and fallen man? I prefer the latter thought, as I cannot easily accept the transference of mankind's darkest deeds to providence, to any divine plan. God may extract good from evil, life from death, creation from destruction—but as part of a divine *process*, not a preordained script. The authorship of evil and suffering must remain a mystery; it is encapsulated in the liturgy of Good Friday.

WEDNESDAY, AUGUST 7, 2002

Listening today to a CD of Bach cantatas sung by a young, silver-voiced Schwarzkopf, I realized that what drew me back to New York that first

Easter at Princeton was the music at St. Bart's, not only the triumphal anthems and resounding trumpets but also those favorite Easter hymns I
could safely join a thousand other worshipers in singing.

Once that sunrise service was over, I still had at least three hours before
I was due at lunch. So I got in my car and drove up to the Episcopal Cathedral of St. John the Divine for the midmorning service. It was virtually the
same, but now with a bishop presiding over all the Anglo-Catholic trappings he could muster for the longest cathedral in the world. The liturgy
struck me as colorful but somewhat stagy. What struck a deeper chord was
Bishop Donegan's sermon, or rather his quotation from St. Paul's epistle to
the Romans, which he intoned with all the majesty of the King James ca-
dences: "For I am persuaded that neither death, nor life, nor angels, nor
principalities, nor powers, nor things present, nor things to come, nor
height, nor depth, nor any other creature, shall be able to separate us from
the love of God, which is in Christ Jesus our Lord."

I heard those very same words, in a more prosaic translation, this past
week at St. Patrick's, and they brought me back again to that Easter Day
and the bishop who had confirmed me six years earlier and who had once
been my mother's rector, long before becoming a court favorite of the
Queen Mother. I don't think that anything Paul or anyone ever wrote better sums up the message of the gospel: it defines good news.

THURSDAY, AUGUST 8, 2002

Yesterday, on my way to morning Mass, I ran into Teri Towe, a former Buckley upperclassman who had his own classical radio show at Princeton—he
called himself the Laughing Cavalier, after the Frans Hals painting; he often
regaled me with musical anecdotes, highly charged opinions, and an inven-
tiveness that allowed him to edit, condense, and splice together all nine
Beethoven symphonies into less than an hour: a tour de force. Our street-
corner conversation took a sudden turn into grief when I mentioned our
mentor Paul Rotella's death, only to discover in his look of horror that he

had not heard. But he recovered with the observation that all personal problems have taken on a new shade since September 11: "At least I wasn't there for a breakfast meeting that morning." By way of illustrating the point, he went on to tell of a ninety-year-old lady he once knew who had survived the sinking of the *Titanic*. Years later she was aboard a cruise ship that sailed into a hurricane and left its passengers very much the worse for wear. A fellow passenger turned to her and exclaimed breathlessly, "Thank God we survived; it could have been a real disaster." She replied, "I've seen worse."

Such words of macabre wit place life and death in perspective. As I look out now on family and friends whose lives have recently been or are about to be rocked by the death of a loved one, those words take me back to a few days after that Easter, when I heard news of the worst family tragedy ever to hit Far Hills. I can still hardly bring myself to describe it, even after more than thirty years.

Early one morning of that Easter week, a lovely couple, parents of three wonderful sons, were found dead in their bed by their youngest. The father had shot the mother with a handgun, and later turned it on himself. They were a model couple in every way and close family friends of ours. Their violent deaths seemed as impossible as the sinking of the *Titanic*, but mental illness is all too often like an iceberg, with only the tip visible.

I returned to Far Hills to accompany my grandmother Scribner to the double funeral at St. Luke's. The last time I had been in our family church (where, within a decade, Ritchie and I would be married) was to hear the Verdi *Requiem* sung by its choir during Lent. That double funeral was something I had never seen before—or after. So much of the imagery—the flowers, the caskets side by side, husband and wife, the assembled members of both sides of the family—evoked a wedding and those binding vows "till death do us part." In death they were still unparted. It was heartbreaking. It was beyond comprehension. Yet despite this act of madness, despite the collective grief, the muted faith and conviction of the gathered mourners recalled the message of Easter even on so dark a day. Yogi's cliché summed it up: it's not over till it's over. The grief and loss would never be over; nor would the life awaiting these two souls.

SATURDAY, AUGUST 10, 2002

Once summer vacation started, my exploration of Catholicism began, albeit tentatively, on several levels. First, one Sunday in Far Hills I went to St.
Luke's, to find that the schedule had been changed for the summer months
and I had missed the morning service. It turned out that down the road, at
the Catholic Church of St. Elizabeth, Mass was scheduled for the next
hour, and so I went. The packed church was visually jarring—a simple,
charming, rustic structure that had been filled with all sorts of polychrome
plaster or plastic statues and eclectic ornamentations. I stood in the back.
The priest was old and ill-tempered; at one point he stopped in the middle of his homily and barked at a young mother: "Either stop your baby
crying or leave." This was not the spirit of welcome I expected. Whatever
happened to "Suffer the little children to come unto me"? I was appalled—
but I stayed.

A small epiphany redeemed the Mass: a few pews in front of me I spotted our lovely and saintly friend Nesi von Meister, an Austrian countess
with the most wonderfully earthy sense of humor. She came from the
Colloredo-Mansfeld family, whose most infamous member was Mozart's
implacable employer, the prince-archbishop of Salzburg. Once a lady of
Rubensian amplitude, she now appeared a waif, in the last stages of cancer.
She had two young teenage sons; it was heartbreaking to think of her ordeal. Yet there she stood, serene and devout, focused on the Mass and not
in the least distracted by all the peripheral detritus that caught my critical
eye. Her presence gave that otherwise unmemorable Mass a dignity and
beauty that transcended its surroundings, and I thought, I want what she
has. How often are frail and suffering souls the most eloquent evangelists—
through quiet witness and example.

Soon afterward, I borrowed a St. Joseph's Missal from our neighbor and
social impresario Nancy Pyne, took it home, and tried to digest in one
night all the Roman devotions, prayers, rules, and the Order of Mass. The

illustrations were the worst of candy-box art and the explanatory text was often childlike—what my father called *sancta simplicitas.* Yet even that appealed to me: its very lack of sophistication and pretense, its preference for clarity over complexity. Not a bad barter. As a more subtle introduction to the faith, Nancy's daughter, Holly, gave me her copy of Graham Greene's *The End of the Affair.* In this novel about a most reluctant saint in the making, a woman in love makes a desperate bargain with a God she does not believe in: she will give up her lover, if God will only bring him back to life after a bomb explosion. When her lover arises and walks—like the boy James in *The Potting Shed*—she feels obligated to keep her end of the bargain, and she pays a painful price for her fidelity and the nascent faith that consumes her agnostic soul while cancer destroys the body.

At the same time, my father recommended that I read Greene's *The Heart of the Matter,* a more morally ambiguous tale, yet firmly rooted in the Catholic faith of its tortured characters and their author. Now hooked on Greene, I began to be slowly reeled into Rome.

SUNDAY, AUGUST 11, 2002

Yet my journey toward Catholicism that summer was not via Rome, but through London as I revisited my favorite Pease cousins.

Before I left for England in June of 1970, my exploratory churchgoing really took off again thanks to Nancy Pyne, who told me of a wonderful Dutch priest, in the mode of Friar Tuck, who said the 10 A.M. mass each Sunday at the parish of St. Brigid's in Peapack, a gem of a medieval stone chapel (like Cram's in Sudbury) that had been built by the Brady family. The original Mrs. Brady was so controlling that she kept the sole key and would lock out the priest if she disapproved of any aesthetic decisions. Her Medici-like patronage resulted in one of the rare parish churches that could rival the Episcopalians' in taste and authenticity.

Into this most welcoming setting Father Verwey entered each week. His warmth, joviality, and relaxed generosity of spirit made him the very model of all that Vatican II had sought to achieve in reengaging the laity. I loved his heavy Dutch accent, like thick warm muffins, early Sunday morning. Patsy and George Richards, who would soon become my new Catholic godparents, introduced me to him. I must have told him of my interest in learning more about the faith, but as yet I had no plans for any formal instruction. I still had purchases to make and a trip to take: each would fill in gaps in my understanding and personal devotion; by the time I returned from abroad, I was ready to declare my intentions.

First, I bought a simple black rosary at St. Patrick's gift shop; I still have it; after several decades in a drawer it now spends more and more time in my pocket, or even in some remote part of the bed, to which it migrates after helping me fall asleep through all those rhythmic repetitions: counting sheep must surely have been a Protestant invention, for those sheep are no match for the decades of Hail Marys as a sleep-inducing, as well as soul-nourishing, aid.

At the same shop, I bought St. Christopher medals for our family cars—an idea that had been planted by my Episcopalian godmother, Patsy Miller, who adored St. Christopher despite those unpoetic literalists in the Vatican who had so unceremoniously removed him from the calendar, merely for lack of proof of his existence. He is the one saint whose existence is most certain, if only as an archetype: his name means "bearer of Christ." How could the early Church ever have survived, much less succeeded in supplanting the Roman Empire, without a real, if now anonymous, army of "Christ bearers"? Is that not the role to which we are all called, no matter how many hours of heavy lifting we may put in at the gym?

My Christophers were unusual on two counts. First, they were French, and hence inscribed *St. Christophe*; second, they had magnetic backings so they could be transferred from car to car. I remember adding one temporarily to the dashboard of the U-Haul van that Uncle Ned had rented for the trip to his house in Maine. I was reading a small book called *Meet the American Catholic*, which told me everything I needed to know about post–Vatican II Catholicism, and I found it persuasive and engaging. But the crucial moment in this gradual conversion (there was no fall from a horse, or bolt of lightning) was my trip back to Woodcott to see the Peases. This time I brought along a rosary.

Cousin Rosie asked with no reproach but genuine puzzlement, "Dear

Charlie, are you becoming a *Papist?*" I might have stepped back into the court of Elizabeth I. Her son Jonathan was less bemused: he recounted all sorts of scurrilous details about my favorite saint, Thomas More, which he had picked up in history class at Eton. I discounted the source, and thought More no less a man for all seasons (if not all denominations). The irony is that thirty years later, that medieval farmhouse at Woodcott has, after a half millennium, a Catholic family dwelling within: my cousin Christopher married a Scottish Catholic, Mariana, and their four children are all little Papists—the youngest, Carola Rosemary, being my only Catholic goddaughter. But back in 1970 it was in London that I finally found the "constant image" of an old faith that appealed to a young heart.

MONDAY, AUGUST 12, 2002

Before I return via flight of memory to that London visit, I find myself lodged in South Beach, Miami, for the first time in my life, having spent a long day reliving my Rubens caper of eleven years ago and recounting it on film for a BBC/Bravo documentary. The sweltering ride from Miami Airport took me to Glasshaus Studio in a run-down section of Biscayne Avenue. As I circled the Bauhaus-era building on foot, looking for some semblance of an entrance, I had a frisson that I had entered a real-life set of a Hitchcock film never made: I later learned that my sense of foreboding was well rooted. In the fifties this place had been a Mafia hangout and the site of several rub-outs.

My first filmed scene was an actual, spontaneous reunion with Special Agents Dave D'Amato and Zach Mann, who had played key roles in the Rubens recovery. They looked the same as a decade ago: it was like meeting them again for the first time—though no longer as strangers. I gave Zach, who was undercover as a taxi driver (toting a rifle) during the takedown at the Ocean Grande, a pair of bright pink fluffy dice, courtesy of our new Stephen King book promotion, to hang on his rearview mirror. Camera rolling, we chatted and reminisced about the intervening years. Dave is now active in counterterrorist operations in the wake of September 11; Zach is in charge of press relations for U.S. Customs Special Operations. The twin girls he and his wife were expecting when we last met for the trial at federal court are now nine years old. Children are the ultimate chronicle of time.

The dice swinging on the mirror of his U.S. Customs car, Zach drove me to the site of the new hotel to be used for the reenactment of the undercover operation. The original and misnamed Ocean Grande was unwilling to permit filming inside: it is allegedly owned by some of the original cast of criminals; no doubt they were less than enthusiastic about having a reunion of agents swarming into the lobby again, guns drawn, for the reenactment of their arrest. In fact, the substitute hotel better captured the atmosphere of seedy elegance and danger, a colorful portal to the underworld. The visit convinced me that artistic license may achieve a deeper level of truth than truth itself: *se non è vero, è ben trovato*—it's better than true.

My account on camera of the experience now depends on the director, Bob Bentley, editing stream-of-consciousness recollections into some semblance of clarity. At least the lighting was Caravaggesque, a rich chiaroscuro that captured this Graham Greene world of shadow and light. At the end of the filming I returned to the reception area, where actors were waiting to be auditioned for a pantomime replay of the adventure. At first I had been underwhelmed by the thought that some stranger was going to impersonate me, but for artistic reasons the director did not want originals mixed in with actors. I caught a glance at a younger man who could have been my look-alike brother. I asked him whom he was auditioning to play: some art expert from New York. I asked him his age: forty, he replied—exactly my age at the time. I was facing my doppelgänger—a decade removed. I hoped he would get the chance to resurrect my younger self. He got the part. Perhaps our paths may cross again. I liked him better than my original—another advantage of illusion over reality.

That point was driven home when, determined to revisit the scene of the crime, I jogged in twilight up the beach a couple of miles from our hotel in South Beach to the Ocean Grande. Except for the aerobic dividend, that was a mistake: time had not been kind to the place. The jukebox was gone, along with several chandeliers; run-down and seedy, it seemed a cross between a welfare hotel and a stage for small-time felonies. In the front there hung a For Sale sign. I should have been satisfied with my earlier snapshots and, more, with mental photography. So I look forward to its television remake—to the triumph of art over nature. As for my one-day excursion into a fantasy adventure, Fitzgerald said it best: "If it was not life, it was magnificent." Or as the director declared at the ending of filming, "It's a wrap."

WEDNESDAY, AUGUST 14, 2002

When I took off for London in July of 1970, I was in part escaping a summer job in New York that I had lined up two months earlier. It was not one of my prouder moments. Through Uncle Tom, I had met a high Anglican priest and friend, Father Korn, who ran a program for helping juvenile defendants get lawyers from the city's top law firms—a high-octane Episcopal version of legal aid. I was to be his assistant and accompany him to court each day. For an early fan of Perry Mason, it was a summer job made in heaven. I really don't know why I cooled to it at the last minute and looked for the nearest escape hatch. Perhaps it was my budding romance with Catholicism and a desire to free myself from any more binding ties with Episcopal clergy. I wanted to be a free agent, if not spirit, that summer.

In London I stayed at the house on Britten Street with Cousin Sandy and his legendary Irish housekeeper, Euna, a favorite of mine from my first visit to Woodcott four years earlier and now my "breakfast guide" to Catholic exploration. She directed me to the splendid little Church of the Holy Redeemer, situated just a few streets away in Chelsea, where Sir Thomas More had lived. His original parish had become Anglican as a result of the king who claimed Sir Thomas's head as the price for refusing to acknowledge him as supreme head of the Church. The pastor of the new Catholic parish, a Spanish don as well as Roman priest, explained to me that his Victorian church was now Thomas More's *spiritual* home and took me to a side altar to kiss a relic of the martyred statesman turned saint. It was the first relic I'd ever seen, much less kissed, but it must have had an effect. The Sunday before, I had accompanied my Pease cousins to a charming village church in St. Mary Bourne and had taken Communion for the last time, as it would turn out, as an Anglican. Thereafter I attended only Catholic Masses, as a spectator waiting for the time when I could soon claim membership in a church that knew no national boundaries.

The first weekday Mass I heard at Holy Redeemer, I sat near the front row and the monsignor asked me to be his server: I had to decline, explaining that I was not yet a Catholic and did not know the liturgy well enough. From there I ventured on to the Catholic cathedral in Westminster. It was a vast Byzantine edifice—well beyond the tempered St. Bart's—very Eastern in feeling (no doubt to set it apart from all those Gothic Anglican churches and the neo-Palladian classicism of Wren). It had an exotic mystical aura beyond anything I had seen in the United States. I returned several times, once to hear a magnificent organ recital of thunderous romantic power that echoed throughout the cavernous space. I am sure that the stylistic similarities with St. Bart's made my translation all the smoother. By the end of a week I was ready to come home.

That renewal of my early attraction to Thomas More had set me on my course. The rest of the summer was spent traveling back and forth between my Catholic Miller cousins in Long Island and my home in Far Hills, where the immediate task at hand was to begin formal instruction in the Church. I had brought back with me an English Catholic prayer book: that took care of devotions. All I now needed was a catechism and a priest. I found both in Father Verwey, who gave me the newly published Dutch Catechism as my textbook and guide into new mysteries. Throughout August I visited him once a week to discuss various parts of it in a most informal and enticing way. What a far cry from the bureaucratic programs of group instruction that parishes now require of would-be converts. I never believed in long engagements; mine was to last only a month. I was fortunate to be found knocking on the door of the Church before it put in place all the post–Vatican Council rituals of communal ventures that today seem more like obstacle courses than inviting paths to Rome. But I have always been a soloist—and an impatient one—at heart. God bless him, Father Verwey kept me at a brisk pace, and I never had a moment's doubt about the destination.

THURSDAY, AUGUST 15, 2002

Today is the Feast of the Assumption, the Catholic dogma of Mary's ascension into heaven after her death, body and soul. The first I had heard of this peculiarly Roman feast day—and the first time I ever kept it by attending the obligatory Mass—was on this day in 1970 in Islesboro, Maine, where I was visiting Uncle Ned. I went down to the small island chapel, where a visiting priest from the mainland said Mass for a handful of Romans. I was still a catechumen—a Catholic in waiting—and not a communicant, but that Mass still holds a special place in memory, for it was the closest I could come to attending Nesi von Meister's funeral at St. Brigid's. She had died during my trip to Maine, and there seemed no way I could get back to Far Hills in time for it. One of the more humane, and at the same time mystical, ideas embedded in Catholic belief is the "communion of saints," a heavenly presence made physical and tangible (and ultimately spiritual) in the celebration of the Mass and reception of the sacrament. I felt Nesi's transcendent presence during that otherwise unmemorable service of stark simplicity and without a note of music.

Alas, if I only had known what I was missing at St. Brigid's that day, I would have driven all night to get there before the doors opened: Flicka von Stade, who had just been signed up to begin her long career at the Met, sang the most glorious "Ave Maria" from the rear balcony ever heard by her home team. It must have sounded as if an angel had broken through the firmament to hover over Peapack. And it must have seemed no less miraculous than those painted images of Mary rising heavenward at her Assumption.

FRIDAY, AUGUST 16, 2002

Yesterday I called my friend Dean Richard Gordon of Georgetown Law, who has just returned home after a sudden trip to the hospital prompted by pneumonia; a few weeks ago he suffered a stroke. Despite his infirmities, his wit shines through, sustained by his rock-solid Catholic faith. Recently he asked whether I remembered what I said to him about our faith the first time we met, twenty years ago. I did not. He said he asked why I had ever become a Catholic, and (I take his word for it) I replied that Catholicism was an impossible religion to live in, but the only one to die in.

That story rang a bell: someone had quipped something similar to me when I was an undergraduate at Princeton, and I loved to repeat it—jesting in earnest. What appalls me now is not the glibness of it, but that up until now I had forgotten what lay behind that quip; or rather, what suddenly lay ahead of me—or so I assumed—that first year at Princeton. When my son Charlie asked me several months ago why I became a Catholic in college and I replied that in writing a book I might discover the answer, I had no idea how long it would take to see the obvious. Only now do seemingly random details—the student strikes over the Vietnam War, the preoccupation with crucifixes and St. Thomas More, the present prayers for the dying—all coalesce into a clear picture of what I have conveniently, if unconsciously, ignored.

For me, as for so many of my classmates, the single most dramatic moment of our freshman year was the published results of the draft lottery. Based on birthdays, it established a ranking among all American males of eighteen years and up. The lower your number, the more certain it was that you would be drafted to fight in Vietnam. My unlucky number meant I would certainly be drafted into the army once my student deferral expired upon graduation—unless Nixon ended the war or the draft. In July of 1970 no end appeared in sight.

I remember thinking: Well, if I have to die in Vietnam I want to have last rites as a Catholic. I don't know where that melodramatic thought came from, but it was real and it seemed simple and obvious. So my summer conversion may have owed more to a lottery than to all the books and art and music and saints that had illuminated the faith into which I felt myself drawn. At the very least, that lottery was the catalyst for thought and for taking action—in this case, for focusing on the sacraments as an antidote to death. Of course, I shall never know how different that year might have been if my number had been on the other end of the scale. Perhaps I'd have remained at the edge of the water, fascinated by the reflections, never compelled to take the plunge.

SATURDAY, AUGUST 17, 2002

The plunge, as it would turn out, was really just a gentle splash. The service of reception into the Catholic Church was a "conditional" baptism— and even its conditional aspect was qualified by the priest's assurance to my parents that he had no doubt that I had already been properly baptized as an infant in the Episcopal Church. So it was really just a renewal of those early baptismal vows by a nineteen-year-old; seventeen years after that first go-round, I could now speak for myself and do something more than tug at the cord of an electric fan overhead.

The quiet service in the Victorian Baroque chapel of the convent school Mount St. John Academy in Gladstone was preceded by two pagan rock rituals that summer. They stand out in high relief in part because they were both so unlikely for me, but more because they have become interwoven with the process of becoming a Vatican II Catholic. The first was an evening trip to Greenwich Village with John Powers and my brothers to attend a concert at that temple of hard rock, Fillmore East. On the way I happened to mention to John that I was planning to join his Church. His reply mildly shook me: Think carefully before you do, he cautioned, because it's a serious commitment—in words similar to those of Lord Sebastian, when he sighed how difficult it was to be a Catholic.

The rock concert was introduced by the virtuoso organist Virgil Fox playing something he called "Heavy Bach": his over-the-top performance was matched by a psychedelic light show. At least I could recognize the composer in this alien setting. I did not fare as well with the ritual of communing: people in our row were successively taking puffs from a small cigarette—or so it looked—and passing it along. When it reached me, near the end of the row, it was just a little smoky stub, and to be helpful I stamped it out on the floor. My thirteen-year-old brother John howled in protest, "You idiot, you just put out their reefer!"

The second event that assumed liturgical significance was the three-hour movie *Woodstock.* To my surprise, I actually enjoyed the vicarious experience of that festival of peace and love without the mud, rain, or hunger pains. Early on in the film one brief clip among the many of arriving fans jumped out of the screen: a group of attractive young nuns in traditional habits beamed with smiles as they approached the festival, and then one of them flashed a peace sign. That fleeting gesture gave, for me at least, the rest of the film—and the viewing experience—a benediction. It was my first glimmer of Catholicism having the power to sacramentalize even the most profane and earthy aspects of human celebration.

SUNDAY, AUGUST 18, 2002

The service was as moving and memorable as it was intimate—just Father Verwey, my parents, my new Catholic godparents, Patsy and George Richards, and me. I have been through that service twice since—for each of our two sons. But it is one thing to play the proud parent, quite another to be the humbled penitent seeking admission into the faith. To the basic act of baptism with water, something shared by all branches of Christendom, the Catholic Church adds several layers of ritual and symbol, each pointing to a healing aspect of our Lord's ministry: the anointing of the forehead with the oil of the catechumens to claim us for Christ, and then with chrism after the baptism to signify membership in the royal priesthood through Christ; the touching of the eyes to grant new vision; the blowing into the ears to open them to new hearing; the presentation of a candle lit from the Easter paschal candle of the Resurrection; the donning of a white robe as the garment of new life.

If I were to undergo such conversion today, this service would no longer be used since conditional baptisms are discouraged, for good ecumenical reasons. Yet I am grateful that I was the beneficiary of this anachronism as it prepared me for our children's baptisms in a way no book or bystander's role ever could. The fact that both the school and chapel were dedicated to St. John the Baptist may subconsciously have reinforced the first of the Christian sacraments. It could not have been a more fitting venue—another happy coincidence.

Before the service concluded, Father Verwey took me into the sacristy to hear my first confession. It was blessedly generalized—how else to fit nineteen years of missteps into five minutes? Afterward the six of us returned home for a dinner cooked by my mother. As I look back on it, my parents were enormously supportive sports about my defection from our family church. As puzzled as they must have been, they never remonstrated: perhaps they recognized that this Latin translation was far less radical than other current trends—from Hare Krishna to the Moonies.

The next morning I arose early to drive back to the chapel for my First Communion. On my way I was seized by a pang of scrupulosity: I had forgotten to include occasions of "drinking to excess" to my list of mortal sins. It had been an innocent oversight, but it troubled me nonetheless, and I went to my First Communion already feeling as morally crippled as a Graham Greene character. I tried to patch the hole afterward, but my first brush with overscrupulosity left a worrisome aftertaste to that First Communion. Confession is an awkward act for a reticent Protestant; in my case, it would take another thirty years before I made a completely open one—a walking confession, side by side more than face-to-face, that filled a three-mile walk with my pal Father Andrew O'Connor from a restaurant in Little Italy to final absolution in the sanctuary of St. Patrick's. But in hindsight the starting point of my ongoing pilgrimage was that chapel at Mount St. John— and the next stop was Princeton, for sophomore year.

MONDAY, AUGUST 19, 2002

Early this morning I had a twilight dream about returning to Princeton as a student again, having a terrible time finding the right room, followed by equal confusion about courses to take and a thesis to write. Only when the stress of putting all these pieces aright was too great for a half-awake mind did I hear myself protest that I already had my degrees and that my thesis had been written and accepted long ago. And so I awoke to the comforting realization that I could return safely as a revisiting tourist, with no further fear of entrapment.

I took a long detour after Mass at St. Patrick's—north through Central Park. I came out on the West Side at the Ethical Culture School, a handsome building with an inscription marking the foundation of that society in 1876, a century after our Declaration of Independence. I had had no idea it was so old. Both its name and philosophical thrust—a stridently secular (even atheistic) humanism—had always bothered me, but strangely not today. What's wrong with ethical culture? Isn't that what all benign religions strive to foster through their creeds? Suddenly it seemed all the more impressive for nonbelievers in God to commit themselves to such an ideal. After all, for them there is no threat of divine sanctions should they fail, or even fail to try. And then I remembered my father saying that if faith is truly a gift, then it is just as senseless to denigrate those to whom it has not been given as it would be to castigate the poor for not owning more possessions.

By now I had arrived at my destination—Lincoln Center—to see whether there were still any tickets left to the two free Mostly Mozart concerts this week. I was in luck: two seats on the highest tier, almost as far from the orchestra as the architect had permitted anyone to sit. But that, too, seemed a gift (as indeed it was, free of charge): I had never sat so high up, and I was intrigued to hear whether Mozart's music would soar to such heights.

My last call today was to Father Weiser, who was as new a chaplain in 1970 as I was a Catholic. One of the first calls I had made upon returning to Princeton was to his rooms on the second floor of the stately brick Georgian house on Mercer Street, headquarters of the Aquinas Institute. In my father's day it had belonged to Thomas Mann. I was visiting the same place my father had thirty years earlier—now to meet a German-American priest, where he had once visited the great German novelist. My disappointed dad had found Mann "pretentious and deadly boring." He never returned. I returned there almost every day of that sophomore year—and all the years that followed in Princeton.

TUESDAY, AUGUST 20, 2002

My two roommates and I had a suite of rooms on the ground floor of Henry Hall, right beside the triple arches that served as a gateway from University Place to the campus. There were two niches high up, facing each other on this Gothic revival façade: one housed St. George; the other, St. Michael—two heroic figures in cast bronze that epitomized an earlier era of muscular Christianity at Princeton. Each morning at seven-fifteen, while my roommates and most of the campus still slept, I walked past them and up the street past the Princeton Seminary and then Trinity Episcopal Church and the governor's mansion, Morven, to arrive at Aquinas in time for the seven-thirty Mass. The undiluted piety of a new convert was already shaping my academic schedule. How very different it was from my son Charlie's schedule thirty years later: he always arranged for his first class never to begin before eleven so that he could sleep late. But then there is a big difference between us: he was born a Catholic.

At the start of that year I still assumed that I would major either in classics or in English. I dearly wanted to get the burden of the social science requirement out of the way and so signed up for a course in anthropology: it was benignly titled "Language and Culture" but turned out to be toxic. The professor, who looked like a caricature of a campus radical, told us that our assignment for the term was to infiltrate an underground group and keep a notebook, Henry Higgins–like, of how they used subcategories of jargon. I could see myself surviving at most a few minutes in my underground role, and I headed straight to the registrar's office as soon as the bell tolled. There I searched the catalogue for a more palatable course.

Eureka—a course appeared that was to change my academic life as well as illumine my new journey as a Catholic: medieval art with Professor Alan Borg. Yet I owe more than I can ever say to Professor Zaretsky of anthropology: he drove me straight into art history. Not art for art's sake, but in this instance art as an escape into history—and into a deeper faith. At home in New York on weekends, Kenneth Clark's *Civilisation* had replaced *The Forsyte Saga* on Sunday evenings. That magnificent series soon confirmed in me the desire to approach cultural history through its visual legacy, a convenient approach for a slow reader who always loved picture books.

WEDNESDAY, AUGUST 21, 2002

Today has been Mostly Mozart in more ways than I could ever have imagined. Walking across Rockefeller Plaza behind Prometheus, as I do every day, I stopped momentarily to look a bit more closely at some of the silver spray-painted old American cars parked (for the summer) around a thirty-three-foot transmission tower. An ensemble of "post video art" by the Korean artist Nam June Paik, it looks like a science fiction vision of a parking lot in the 1950s after a nuclear attack—the empty autos frozen in time like industrial tombstones to a once mobile society. At other times, it seems too close to home—resembling, but for the dates of the cars, those images of ash-covered autos abandoned on the streets around the World Trade Towers after their fall. In each case: a funereal intrusion into this center of broadcasting, business, and tourism. But for the first time, today, I paused long enough to hear the music coming from various points under the auto-tombs: the Kyrie from Mozart's *Requiem.* I was dumbstruck and went over to one of the guards and asked him why they were playing Mozart's *Requiem.* He said it plays all day long, nonstop, over and over. He said it's part of the show and suggested I read the program.

There I found a partial answer: the sixteen cars are from Paik's "elegiac" *32 Cars for the 20th Century: Play Mozart's Requiem Quietly* (some title!). I read on: "Each car is painted silver, stripped of its engine and filled with defunct audio-visual equipment. Near the cars one can hear Mozart's *Requiem*, the composer's final, unfinished work. . . . His updated take on Mozart's *Requiem* is a clear-eyed, unsentimental ode to the 20th century. . . . It is a poetic commentary on the nature of consumer culture, technology and obsolescence." All well and good, but it left me hungry for one missing piece of information. *Whose* performance was I hearing? No credit was listed in the program. If I were more patient, or more of a masochist, I might stand beside those cars and listen until I came up with a short list of candidates. But I am too impatient, and besides I needed to get home in time for the Mostly Mozart concert this evening.

Ritchie had grave doubts about climbing so high into outer space, as she described our seats on the highest tier. But they offered an awesome view of the hall and stage below. And once the instruments started to play the overture to *La Clemenza di Tito*, a favorite on my list of underrated operas, I knew how lucky I had been to come to the box office so late. It was the musical equivalent of this morning's gospel parable about the late laborers who get the same wages as the early ones: "The first shall be last and the last first." I have never heard the music in this hall with such resonance or clarity as in those remote seats; it seemed a miracle that sight could be so diminished by the distance while the sound made the instruments seem within touch.

Once home, I found a CD of Haydn's *Missa Cellensis* outside the front door. It has just finished playing, and I finally understand why Mozart revered Papa Haydn so unreservedly. In the program notes I found a powerful and evocative description by Maestro Burdick of the "maelstrom" around Trinity Church on September 11 that "blanketed the graveyard" with debris and "fine ash-like pumice." This strange juxtaposition in one day of Mozart and Haydn, of masterpieces and of graves, offers yet another reminder of the power of music to rise above ashes (or even metal auto-tombs) as a foretaste of a greater resurrection.

SATURDAY, AUGUST 24, 2002

Mozart's *Requiem* has become an obsession: this morning I listened to the different edited versions while I reread chapters of Robbins Landon's book about Mozart's last year. The accumulation of documentary evidence over the past two centuries makes it clear that Mozart had left precise instructions to his pupil Süssmayr about how he wanted all the remaining movements of his *Requiem* completed and orchestrated if he were to die before finishing the score himself. Late in her life, Mozart's widow Constanze said that anyone could have done what Süssmayr did, given the composer's detailed directions. The last thing he did before he expired was to mouth the sounds of the kettledrums.

What bad luck, illness, and a tragically untimely death did not do to poor Mozart and his young wife, Constanze, modern authors have wrought with a vengeance. I wonder whether my sons and generations to come will picture him as other than the crude caricature of Shaffer's *Amadeus*, a drunken imbecile with a God-given talent and a dippy wife. Even when I was at Princeton, the common wisdom was that Mozart's religious music was strictly "for hire," something he knocked off to earn a living so that he could write the music—operas, symphonies, chamber pieces—he really loved. What a surprise then to read that his widow said that his favorite genre of all was church music. As for his poor choice of a spouse, this portion of a letter to his father—shortly after their wedding—struck me as especially poignant: "For some time before we were married we had always attended Mass and gone to confession and received Communion together; and I discovered that never had I prayed so ardently or confessed or received Communion so devoutly as by her side; and she felt likewise. In short we are made for one another: and God who orders all things and hence this too, will not forsake us."

SUNDAY, AUGUST 25, 2002

This evening I went to Mass at St. Vincent's, happily accompanied by son Charlie. That church was the first in New York where I attended Sunday Mass right after my conversion in September of 1970. I found myself sitting across from John Powers and his parents on that day—I had come full circle back to my first Catholic friend at Buckley. But soon afterward I heard from a family friend that I should go uptown to St. Thomas More on Eighty-ninth Street, where the choir sang Gregorian chant at the Sunday High Mass.

So I ventured north and discovered that gem of a church, well-named after my adopted patron saint, Thomas More—a small London Gothic church transplanted across the Atlantic. It was unusually tasteful, with beautiful and intimate proportions, stunning stained glass windows, and restrained Catholic furnishings. I felt immediately at home—and soon discovered why: the church had originally been built by Episcopalians, and had been taken over by the Catholics only a year before my birth. It presents, in a sense, the mirror image of those London Catholic parish churches, like Sir Thomas's own in Chelsea, that became Anglican at the behest of King Henry. So I got to change my church and keep it, too. Perhaps church may be the one exception to Thomas Wolfe's dictum that "you can't go home again." No matter where it is, or how renovated beyond recognition, it remains a spiritual home for all who seek it.

MONDAY, AUGUST 26, 2002

Another of the extracurricular activities I undertook that sophomore fall term, in the first flush of conversion, was a weekly evening class sponsored by the CCD—the Confraternity of Christian Doctrine—held in the basement of the Catholic parochial school a few blocks south on Nassau Street. I was back at another St. Paul's School, and the course was in the Old Testament, with lectures given by a very animated young priest named Father David Fulton. It was like being back in third-form sacred studies—only with no tests and no grades, the ultimate blessing of continuing education! These courses grew out of the Second Vatican Council's mandate to reemphasize the Bible and to foster biblical literacy among the laity after centuries of neglect. Martin Luther and the other early Reformers had finally left their mark on Rome, and I was one of the new beneficiaries.

Meanwhile, my favorite surprise course—medieval art—also took me back to basics in a way those first Protestant Reformers would have applauded: the Reformation had in large part sought to recapture the purity and simplicity of the early Christians. Our survey of the Middle Ages began with an in-depth study of early Christian painting and sculpture. It was the perfect baptism in a new field and discipline, for the images were simple and easy to read; there were no names and dates of artists to memorize—they all were blissfully anonymous. The main thrust was iconography—a historic tradition in Princeton's Department of Art and Archaeology—and for me it was the perfect approach: a literary and theological one, an exegesis of imagery, so to speak. What does the picture mean? What is the text it illustrates? How does it interpret that text symbolically? It was the art of reading images as though they were a language, the perfect detour down a picture-perfect route for someone who had tired of carrying around his Latin and Greek dictionaries.

I soon fell in love with the world of the early Christians—mainly Rome, and later Ravenna, that glorious seaport south of Venice that for a brief shining moment in the fifth century was the capital of the late Roman Empire in the West. The catacomb wall paintings with their Matisse-like simplicity held me in awe, probably as much for the romance of their underground settings as for the pictures themselves. My favorite medium was mosaics, the primary form of glowing decoration throughout the Constantinian churches of Rome—Santa Maria Maggiore, Santa Pudenziana, Sant'Agnese, Santa Costanza, and on and on. I knew that before the year was over I had to go to Rome as a pilgrim and visit every one of these textbook places in the flesh. Meanwhile, they came alive liturgically every morning as the priest recited the litany of these earliest saints during the Roman Canon of the Mass: "thy blessed apostles and martyrs Peter and Paul, Andrew, James, John, Thomas, James, Philip, Bartholomew, Matthew, Simon and Jude . . . Linus, Cletus, Clement, Sixtus, Cornelius, Cyprian, Lawrence, Chrysogonus, John and Paul, Cosmos and Damian." The very list itself conjured up the places of their veneration in that Eternal City. It was as though I had become a Catholic to go back to square one. And when on the midterm test we faced two alternate apse mosaics of the Transfiguration— one at the monastery of St. Catherine on Mount Sinai, the other at Sant' Apollinare in Classe outside Ravenna—I recalled my first: the apse of St. Bartholomew's in New York. Through art, I had again come full circle.

WEDNESDAY, AUGUST 28, 2002

Realizing that today would be my last chance to solve the riddle of the *Requiem* beneath Haik's autos, which are scheduled to disappear this Sunday in time for Labor Day, I arrived at the plaza armed with my CD Walkman and the Levin edition as performed by the Boston Baroque. *Ecco*: the voices, instruments, and tempo were a perfect match, and upon the third repeat there was not a shred of doubt left. My only slight regret was that this convenient fluke—the recording was obviously stuck in a repeat mode—meant that tourists and passersby would hear nothing of Mozart's masterpiece today except for an appended Amen. But I was elated that the musicians were no longer anonymous under those decaying bodies of motorcars.

As I left Rock Center on my way home, that same Amen playing endlessly, while the rest of the *Requiem* remained frozen in digital limbo, I mentioned it to a guard, to pass along to the sound engineer when he came by at the end of the day. "You mean it's like a broken record," he volunteered. "Yes," I replied, grateful for the image of those earlier years of vinyl discs and warmer sounds when a problem like this one needed only a gentle nudge to get music and life back into the next groove. But as I walked home I had the inescapable sensation that the endless Amen signified, however coincidentally, something amiss—an unresolved prayer, a metaphysical limbo. When I got to Long Island and called Aunt Patsy to ask her for dinner tomorrow night, I learned that she was not at home but rather at a hospital keeping a vigil for her son, Garrison, who had been given last rites and was—according to the doctors—within hours of death. I had prayed earlier today that God might soon take him home after so long a brave ordeal; perhaps my encounters with Mozart had more to do with prompting that prayer than I suspected: *"Requiem aeternam dona ei, Domine, et lux perpetua luceat ei."* May the good Lord grant him eternal rest and light perpetual. *Amen.*

FRIDAY, AUGUST 30, 2002

Today I got to St. Vincent's early, in time for the communal friars' Mass. The young Dominican who officiated gave a very crisp and engaging homily on the story of the wise and foolish virgins, the moral of which is "Be prepared, for you know not when the bridegroom approaches." We were reminded that our preparation as Christians is to be of joyful expectation. The challenge this morning was to square that sound view with the dark reality of my cousin Garrison lying in limbo betwixt the chains of terminal decline and the interior light that must already be breaking through the cells of consciousness.

Last weekend at this very time I was reading the all too lurid, if clinical, description of Mozart's last hours as his body bloated into a cruel caricature of self. The reports I heard today from my cousins sadly confirmed that two centuries of medical revolutions have left untouched the pathos and despair in viewing our "too, too mortal flesh" before it releases the ineffable spirit at the final moment. In Garrison's case, his suffering is by now all past, but not past reflection in the eyes and hearts of the loved ones gathered about his bed. At the end of the Mass I went up to the Rosary altar and there felt he was already among the saints enshrined in gilded niches. It was more, I am sure, than wishful thinking: he was joining this mystical communion while his family sat vigil and watched with utmost pain the remnants of life and the aura of love fade from his swollen body. Perhaps it was a proleptic epiphany—the revelation of a future state as seen through the prism of the present.

Theologians teach that God's time is telescoped, synthesized, and reconciled into an inscrutable simultaneity. Our time is not his. Ours marks decay; his distills in a flash of light or a blink of an eye the essence of eternity. There is no doubt that we stand, with the exceptions of a few mystical saints like Teresa and St. John of the Cross, on this bleak side of the final equation. It's hard to see the sunlight through the eye of the storm.

Science and theology are walking down a new path and together promise epiphanies to the faithful and unbelievers alike. It's sure to be a long exploration, an odyssey into the very heart of space. For the rest of us, we must turn back to the age-old agents of love and faith to fashion a model of reconciliation, perseverance, and, above all, hopeful expectation. It's a hard path of prayer, but the softer cushions of despair offer but a respite from which we may never arise: the sleep of oblivion. The road to communion is longer and fraught with doubt, but well-trod for two millennia by our Lord himself, his apostles, saints, and sinners—the best company a soul might seek on the darkest of days.

SATURDAY, AUGUST 31, 2002

The last day of August. When I picked up my mother this morning she told me that Garrison had died in the night. I called and learned from his brother-in-law Gary that he breathed his last around one in the morning—as it turned out, just as I was completing last night's entry in this journal—another small piece in a mosaic of coincidences I no longer feel able to understand, much less explain.

A day before the Labor Day migration along the Long Island Expressway, it was good to be back at St. Jean Baptiste on a Sunday evening when the days are still long—and light—enough to illumine the window of *Moses and the Manna*, high above the transept. It's my father's window (recently restored in his memory) and I love to look at it during the Mass. As I did so tonight, I recognized what it was that halfway through my sophomore year caused me to commit myself to art history as my major: art as a *window* into history—images, sculptures, artifacts, and entire buildings as the means of re-creating a past. Re-creation as the ultimate recreation: it was as fun as engrossing. And so for the second term that year three of my four courses were in art history: a survey of Western art, medieval architecture (again taught by Professor Borg), and Italian Renaissance art.

I don't recall my father's reaction to this sudden downpour of art history—and equally sudden disappearance of classics and English as probable majors. Perhaps the fact that we had all become addicted to Kenneth Clark's *Civilisation* made my lunge toward picture books less disturbing to this master of ancient languages and the written word. Besides, he had been the one to bring me an art book while I was writing my paper on Gunn's poem. He said that one of his favorite courses at Princeton had been in the art department. So perhaps my major offered him a vicarious curriculum— just as my son Charlie's recent decision to major in history gives me the chance to explore a new academic path. Last week on my way to work, halfway down Park Avenue, I stopped at a red light and thought how much fun it would be to return to Princeton and earn a degree all over again— but in another department. Like the Magi returning by another route.

THURSDAY, SEPTEMBER 5, 2002

Tomorrow morning I drive down to Princeton with Charlie and a carful of belongings as he begins his junior year. He is now half a year ahead of his dad, as I still find myself stuck in the winter of sophomore year—but I shall catch up with Charlie all too soon, alas, as I begin to press ahead to the present. So I may as well enjoy being the younger of us two Princetonians for the next few days.

Along with my new church that sophomore year, I acquired a new holiday to celebrate: St. Patrick's Day. As a freshly minted Catholic, I secretly regretted that I could not claim any Irish ancestry, but still I wore to class that day a green-dyed carnation in my lapel. One of my preppier classmates chided me, "Scribner, take off that flower—you're no more Irish than I am." All I could think to answer was, "Every Catholic is spiritually Irish today, for Patrick is our saint." Glib—but it got me to class still sporting the green.

I was by now so settled into a new life at Princeton that, for the first time in memory, I chose not to go with my family south for spring break; instead I stayed on campus. One unseasonably warm day, I set out for a long walk around the town. My destination was the house of Sir Hugh Taylor, a distinguished scientist and retired dean of the Graduate College, whom my father had urged me to visit sometime. But I had a more precise objective: to ask him to be my official sponsor at my upcoming confirmation in the Catholic Church later that spring.

A Scotsman who had spent much of his academic life in the Chemistry Department of Princeton, Sir Hugh was the scientist who discovered how to create "heavy water," an essential ingredient in producing the atomic bomb during World War II. He was also a devout Roman Catholic and a member of the Pontifical Academy of Sciences. But what really caught my attention was the remark by Father Weiser that he was the only man to be knighted by both the queen of England and the pope; he had *two* knighthoods—one Protestant, one Catholic. To a young monarchist and new papist, this was too good to be true. But he wasn't: he was the real thing, a model of professorial preeminence. He was also delightful company, and every time I come upon my confirmation program with Sir Hugh Taylor listed as sponsor, I am grateful I followed up on a suggestion of my father. I hope my children may ponder this unthinkable thought.

SATURDAY, SEPTEMBER 7, 2002

This morning at Garrison's funeral Mass, at the Church of St. Thomas More (another divine coincidence?) in Darien, I heard a recapitulation of these very same human qualities, as Garrison's all-too-brief but incomparably full life illuminated that modern church in the round, even more than the bright sunlight streaming in. Garrison had planned this funeral four years ago, when he first learned that his cancer was terminal; then he fought the good fight and extended his life and his gift of presence to family and friends by a full two years beyond the most optimistic predictions of medical experts—by sheer force of will. I dreaded the sorrow and sadness of this funeral, but I should have known better: it wasn't sad; it was Garrison. Even his decision to forgo a casket—which ran against my traditionalist grain—proved to be pitch perfect: the focus was shifted from the remains, from mortal flesh to the life of the Spirit.

SUNDAY, SEPTEMBER 8, 2002

Hearing, for the first time, Garrison's nickname, "the King," in the midst of a memorial Mass brought back to me a sequence of variations on a religious theme during my first Catholic year, a theme I had long forgotten: Christ the King. (Perhaps my recollection was reinforced by recent late-night reading in Father Greeley's prayer journal, where he often mentions events and reunions at his old Chicago parish, to which he simply refers as "CK"—Christ the King.) My first introduction to this epithet was at a Sunday service back in the fall of 1970 in the Princeton University Chapel, where I had gone to hear as the guest preacher Archbishop Fulton J. Sheen. He was the first and—up until Pope John Paul II—the most charismatic Catholic prelate to harness the power of television for the faith. I already owned a copy of his book *This Is the Mass*, with magnificent photographs of him celebrating it in his private chapel of gilded New York Baroque. I brought along the copy for him to sign.

I'll never forget his sermon, nor his mesmerizing eyes and voice—both of which had successfully converted such worldly folk to the Roman faith as Claire Booth Luce and Henry Ford. He announced that this day was the Feast of Christ the King (a new feast to my ears), and then thunderously proclaimed that our King ruled not from a throne but from a cross. That woke up the mostly Protestant congregation. He quoted our Lord's announcement "I have come not to bring peace but the sword," and then he explained that people who were not at war with the sin within themselves invariably turned their swords outward to strike at others. He said that whatever the Church forgets—or neglects—the world appropriates and inverts. We neglect the cross, and right outside our chapel stand three large sculptures of "peace symbols" (the old ban-the-bomb circles), which he scathingly described as "the cross broken and turned upside down." Just as nuns abandoned their rosaries, he added, hippies took them up and wore them around their necks as beads. It was very colorful and provocative, to say the least: I cannot think of another sermon I can recall so vividly after more than thirty years. Afterward, I got a chance to meet him outside the chapel, and he inscribed my book in a script as bold and theatrical as his rhetoric: "To Charles—whom God has called into greater intimacy with Himself..." It was an original gloss on what my conversion to Rome was all about. I pray the romance may continue.

A few weeks later, perhaps in an afterglow of that new feast day, I chose as the topic for my first term paper in art history "Christ as Emperor in Early Christian Art." In the spring I followed up my study of royal iconography with a survey of early Christian basilicas (the term derives from the Greek word for king): imperial halls adapted to the worship of Christ the King, wherein the altar, under a royal baldachin, replaces the throne. I suppose I was still a classics major manqué: not for me the dark massiveness of the Romanesque or the lofty intricacies of High Gothic. No, I was firmly rooted in the late Roman Empire, in the formal simplicity (if sheathed in gleaming mosaics and marble) of the early Christian era.

MONDAY, SEPTEMBER 9, 2002

All day I have been hearing radio ads for a performance of the Verdi *Requiem* in two days, in memory of the victims of 9/11. Late this evening, Chris came in the door a few minutes ahead of curfew, carrying a FedEx package and announcing, "Delivery for Dad." I took one look at the sender, the JFK Library, and knew that the day would indeed end with an epiphany. I was not disappointed.

The grainy black-and-white video of the NBC broadcast from the Sports Arena in L.A. on Sunday, November 24, 1963, captured the most moving and passionate "Libera me" I have ever heard and certainly have ever seen. After my initial confusion over the operatic bombast of Verdi's *Requiem*—or so it sounded when I first heard it one Sunday of freshman year at St. Bartholomew's—I soon grew to love it more than any other choral work. I collected various recordings as far back as the Rome performance conducted by Tullio Serafin on the eve of World War II; I listened to all of them religiously. But no recording has excited me more than this broadcast on the day before our president was buried at Arlington.

The young Zubin Mehta conducted with all the animation and intensity of Toscanini; even more, this is the best visual and audio record I have ever discovered of Mary Costa in performance, with all the expressiveness of a Guido Reni saint looking heavenward as she sang, *"Libera me, Domine, de morte aeterna, in die illa tremenda, quando movendi sunt caeli et terra."* The heavens and earth are already moved with pity long before that day of wrath and judgment—thanks to Verdi's music and the voice of an angel. I shall look at the video one more time tomorrow morning, as an antidote to the renewed horror of 9/11 that the approaching anniversary cannot avoid evoking. Then I shall send this tape to the soprano, with special gratitude that she undertook that assignment within minutes of her stage entrance as Musetta across the city at a matinee of *La Bohème*. Act two was delayed to allow the police escort time to whisk Mary from the Sports Arena to the opera stage at the Shrine Auditorium. Among the members of the audience who waited was a virtuoso young pianist—Van Cliburn. If this were not all verifiable, would anyone believe me? I have often wondered whether I would ever have the inclination to try my hand at fiction. I doubt it: I cannot invent things; I find the unvarnished truth much too mysterious and engrossing. Fortunately I don't need to explain it; that is the domain of its Author.

WEDNESDAY, SEPTEMBER 11, 2002

As I write, Verdi's "Libera me" is playing on the radio, bringing to a resounding conclusion the *Requiem* performed as a memorial to the victims of
9/11. The day turned out to be one of subdued and seamless tribute and
remembrance; the greatest drama was getting Chris out of bed and his new
dorm room unpacked and ready for a final year of Eaglebrook. Back in
New York, as I took an evening jog in Central Park, I looked up and
glimpsed, over the crowns of the midtown skyscrapers, a silver sliver of
moon punctuating the still-blue sky; it looked like a celestial apostrophe, a
possessive mark over the urban skyline: But whose are they? Whose are we?
The void around the mark of the moon suddenly seemed to suggest the obvious—Whose, indeed? "I Am Who I Am."

FRIDAY, SEPTEMBER 13, 2002

Safaris were my grandmother Scribner's passion. By the time she died I had
lost count of her trips to Africa. Her family entourage this time included
my two cousins Mary and Anda and a Princeton classmate. Our guide was
an Englishman who looked and sounded like a young David Niven (and
who later married Mary).

   We spent the first night en route to Nairobi in Rome, where we were
treated to a magnificent *son et lumière* in the Roman Forum that covered the
entire ancient history of the Eternal City from its legendary founding by
Romulus and Remus to the fall of the Caesars. The interplay of lights and
sounds over the ruins was sheer magic. Over the past thirty years of revis-
its I have sought but never found another such show there; yet I refuse to

believe it was a dream. The next morning we dashed off to St. Peter's. Mary and Anda didn't get farther than the gates since their miniskirts precluded admittance into the basilica. I longed to return on my own, as a true pilgrim and not a frantic tourist. "All roads lead to Rome." I prayed the dusty roads of Kenya and Tanzania would be no exception.

Oscar Wilde said that "experience" is the name we give to our mistakes: that African safari was quite an experience. In Nairobi, before setting out into the wilderness, I went to Mass at the Catholic cathedral, a modern translation of Gothic vaults into concrete, hovering between a basilica and an airplane hangar. But the Mass was the Mass, however far removed from cultural constants, and that was the most precious epiphany Africa was to offer: my adopted Church was truly catholic after all; anytime I was at Mass I was at home—or at least on my way home.

The books I took along with me as we motored up into Samburu country included Waugh's *A Handful of Dust*, in which I could identify all too closely with the protagonist, who is doomed to be a captive in the Amazon jungle for the rest of his life—reading the same books over and over to his insane captor. Then I moved on to C. S. Lewis's *Surprised by Joy*, the best account of Christian conversion and grace in the face of suffering and loss that I have ever read. Down at Treetops, where two decades earlier Princess Elizabeth learned she had become queen, I spent my time not watching elephants and rhinos gathering below but following Father John La Farge's journey as a Jesuit in his memoir *The Manner Is Ordinary*. It was a long and dense tome Uncle Ned had given me, but it proved consoling company through the African nights.

The main course, once we reached the main game parks such as Fort Ikoma, and Lake Naivasha, and the Serengeti, was Greene. I had bought a bunch of his paperbacks en route; they perfectly suited my dark mood and my quest for some transcendent mystery and intervention. *A Burnt-Out Case*, about a doctor who is destroyed by his missionary work with the lepers in the Congo, was offset by *Our Man in Havana*, a light comedy about a witless vacuum cleaner salesman in Cuba who invents a role for himself in international espionage. That novel I read in the bathtub at Fort Ikoma all night long, since my hut had been invaded by a column of army ants. *Brighton Rock*, one of Greene's early novels, about a street thug named Pinky, I read during an entire day toward the end of our safari. While the rest were all out in the Land Rover chasing their hundredth herd of zebras, I sat under an umbrella table with a glass and an ice bucket and a bottle of vodka to lend ambience to the seedy world of Greene's teenage gangs. The revelation under that umbrella was a single line, when Pinky is about to experience mortality, quoting the old adage that repentance and salvation are still possible "betwixt the stirrup and the ground." With God, it is never too late. Graham Greene reminded me that Catholicism is the only faith to die in, however impossible it might seem to live in.

Before the end of the safari, I had purchased an African statue of a Madonna and Child to take home to the States. My grandmother insisted on referring to it as my "idol." I countered, in a lapse of Christian charity and deference, "Granny, people have been burned at the stake for comments like that!" But she stuck to her term. I decided to give it to Father Verwey when I returned, for he surely had the sacramental power to cast any idol into a venerable icon worthy of devotion.

SATURDAY, SEPTEMBER 14, 2002

After the game parks of East Africa, Rome was Easter after Lent. I was ready for a feast—and I found it. There my first quest was to find and visit every early Christian church and site that I recalled from my first Princeton art course. I saw all five of the major basilicas, beginning with Santa Maria Maggiore and its magnificent, if dimly lit, early Christian mosaics along the nave. From there, I proceeded on to the Lateran, where I climbed the *scala santa* on my knees and earned, I hoped, the promised indulgence. Santa Croce in Gerusalemme was a bit gloomy, even if it did contain a piece of the True Cross, thanks to the empress Helena. St. Paul's Outside the Walls was a nineteenth-century rebuilding of the early Christian original destroyed by fire, but more than any of the others it conveyed the sense of its original time and place—like a classic Cecil B. DeMille set.

St. Peter's, the reigning basilica, stood apart, since its predecessor had been demolished to make way for the new grandeur of High Renaissance and Baroque aspirations. I felt suitably awed by its status as the de facto cathedral of the universe, a role supported by extravagant gilded bronze and shining marble personifications twice life-size. I felt like Dorothy approaching Oz: this was not Kansas. As mortals were transfigured into celestial beings before my eyes, I yearned for the scale and simplicity of the early Christian era.

At San Clemente, with its three descending levels of worship throughout its first millennium, I fell in love with the uppermost mosaics, especially the apse that set our Lord in a serene equilibrium from which he fulfilled the task of redemption without any of the contortions and grimaces that might offset his gracefulness in paying a mortal debt to achieve immortal victory.

The converted emperor Constantine had unleashed an enormous energy among sculptors, painters, and architects, to fashion physical persuasion at the invisible core of the new faith. After visiting San Clemente, I found my architectural favorite via a long cab ride outside the Roman walls to the little round church of Santa Costanza—a funerary chapel built for the daughter of the emperor Constantine. Only two millennia before its time, it captured the modern aesthetic of simple circular forms, a centralized focal point, life-affirming, almost whimsical vines and flowers, recalling our Lord's declaration that he is the true vine. As a burial chapel site for regular worship it replaced hierarchical features with communal ones for all who gather around the table of the Lord. Here I found the perfect Roman—and romantic—setting for those wandering agapes, those Eucharistic love feasts at St. Paul's two years earlier, on the eve of Woodstock.

There was still enough of the early Christian sensibility in me—fostered through a childhood at St. Bart's—that thrived on these quiet epiphanies punctuating the grandeur of Rome. My reaction to the High Baroque churches of the Gesù, Sant'Ignazio, and Sant'Andrea della Valle was much like my first response to the Verdi *Requiem*: why all the flash and noise and confusion? The modern architect Mies said "less is more"; the architects of the Roman Baroque seemed to agree with Mae West: "Too much of a good thing is wonderful." I returned to Princeton full of blessed medals, rosaries, books, artifacts, from my whirlwind baptism into Roman Catholic culture, but with a lingering sense that my signing up for Baroque art that fall term had been a mistake, even if the professor was the most celebrated lecturer in the department.

But John Rupert Martin won me over from the start. There can be no overestimating the power of professorial enthusiasm that breathes new imagination and passion into young doubting Thomases. There is no student like a newly converted one. A few lectures into Martin's course, I was ready to "go for Baroque"—wherever that might take me.

THURSDAY, SEPTEMBER 19, 2002

One of our early assignments in Martin's course was on Rubens's two great triptychs in Antwerp's cathedral: *The Raising of the Cross* and *The Descent from the Cross*. The second, though less dramatic than the first, was the more thought-provoking, for it incorporated a sophisticated theological program of imagery—of iconography—that represented a brilliant continuity with the traditions of medieval art while, at the same time, recasting the figures in a thoroughly modern, heroic mode of naturalism tempered by Renaissance classicism. Rubens achieved here as in so many other masterpieces an inspired synthesis of theology, devotion, and emotion. The three biblical scenes on the inside of the altarpiece were thematically coordinated with the scene on the outside shutters showing the muscular St. Christopher carrying the Christ Child across a river. This legendary encounter between the sainted giant and the Child God provided the key to the meaning of the other scenes: in the main frame, the descent, or lowering, of Christ's body from the cross following his death; on the left, the visitation by the Virgin Mary "great with child" to her old cousin Elizabeth, also pregnant (with John the Baptist); on the right, the presentation of the Christ Child in the temple, where the baby is held by the old priest Simeon and receives his name. Every scene is linked by the saint's Greek name, *Christophoros*, which means "carrier of Christ." In each case, we see someone fulfilling that sacred role of being a Christ bearer: the disciples who lower him from the cross, his mother who carries him through to birth, the priest who carries him in the temple, and finally Christopher himself. I no longer minded my father's speculation that St. Christopher, who had recently lost his official place on the church's calendar for lack of historical evidence, was really a mythical Christianizing of the pagan hero Hercules. The Rubens triptych made it clear that the allegorical meaning of his name alone was reason enough to posit his sainthood—if not his very existence. The central task of the Christian is to be a Christ bearer, a carrier of Christ to and for others. Perhaps the study of that Rubens triptych thirty years ago is what prompted me to wear a medal of Christopher instead of a more historical saint. Sometimes myth can convey a greater truth than fact. It can certainly be the bearer of grace. As I wear my new medal I reflect gratefully on the young Rubens's triptych that convinced me beyond doubt that I had found a Christian artist worth exploring.

Another assignment was to compare two prints from the Passion of Christ: first, an engraving of Rubens's so-called *Coup de Lance*, the moment after Christ dies on the cross and a centurion pierces his side with a spear, while the heavens are shrouded in darkness; second, an etching by Rembrandt showing the solemn and silent transporting of our Lord's body to its tomb. The Rubens was triumphant and heroic; the Rembrandt, a quiet study in pathos. I was enthralled by the Rubens as I attempted to tie every detail to a reference in St. John's gospel account—a pictorial and biblical exegesis. When I got the paper back, Professor Martin wrote that he was pleased I had "avoided the temptation to exploit the Rembrandt at the expense of the Rubens." If he had only known: I had only to make sure I didn't gloss over Rembrandt too quickly. Rubens had already claimed me.

FRIDAY, SEPTEMBER 20, 2002

As first-year majors in art history, we all met once a week for our Junior Seminar. The painting I chose for my iconographical term paper was Rubens's *Christ and the Penitent Sinners,* in the Alte Pinakothek in Munich. As soon as I saw the color photo of this painting posted on the wall of the study room, I knew I had found my favorite Rubens—and so it remains today. The canvas is filled with five figures. On the right is an imposing Christ who might be mistaken for a classically ideal Jupiter or Apollo, partially draped in a red toga and with a physique to rival any Calvin Klein model. Facing him are four famous penitent sinners from the Old and New Testaments: closest to him, a radiantly blond Mary Magdalene, behind whom stand a weeping St. Peter, the Good Thief (holding his cross), and King David. An allegory of the Catholic sacrament of penance, it reveals Rubens as the most inspired painter-propagandist for the Counter-Reformation. To me it represented a seductive fusion of beauty and theological content. There is an erotic aspect to Catholicism (in the best sense, Father Greeley would insist), and this painting epitomizes Rubens's ability to capture it in paint, as Bernini would later do in marble and bronze.

SATURDAY, SEPTEMBER 21, 2002

This weekend I took home some homework, something I have not done for years: a partial manuscript of a book we have signed up—a brilliant, original reinterpretation of Shakespeare's plays as the work of a Catholic, who, like Hamlet, had to disguise the subversive (in the eyes of the persecuting officials) elements of his plays while conveying them to his intended audience. I am not yet far along enough in this complex but illuminating study to summarize it adequately, but the author, Cynthia Asquith, has assembled compelling evidence that the very thing we Catholic students jested about with wishful thinking at Princeton—that Shakespeare was a crypto-Catholic—may actually be true. I never realized that even at the height of Elizabeth's reign, the majority of Englishmen were still Catholic, and that out of political necessity they had to hide the light of their old faith under a bushel, as the penalties for recusancy were as harsh as any the Soviets later devised for those who did not adhere to the party line.

Thirty-one years ago, as a junior, I took Tom Roche's Shakespeare, the last English course I ever took—and the best. His approach to Shakespeare had the same iconographic and contextual integrity as D. W. Robertson's explication of Chaucer. Although a devout Catholic himself, he never gave

Shakespeare an overtly Catholic spin, but rather presented the plays within the continuum of Christendom as it evolved throughout the Middle Ages and the Renaissance.

I often sat next to Tom in one of the choir stalls of our cathedralesque chapel during the 4:45 Sunday Mass—or as he termed it, with Shakespearean color, the "drunkards' Mass." Indeed I often was not able to arise much before that time on Sundays. Today he is a trustee of the F. Scott Fitzgerald literary properties, and that is what we now work on together from our respective sides of the Hudson.

SUNDAY, SEPTEMBER 22, 2002

At a dinner party last night I sat next to the general counsel for American Express, and in a very short time we segued from those ubiquitous green, gold, and platinum cards to music. She told me that years ago, when she took the Johnson O'Connor course in choosing careers, she learned that the one aptitude that could not be suppressed without causing unhappiness was in music. People with a love of music must pursue it—or else.

That spring term of junior year at Princeton I exercised some similar self-indulgence in the choice of another music course—this time devoted entirely to Haydn and Mozart. We listened to symphonies, chamber pieces, choral works, and operas by the two towering giants of the classical era. When it came time to choose a topic for my paper I turned back to church music, and to a work I had sung (in part) during those years of the Buckley Glee Club under Paul Rotella: Mozart's *Vesperae Solennes de Confessore*, with its twilight "Laudate Dominum." My mission, as I saw it, was to prove that Mozart devoted all his God-given talent and efforts to his Salzburg church music—however much he might have chafed under his boss, Archbishop Colloredo. In other words, the pervasive notion that he dashed off these sacred commissions with secular abandon was simply untrue: his church music was as carefully composed as anything else, and he paid special attention to the texts of the psalms and canticles that made up the chanted sequence for his vespers.

Father Kelly, a Benedictine who had earlier given me a daily itinerary for my first tour of Rome, now provided me with a detailed description of what an eighteenth-century service of vespers would have been like, and with that I was able to fit Mozart's movements into a liturgical context— something we miss in recordings and concert performances. I found the technical analysis a daunting task: I much preferred listening to the score to reading it, but I came upon that paper this past weekend and I was impressed by the young man who once could explain compositional intricacies that his middle-aged counterpart can now only admire—and enjoy. Yesterday I discovered a CD of the work on sale and bought it, to recreate the sensation of those original listening sessions. Much to my surprise, the soloist was a very young Kiri Te Kanawa, and her recording was made that very same year: 1971. *Laudate Dominum!*

TUESDAY, SEPTEMBER 24, 2002

Today, before singing at the noon Mass, I had a brief reunion outside the rectory of St. Pat's with Dony MacManus, a young Irish sculptor I had met inside two years ago, who has been living and sculpting in Rome for the past year. This time last year, I had urged him not to try to set up his own studio there, as I thought it would be too expensive, unrealistic, unwise. Better to find an established studio and join forces as apprentice to another sculptor, I said, playing it safe. But he believed in aiming high. When I saw the photos of his studio, I couldn't believe my eyes: he had been right. He had found a perfect place to set up shop and already was at work on commissions. How fortunate Bernini was not to have had me as an adviser: I probably would have told him to stay put as an assistant to his father, Pietro.

When I got home this evening, I found the package containing the first sculpture I ever bought, that lithe German crucifix, now set into a new wooden base. What a difference a small piece of dark-stained, tapered wood makes—a vast improvement on the original. How lucky I was that I had thrown that once-broken base out: the new proportions favor the bronze sculpture, like a frame that no longer distracts from the painting. Thank God I did not specify the original dimensions to the craftsman, but instead asked him to fashion a new base according to his own lights. I hope I remember the benefits of leaving artists alone, however tempting it may be to do otherwise.

I got an e-mail from Charlie saying that he had eight hundred hours of reading to do for history; all I could write back was that that was why I chose to major in art history: I was a slow reader and much preferred the illustrations! When it came time to pick the subject for my long junior paper in the spring term, I chose the supper at Emmaus. I am sure the idea was originally planted by an assignment of Professor Martin I once spotted on the walls of the study room, comparing the Caravaggio and Rembrandt treatments of this subject—a year before I took his course. That juxtaposition stuck in my mind's eye, and now I sought to trace the evolution of artistic renderings of the scene throughout the Renaissance and Baroque. But I think I may equally have been influenced by the sheer beauty of the biblical story of the journey to Emmaus on the afternoon of that first Easter Day. Like the journey of the Magi, it ends in a simple lodging—a proper inn this time—and in an epiphany: the revelation of the risen Lord. In its own way it is as intimate a scene as the Babe in a crèche; here the intimacy is Eucharistic as Jesus reveals himself suddenly in the blessing and breaking of bread.

WEDNESDAY, SEPTEMBER 25, 2002

Why did the story of Emmaus so captivate me thirty years ago—as it still does? I told Father Andrew O'Connor over dinner tonight that it was my favorite biblical story. But why? Perhaps because it represents the first Mass, the first Communion, with Christ presiding, after the Resurrection? It is also, literally, the Last Supper of St. Luke's gospel—even if shared only by two disciples, only one of whom (Cleopas) is named. But what gives this evening meal at Emmaus its poignancy is its combination of revelation, recognition, and reunion all in that instantaneous act of Christ's "breaking of the bread" with his companions. That coincidence of acts lies at the very heart of each Mass celebrated since that time, over the past two millennia: revelation, recognition, and reunion—all through communion.

St. Luke never explains why the two downcast disciples who meet the resurrected Jesus along the road to Emmaus fail to recognize him. The New American Bible simply says that they "were restrained from recognizing him." It is the same element of mystery that injects itself into St. John's account of Mary Magdalene's encounter with Christ outside the tomb on Easter morning, when she mistakes him for the gardener—even after he speaks with her. Those temporary failures of recognition by people who should have known better—they certainly knew him better—give the eventual epiphany its emotional power. In each case that epiphany is fleeting. Jesus tells Mary in the garden not to cling to him, but to go off and tell the other disciples what has happened (something our Lord could surely have accomplished more persuasively himself, yet delegated to her). No sooner do the disciples recognize Christ beside them at the table at Emmaus than he vanishes from their sight completely—and, again, leaves them to go and tell the others. But not before a moment of reflection, as they ask each other, "Were not our hearts burning inside us as he talked to us on the road and explained the scriptures to us?" In other words, we had the clues, we just didn't follow them to the conclusion.

That sequence—the explication of scripture followed by the meal, the breaking of bread, the revelation of Christ's real presence, and finally a moment of reflection before going back out into the world—is nothing less than a synopsis of the Mass. Past and present are forever bound together in each reenactment of that crucial epiphany: maybe that is why, of all the subjects in Christian art, I chose to explore it throughout the Lent of my junior year. After my father read the paper and gave me yet another at-home course in editing, I had it typed and bound. I still have it on the shelf, and each time I pull it out and flip through the pages I am reminded of all those happy hours, days, and weeks spent at Emmaus—while sitting at a study carrel in the basement of Marquand Library.

THURSDAY, SEPTEMBER 26, 2002

Today in a confessional of St. Patrick's I met a wonderful Jesuit priest who had been chaplain to the navy Seals during the Vietnam War and is currently chaplain to the New York Yankees. I learned that the entire infield, but for one good Baptist, is Catholic. Before I'd finished our extended and ever livelier conversation I saw him expertly swat and kill a giant cockroach crossing the confessional floor. What the people waiting outside must have thought, I dread to think. Perhaps they assumed an exorcism was taking place behind that closed carved door, or at least the absolution of cosmic sins.

FRIDAY, SEPTEMBER 27, 2002

During Lent of 1972, while I surveyed the road to Emmaus in art, I had given up drinking. But with Easter came the break of fast (fortunately most of my paper had been written by then). I borrowed a full rabbit's costume, got in my car, and drove to the Millers in Locust Valley, where I spent a raucous Easter Day in costume. By evening the rabbit was wobbly from the countless daiquiris that fueled him.

By Monday morning it was clear that I could not make it back to Princeton for classes. I recuperated at home in New York in time to meet the Pynes for an evening at the opera, where I saw for the first time Verdi's *Otello*. It was the new Zeffirelli production, and even with a hangover, I was swept away; it became my instant favorite among operas. Just the week before—Holy Week, as it happened—Professor Roche had devoted both lectures and the precept to Shakespeare's *Othello*, so I had been well primed for its transformation into nineteenth-century opera by Italy's greatest master.

Two days later I was back in T. P. Roche's lecture hall; I dashed up to the front to inform him that I liked Verdi's *Otello* even more than Shakespeare's original, and that I thought his librettist Boito's addition of an evil "Credo" sung by Iago (to supply the motive missing in Shakespeare) was a stroke of dramatic genius. Tom, bless him, did not take umbrage but replied that my enthusiasm for the opera was understandable and that he agreed about Iago's "Credo." An opera libretto is so skeletal compared to a fully fleshed-out drama that it must sharpen the focus on every character and action; Iago needs a motive to be a credible foil to Otello; by singing his belief in "a cruel God" and his dedication to evil, he leaves no trail of ambiguity to diffuse or dampen the power of Verdi's score.

While I still enjoy listening to *Otello*, I no longer enjoy seeing it staged. The cruelty and injustice in the story overshadow the transcendent music; perhaps all the attention in the press to spousal abuse over the intervening decades has taken its toll. It is no less a great work of art in my ears, but I can't bear to watch it unfold. Mozart's Queen of the Night does not bother me in the slightest: I have a strange affection for this caricatured tyrant of a mother. But Otello and Iago are all too real and make me yearn for the more benevolent world of *Figaro* or *Der Rosenkavalier.* Yet I remain grateful that when I was Charlie's age, I could enjoy them all equally—and innocently.

SATURDAY, SEPTEMBER 28, 2002

I am still searching to find the right placement of the voice where expression and intonation may meet naturally. This, too, is a journey, a pilgrimage of sorts; the challenge is not to become discouraged but rather to savor the process, however slow and tedious. Bernini used to say of his favorite creation in Rome, the Church of Sant'Andrea al Quirinale, that it was the "work that displeased him least." That expression came back to me as I listened to today's practice tape of two Schubert lieder I made at Mason's: so far it is the one that displeases me least—but I hope not for long. Next week will offer more takes. I returned from Mason's with the realization that, despite my glaring limitations, nothing gives me more pleasure than these exploratory rehearsals and coaching. When I sent Dame Elisabeth my book *Bernini* a year ago, she wrote back that, for her, the happy process of recording at the EMI studios was a matter of "sculpting in sound." I finally have a glimmer of what she meant. There is still so much polishing and detailed carving to do after the initial blocking and heavy chiseling, but it is a delight to anticipate; and here perfectionism appears an ally, not an adversary; I don't quite know why. Perhaps because it points the way to beauty. I have never minded the open-ended process of editing—a form of sculpting with words, I suppose—and so perhaps that is why the musical equivalent seems more an opportunity for small epiphanies in sound, a means of giving words a life beyond print, even speech. Music is a mystery and a miracle; no wonder the ancient Greeks had Orpheus making trees by playing his lute. But it is when words are conjoined with the notes that the highest form of communication is approached, if never reached entirely, here on earth. No doubt that is why angels sing.

SUNDAY, SEPTEMBER 29, 2002

For that final summer vacation as a Princeton undergraduate, between junior and senior year in 1972, I decided to return to Italy—solo. It was more a pilgrimage than a tour, first to Rome again, where I had found such exhilaration the previous summer; then onward to Florence, Ravenna, and finally Venice. I think I must have wanted to absorb as much as possible of the originals I had studied over the past two years in the art department before my final, senior year and the inevitable thesis. Why I did not arrange to travel with a friend is beyond me now; perhaps the reason was my awareness then that no one I knew would ever agree to the frantic pace I had set for myself in Rome those final three days of endless sightseeing the year before. It was a mistake.

Toward the end of my stay in Rome, I had dinner on the Eden roof with Father Weiser, who had been attending a conference of theologians and priests. Afterward we went off to the Baths of Caracalla for an alfresco per-formance of *Aïda*—complete with marching elephants across the stage of grand imperial ruins. Next to us sat a Scribner author, the Scottish theologian John Macquarrie (a Presbyterian "crypto-Catholic," according to Weiser). No production of *Aïda* has ever rivaled that Roman one for me. I've never been tempted to go to Egypt: Verdi and Caracalla brought me close enough that magical evening under Roman stars.

MONDAY, SEPTEMBER 30, 2002

The day before I set out for Florence I was standing in St. Peter's Square af-ter a farewell visit to the basilica and ran into a group of American students; the two guides were friends from Princeton; within their charge of teenagers was my brother Blair. I suppose that meeting one's brother unexpectedly outside St. Peter's is less than miraculous, but it was memorable. As it turned out, they were off to Florence, too, and we agreed to regroup once we all got there. I boarded a tourist bus the next day and headed north, stopping for lunch at Assisi, where I quickly visited the dark Basilica of St. Francis and saw the famous frescoes by Giotto. Once in Florence, I unpacked at my ho-tel and dashed off to Santa Maria Novella, the first of the many must-see churches on my list culled from the past term's course in Renaissance art.

Florence is a Renaisance city. I missed the Roman ruins, the early Chris-tian legacy of Rome, and its Baroque flowering. I felt I was trapped in Boston, longing to return home, but I stuck to my itinerary. The one saving grace was not in fresco or stone or on canvas, but rather on the stage of the small opera house, where I bought a single ticket to hear *Tosca* for the first time.

At my hotel was a very kind old man from the States who came there every summer and whom the staff called "the professor." He was, he ex-plained, a high school teacher from New York and as we sat at the hotel bar early that evening he gave me a detailed synopsis, scene by scene, line by line, of the opera. By the time I took my seat in the audience I no longer felt a stranger to Puccini's characters: once his exquisite music engulfed me, *Tosca* instantly became my new favorite opera. As my father liked to say, "There's no friend like a new friend."

I was to return to Florence only twice again, during each of the next two summers, but I never saw the magic until fifteen years later, and not in person but vicariously through the lens of Merchant Ivory: *A Room with a View.* If only I had seen that city for the first time in the company of Maggie Smith, Denholm Elliott, Helena Bonham Carter, and Julian Sands. Or perhaps if I had only seen that magical movie first, then nature might have imitated art. But not for this solo tourist in 1972.

During the train ride to Ravenna I sat across from a young American priest of some obscure Catholic order. He was very friendly, but aloofness kept me from more than polite conversation. We had one dinner together at the hotel in Ravenna, but I went to Mass alone, and ventured forth alone to see all my favorite mosaics. My cult of independence was extreme; I was thrilled to see all those color textbook illustrations face-to-face: the tomb of Galla Placidia, Sant'Apollinare Nuovo, the baptisteries, and above all, San Vitale, where I returned one evening for a thrilling organ recital under its Byzantine dome. Then I took a bus to the former imperial seaport of Classe, to see my favorite of all mosaics, the apse of the Transfiguration in the Basilica of Sant'Apollinare—right out of my first midterm test in medieval art. There was one young couple, probably American students, on the bus with me, but once again my self-imposed isolation was absolute: I felt too shy to impose upon them, but I would have liked to share the excitement of seeing those mosaics in that early Christian church that seemed untouched by the fifteen hundred years since Ravenna was, ever so briefly, the capital of the Roman Empire in the West. The next day I boarded a bus for Venice.

TUESDAY, OCTOBER 1, 2002

When the humorist Robert Benchley arrived in Venice for the first time he reportedly cabled his agent back in America: "Streets full of water—please advise." Upon my first arrival in that city suspended between the blues of sky and water, I felt claustrophobic. There was no escaping the hordes of tourists, especially in the Piazza San Marco, the only place I recall visiting: its basilica was dark and dirty and depressing. The first evening I stood there looking out over the lagoon at the café-au-lait evening sky, I bumped into my priest acquaintance from the train. But by this time I was too dis-enchanted with my travels to share more than a short greeting. My hotel, the Londra, was a bedlam of tourism and bore no resemblance to the city of its name; it offered little solace. I wanted to leave the Londra for Lon-don. I bought a paperback of Greene's *Travels with My Aunt* at a bookstall outside the Doge's Palace and then boarded a motorboat to take me as quickly as possible to the airport for the first flight to England.

Greene's comic novel quickly pulled me out of the doldrums as I sat in the waiting room of the Venice airport and read of Aunt Augusta's crema-tion, as recounted by her nephew in chapter one. From then on, Greene provided enough vicarious traveling for this worn-out armchair tourist, soon ensconced in a spacious, cheerful room overlooking Hyde Park.

There I made one marathon phone call—to James Greaves, who was then convalescing at his parents' home in Bedford. It was the last time I ever heard his voice, full of melancholy resignation. In a final letter, a few weeks later, he wrote, "I agree that traveling alone is unsatisfactory. In my various jaunts around Italy I always had someone to talk to about the things that we saw." I took those words to heart: it was a mistake I was determined not to repeat. But as I look back, if I had not made it that summer, I would have had no reason to escape to familiar London, and I would have missed that chance to speak to him one last time. Two months later he died.

WEDNESDAY, OCTOBER 2, 2002

When I returned to Princeton in September I felt I had come full circle— to a spacious single room in a Gothic dorm just down the hall from my friends (and last year's roommates). It was like being a sixth-former in Brewster all over again, except without James Greaves and without third-formers in my charge.

I knew that I wanted to write my senior thesis on some aspect of Counter-Reformation art, as an extension of my two junior papers, and so I signed up for a course in the history and theology of the Reformation and Counter-Reformation, taught by a most engaging English cleric and scholar, Horton Davies. He was, like my Puritan ancestors, a "noncon-formist" in English parlance—a Congregationalist. But he also had a pro-found love of art and sacraments that suggested a crypto-Catholic. His course began with Luther and then followed Calvin, Zwingli, and the more radical Protestant sects such as the Anabaptists, and then proceeded to the Counter-Reformation under the Jesuits and mystics like Teresa and John of the Cross. He was sympathetic to each nuance of faith, and offered a gen-uinely ecumenical approach to a period marked by tragic splits and conflicts within Christendom. His sympathy was contagious and, in a real sense, pro-vided the most lasting appreciation of diversity and tolerance that I drew from my Princeton experience. He made it possible to reconcile my Protes-tant past with a Catholic present, for I could now see the merits of both. The challenge now was to find a convincing thesis topic.

My first plan was to expand my recent survey of the supper at Emmaus into a full study of the Last Supper in art, with special focus on the period of Reformation and Counter-Reformation. But as I started to compile a list of paintings I grew dissatisfied. I yearned for a fresh problem to tackle, a mystery to solve. One day in the stacks of Marquand Library I came upon a reference to a large cycle of tapestries designed by Rubens and called *The Triumph of the Eucharist*. From the moment I saw the title I was intrigued; it sounded almost too good to be true—the very model of a Counter-Reformation epic, something Milton might have written had the Reforma-tion never taken root in English soil. I went to Martin and asked him about that tapestry cycle (of over twenty pieces). He said that it had been a very important commission for Rubens but it had not been much studied by scholars and that there were several problems with it, beginning with the in-tended location and function of these magnificent tapestries. That was enough for me.

THURSDAY, OCTOBER 3, 2002

I have never understood scholars who devote their talent and time to a minor artist or minor work in order to position themselves as sole custodian
of some (usually justly) obscure niche of scholarship. I have always considered it the intellectual equivalent of an eccentric collector, whether of bottle caps or trading cards. If I had been an English major, I would have
written my thesis on Shakespeare; if a music major, on Mozart. In Baroque
art, Rubens was my master; I soon discovered to my delight that his Eucharist tapestries qualified for several superlatives in the art of the superla-
tive. Not only was this commission the largest and most complex of the
four series of tapestries he designed over his career, but it was also his most
sumptuous and complex religious commission. My good fortune in finding
it so widely understudied was due to its location not in a major museum
but in a royal convent in Madrid.

MONDAY, OCTOBER 7, 2002

In Madrid, during Election Week recess, my mother and I stayed at a hotel
only a few blocks away from the Prado. There we passed from Rubens to
Rubens—I could not believe that so many of one artist's works could be
gathered in one place. It was a feast of flesh and color. At the Descalzas
Reales, we had to join a guided tour as no one was allowed to wander alone
through the convent museum. The tapestries hung in a converted dormitory, blazing with spotlights; the ceilings were high, but not quite high
enough to accommodate these huge hangings that rolled out and onto the
floor. Clearly they were designed for a grander space, and could never have

been intended for the narrow corridors of the rectangular cloister. The one space on our tour that could contain them and allow the viewer to stand back in wonder was the chapel. I was determined to return and study it long enough to sketch a plan. That meant a visit to several government offices to get the required stamped letter of permission.

My brief exposure to Franco's bureaucracy was as comic as frustrating: no one quite knew how to cut red tape. Finally, I just returned on our last morning in Madrid, and offered the nun at the desk a few crisp bills as a donation to match my desperation; that worked as well as an official permit: I was allowed back in the chapel alone for a few minutes. There I paced off every area, and sketched my own blueprint.

On the plane home, I used these sketches to draw a clearer diagram, into which I would later attempt to reconstruct Rubens's tapestry cycle. Somehow the definitiveness of the ruled lines and dimensions (still in "paces") created the comforting illusion of a reliable plan. Nixon won his landslide reelection in a walk. I hardly noticed; I was more intent on translating my paces into feet and inches—which was the first thing I did when I got back to my dormitory hallway the next day. Anyone watching me pace back and forth past my room, marking the floor with chalk and then carefully measuring it with a tape, would have concluded I was already a candidate for a mental ward. But the trip had been a success, and I came back fired up to complete my research by Christmas. It was the only time my mother and I ever took such a trip together; for that alone I have Rubens's Eucharist tapestries to thank—and rightly so, for the Greek word "Eucharist" means thanksgiving.

TUESDAY, OCTOBER 8, 2002

Yesterday I received in the mail the literary antidote—or at least antithesis—to Rubens's Counter-Reformation tapestries: the very first book published by my great-great grandfather's fledgling press in 1846—Edwin Hall's *The Puritans and Their Principles.* The first location of Scribner's publishing house was an unused chapel of the Brick Meeting House on the corner of Nassau Street and Park Row, where Pace University now stands. It was our family's Presbyterian house of worship and that first book was as devoutly Protestant a tome as any I have ever seen. Hall had nothing good to say about the Catholic Church or even Episcopalian bishops.

> *O what emotions often fill my soul, when, on the very soil on which the early fathers of New England trod, and looking abroad over the hills and waters on which they once looked, and while walking amid their graves, I think of the hand of God so clearly revealed; and on his great designs in bringing such a race of men to people the shores of this great continent! What other people on earth can point to such an ancestry as the people of New England? . . . Under every earthly disadvantage, with incredible toil, in the midst of appalling dangers, obstructed by the jealousy of the mother country, and at last compelled to encounter her in arms, in two centuries the people, rich in nothing save the principles of the Pilgrims, have turned this wilderness into a fruitful field; and made it the moral garden of the whole world.*

I soon found myself succumbing to his passionate apologia for the Calvinistic Puritans. I suppose enough of that Puritan Protestant blood still courses through my veins to make me wonder how I ever succumbed to the lure of Rome. Only the cold and rigid doctrine of predestination reminds me why I could never return to that faith of my fathers. Yet enough of Professor Davies's course that senior year remains fresh to keep me sympathetic to the genuine reforming impulses of the Protestant sects that arose in the sixteenth century; none of us can ever corner the market of revelation, and I am certain only of one thing: that true ecumenism and inclusiveness is the only hope for our beleaguered, fragmented Christendom of the twenty-first century. We must all come back to the same Christ, by whatever route, highway or byway, we find ourselves on.

As I arrived at St. Patrick's today and saw Monsignor Clark waiting to preside at the noon Mass, I knew what now, after thirty-two years, still binds me fast to the Roman route: the company and extended family of fellow worshipers I have gained along the way. In the end, it is not so much a matter of rule or ritual, but of community and communion. The Mass today was unexpectedly stressful, as a fellow cantor stood chatting with the organist throughout the entire service and I spent all my nonsinging moments worrying whether the organ would sound at the key moments. By the time I arrived at my voice lesson with Natasha Lutov, discouraged about the amount of work I needed to do on pitch and intonation, I knew that I wanted to do that necessary work, however long it took—not walk away from it. Perhaps revisiting the process of assembling those tapestries had reminded me that important projects in life are undertaken piecemeal, note by note—whether the footnotes of a thesis or the fleeting notes of a new song. Every pilgrimage is a succession of small steps.

WEDNESDAY, OCTOBER 9, 2002

When I returned to Princeton after that last Christmas break I had become so absorbed in my scholarly adventure that I decided to apply to graduate school in art history—but only to one school, Princeton. I had no interest in expanding my horizon; I wanted only to continue our collaboration and to eke out a few more years of Princeton Paradise. Now that Nixon had ended the draft along with the Vietnam War, it was safe to stay a student; yet I was ambivalent, for my forebears had all gone from graduation straight into the family publishing house, and a part of me wanted to maintain that tradition and return home to New York. More than anything, I wanted to postpone the future, extend the present, and buy time—a tall order. It still is.

THURSDAY, OCTOBER 10, 2002

That last spring term at Princeton had a natural Dionysian strain running through nature and through students who strove to alternate academic intensity with revelry. The highpoint was Martin's course on Rembrandt. I had been well prepared by Horton Davies to appreciate the quiet, reflective approach of this profoundly original artist in capturing the spirit and inner light of his subjects in a genuinely Protestant frame of faith. I took my theme from the previous spring, the supper at Emmaus, and now revisited it through the eyes of Rembrandt. Just as the disciples find their eyes opened unexpectedly by the Lord at table, I found my own eyes opened again to recognize an entirely different facet to this miracle, with Catholic sacramentality now replaced by Protestant reverence for the power of the word. Martha might be the classic Catholic saint as she busies herself in deeds for our Lord, while her sister, Mary, simply sits quietly at his feet and listens. He does not scold Martha, for her intentions are sound, but he gently suggests that she is missing the main course, and that Mary has chosen the better part. Rembrandt's art conveys the quiet epiphanies that come from those humble moments of prayer, silence, meditation, and small acts of kindness. We Catholics, attuned to blaring trumpets and Olympic saints, have much to gain from the more human and muted hues of the Protestant Rembrandt as he strove to encounter God within the shadows of daily life.

FRIDAY, OCTOBER 11, 2002

The final course taken that spring was Professor Knapp's choral music—audited purely for pleasure, a recapitulation of freshman spring. We studied Bach's *St. John's Passion*, Handel's *Messiah*, and Verdi's *Requiem*; the last two have remained perennial favorites, but I have neglected to return to the Bach all these years—a major oversight that must be corrected next Lent. I am reminded by my father's urging "to do a favor to the person you will be decades from now." I don't think those four fleeting years at Princeton were so much a matter of "higher education" as a sound investment: the modest deposits of intellectual and cultural treasures have paid extraordinary dividends down to the present day.

The strangest realization of all is that I cannot recall why I was so conflicted about my future beyond that fast-approaching graduation day. When the news of my acceptance by the Graduate School had arrived in the morn-

ing's mail, I agonized over what to do. After days of indecision I mailed back
the postcard with the box checked that I was declining the offer. I told Professor Martin I needed to talk to him about my plans for the next year. We
walked into the Art Museum and sat down on the first bench. As soon as he
said that he hoped I would be continuing my studies with him in the fall, I
knew that I couldn't tell the truth—that I had notified the dean I was not
coming back. It had now become a personal invitation I could not bring myself to decline, face-to-face. I dashed off to Nassau Hall and explained to
the secretary that I needed to find the card I had just mailed in, since I had
"a terrible feeling I might have made an error and checked the wrong box."
She found the card, and lo, my fear was well founded—but easily corrected
with a single stroke of a pen.

TUESDAY, OCTOBER 15, 2002

I never considered moving to the Graduate College, a beautiful neo-Gothic,
cloistered copy of an English college. It was by far the most beautiful assemblage of buildings at Princeton, but it was way up on a hill overlooking the
golf course and deliberately separated from the undergraduate campus as a
result of a historic battle between Woodrow Wilson and Dean Andrew
West. West won, Wilson lost—and as a result he left Princeton for the
governor's mansion and then the White House. But we undergraduates
had called it the Goon College—such was the social view of graduate
students—and I was unwilling to exchange my present status for those academic gowns worn in the graduate dining hall at dinner. Instead I found,
through Father Weiser, a room in a private house on Cleveland Lane, a few
doors down from President Wilson's former home.

My landlady, Winifred Humphrey, was a delightful Englishwoman who
had been widowed three years earlier and now rented out a room in her home.
She was from an old English Catholic family by the name of Eyre (made famous by Charlotte Brontë); we were soon to become such close friends that I
kept the room for three years after my last graduate classes ended, by which

time her whole family had become an adopted extension of my own. But that was well in the future. The more immediate question was what to do with the summer following graduation. Safaris were out, as was traveling solo. When our neighbor up Holland Road, "Princess" Pyne, who had for years organized the social lives of her children and their friends with all the aplomb of Auntie Mame, proposed that I take her lovely daughter, Holly, along with the two belles across the road, Andrée and Ritchie Markoe, on an art history tour of Europe, I leapt at the opportunity. My sons should be glad I did, for six summers later our foursome would regroup as two bridesmaids, bride, and groom—all thanks to the only tour I have ever led.

WEDNESDAY, OCTOBER 16, 2002

At the National Gallery in London, Andrée stood marveling at Uccello's *St. George and the Dragon*, a small Renaissance gem, and announced to us all that it looked just like Walt Disney. In fact, she was right—and prescient: several years later she designed a program at the Metropolitan Museum in New York for schoolchildren; two decades later she created a children's museum in Chattanooga, Tennessee.

Our next stop was Amsterdam, where we saw all the Rembrandts in the Rijksmuseum. As we were leaving Rembrandt's house, Ritchie said she saw my brother John coming toward us down the street. I said her imagination was working overtime, and then found myself facing my sixteen-year-old brother, whom I reluctantly recognized. He was touring Europe with a school group and we took him out to dinner along with our cousin Blair Villa. The two of them consumed more tankards of brew than a pair of Frans Hals revelers.

In Antwerp I gave full rein to my obsession with all things Rubens. As I had never been to Rubens's hometown, I was like a drunkard in a brewery: the cathedral with the two great triptychs, the Plantin-Moretus Press, the Jacobskerk with Rubens's grave, the former Jesuit church to which Rubens contributed altarpieces, sculpture, and even the façade, the Royal

Museum with rooms and rooms of wall-to-wall Rubens paintings, and above all Rubens's house and garden—a small palace. At the Royal Museum, Ritchie whispered to Holly that she found Rubens's Christs an erotic epiphany (my euphemism): I was momentarily shocked, but as an artist herself she saw through to the heart of the matter without any scholarly gloss.

THURSDAY, OCTOBER 17, 2002

The final city, Rome, was well saved for last. It more than compensated, as it always does, for the shortcomings of other cities. Our hotel was just behind the Piazza Navona, where we discovered *la dolce vita* at the Tre Scalini bar each night, thanks to the Italian fiancé of a neighbor back home. He introduced us to Rome's "black nobility," the old papal families Corsini, Barberini, and Massimo. Prince Carlo Massimo, whose palace has stood at the far end of Piazza Navona for half a millennium, took us out to his family's crumbling castle on the border of the old kingdom of Naples, outside Rome, and gave us a grand tour of its faded frescoes and cracked stuccoed ceilings. At one point he turned and asked us, "Are you boring?" Andrée replied in alarm, "I hope not!" But a quick retranslation of the question saved the day. No, nothing in Rome bored us.

At the baths of Caracalla, we heard Puccini's *Tosca* and saw it staged with a magnificent fidelity to the three Roman settings that has been rivaled only by Zeffirelli at the Met many years later. At one early Christian basilica, I decided to try Scarpia's ploy on Ritchie, and dipped my fingers into the basin of holy water, then extended my hand to her so that she would have to touch it to share the water for the sign of the cross. It worked better on the devout Tosca, who was Catholic and knew the routine.

Thanks to Holly, I discovered Bernini that August in Rome. She pointed out every sculpture and fountain by him as we passed and introduced me to an artist who was soon to captivate me as much as Rubens had. By chance, one of the regulars at Tre Scalini late at night was an American expatriate, Jules Wright, who had written his doctoral dissertation at Yale on several plays by Bernini. He was straight—well, not so straight—out of a Fellini film, but wonderfully entertaining, and his many tales of Bernini over glasses of Sambuca Romana whetted my appetite to pursue my own research once I returned to Princeton. Jules, in turn, introduced us to the young Prince Barberini, a descendant of the papal family who had given Bernini full rein to transform Rome into a Baroque city worthy of their pope's adopted name—Urban. We had a farewell dinner on the Eden roof before leaving that magical city for the States. I didn't need to throw any coin in the Trevi Fountain to ensure I would return—often.

FRIDAY, OCTOBER 18, 2002

The summer romance that had begun in Italy continued through August once Ritchie and I returned to Far Hills, but in September she left for a year of college in France and I moved south to Princeton once again, now with profound ambivalence about the near future. But I decided to hang on for the fall term and make the best of a bad choice. Outside the art building, I took a crash course in reading German so that I might pass the departmental requirement at the end of the term. But my favorite course had nothing to do with my graduate career: it was Professor Knapp's course called "Opera as Drama and Music," cotaught by Professor Daniel Seltzer of the English department. It treated in depth my two favorite operas at the time: Mozart's *Marriage of Figaro* and Verdi's *Otello*.

SATURDAY, OCTOBER 19, 2002

By a strange coincidence, that brightest of Mozart's luminous operas was juxtaposed with the darkest of all my weekends as a Princeton student. I see myself sitting in a living room chair at 791 Park one Saturday in October, a month into graduate school. My Princeton pal Ted Gamble had come into New York with me for the weekend. I was doing my homework for Professor Knapp and the two of us listened to the first two acts of *Figaro*, as I followed the vocal score and Ted humored me. My parents were away for the weekend with our family physician, Dr. Frode Jensen, and his wife. He had had a heart attack back in March and had had two bypass surgeries since then, the first one having failed. Shortly before dinner, the phone rang. It was my father. He said that Dr. Jensen had just died of a heart attack. His death was a terrible blow to me, and even worse for my parents, who had been with him at the time. In fact, he died in my mother's arms as she tried to stop his collapse during an after-lunch tour of his club library while my father and Mrs. Jensen remained outside enjoying the bright autumn day.

I returned to New York a few days later for the funeral at the Columbia University chapel, where I served as one of the ushers. I remember we sang "For all the saints who from their labors rest," and it struck a chord—but one that was not to be resolved for another few weeks. I returned to Princeton to write condolence letters and sink into an even deeper depression about being there. Then, quite as suddenly as that Saturday phone call from my father, the cloud vanished and my spirits lifted. It happened on All Saints' Day, at the end of the noonday Mass in the chapel. I caught sight of Peggy Goheen, wife of my father's friend and my first Princeton president. As we chatted and I asked about her family, she told me about a child who had just suffered an attack of depression, and that she had come there to pray for her. Something about her grace and faith struck me deeply. I felt enormous gratitude to encounter her on All Saints' Day and, beyond that, to be in Princeton. My own depression seemed suddenly trivial and self-indulgent—something to be disowned that very moment. Peggy personalized Princeton for me in a way that I cannot describe; the words "sacrament" and "epiphany" come close, but what they mean and how they work must remain a mystery. For the first time I returned to my room on Cleveland Lane feeling that I was exactly where I was meant to be. I began work soon afterward on my first seminar report—a survey of the "Landscape of Paradise" in northern Renaissance art and, by extension, at Princeton.

SUNDAY, OCTOBER 20, 2002

This evening when we arrived back at the apartment in New York I found amidst the weekend mail a package from Boston; it contained the CD of Van Cliburn's *Emperor* Concerto, which I have just finished hearing—I wish I could say playing—for the first time in over thirty-seven years. I have listened to his RCA recording of that work, under the baton of Maestro Reiner, so many times that no live recording could fairly compete. The excitement of hearing the Tanglewood broadcast as I exercised on a Nordic-Track for the duration (just over an hour) was in returning back to that audience of 1965 and trying to imagine the sensation of hearing it again for the first time that late summer night. So much of the excitement was visual as we watched the virtuoso golden boy of the keyboard dazzle us with his vitality and passion. The CD, on the other hand, is cold and unforgiving; it captures every technical imprecision and tonal smudge, yet nothing of the ambience or thrill of an audience of over fifteen thousand—the third largest to date in the history of that summer music festival, according to the announcer. I shall listen to it again tomorrow, and try to get a better sense of the performance as a whole, not just the details that distracted me as I sough to rediscover the perfection preserved in a child's memory.

Perhaps I have long confused passion with perfection; they are not the same, though the former may conjure up the illusion of the latter. The most exciting moments of listening came at the end, when Cliburn took several curtain calls, alone and with Leinsdorf, as the audience refused to let him depart in peace. I strained to hear my voice in the crowd crying "Encore" before the announcer mentioned that Cliburn was again sitting down at the piano: "Let's see what happens now." Van launched again into that rondo at full tempo; it was as surprising now as then, and equally exhilarating. After that final finale, the announcer seemed nonplussed, uncertain as to whether such an encore had ever been heard before at Tanglewood. For me, the lesson tonight is that what made it the most memorable concert of my life lay not so much in the playing but in the power of Van's performance, as much visual and visceral as auditory. It makes me grateful that we do not have a tape of the Sermon on the Mount. There is no substitute for presence.

TUESDAY, OCTOBER 22, 2002

When I returned from Christmas vacation I plunged into my first Bernini paper, an architectural study of Sant'Andrea al Quirinale, in Rome. Of all his creations, Bernini considered this the one that "displeased him least." Today that oval theater of sacred space is a perennial favorite for weddings; it soon became my favorite Baroque church in Rome, despite my lingering affection for the earlier Sant'Andrea della Valle, where Puccini set his first act of *Tosca*, bathed in gilded light. The next term offered a series of recapitulations of earlier courses: a survey of early Christian art and architecture, Martin's seminar in Rubens, a seminar in Hellenistic portrait sculpture, and Irving Lavin's colloquium on Caravaggio. By this time I had fully gone for Baroque and somehow managed to tie these courses all together to further my pursuits of Rubens, Bernini, and Caravaggio.

Lavin's colloquium took as its starting point his radical new interpretation of Caravaggio's first altarpiece of St. Matthew as representing the first evangelist as a Christian Socrates. Following his lead, I returned to Caravaggio's *Supper at Emmaus* and sought to discover the meaning of that revolutionary artist's representation of Christ as a beardless youth, as unexpected to the viewer as to the two disciples at Emmaus. In the end it came down to a matter of both rationalizing and *sacramentalizing* the miracle of recognizing the risen Christ.

By substituting the face of a beardless youth for the more usual visage of Christ (as recorded on Veronica's veil), Caravaggio presented a visual explanation for the disciples' failure to recognize him along the road. He did not look like the man who had been crucified three days earlier. At the same time, he made it clear that they now recognized him not through familiar features but through the sacramental act of blessing and breaking the bread: in other words, his Eucharistic body opened their eyes to his identity. It was a paradox-ically orthodox meaning: only in the sacrament, or Eucharist, may we fully recognize Christ. The more I probed this painting the richer it became. Car-avaggio had not chosen an arbitrary face for Christ, but rather had reverted to the first depictions of the Savior in early Christian art and, simultaneously, re-called Michelangelo's beardless Christ of the *Last Judgment* in the Sistine Chapel. So in that instantaneous revelation of our Lord we, along with the disciples, are granted a glimpse into the Second Coming at the end of time.

Finally, I stumbled upon a scriptural source for Caravaggio's original rein-terpretation of that epiphany at Emmaus: at the end of the gospel of Mark there is a brief reference to Christ appearing to his disciples along a road "in another guise" (*"in alia effigie,"* as the Vulgate puts it). It offered the best Lenten lesson of that term—and long afterward: how often do we encounter Christ *"in alia effigie"*—in another guise, form, or face? The simplest yet hard-est challenge of our faith is to do just that: to recognize him in one another.

WEDNESDAY, OCTOBER 30, 2002

During my last term of classes the next fall, I came down with the worst sore throat of my life. By the time I got into New York to see my new doc-tor (with the encouraging name of Fein), I was weak and feverish and could hardly swallow. I was referred to a throat specialist for some tests, and on my way home I stopped off at St. Jean Baptiste for some last-ditch prayers: I was convinced I was dying. I took to bed, unable to swallow more than a few sips of water or tea. I had never felt so sick in my life. My bed faced my piano, which prompted thoughts of Chopin's and Mozart's last days. I was too weak to walk more than a few steps, but my sense of melodrama was as strong as ever. Yet there was no sense of panic, only an unexpected resignation and peace: I was glad I had had time to become a Catholic.

Within a day or two, the report came back that I had a severe case of mono, compounded by a throat infection. I had never missed more than a couple of days of school; now I was to miss several weeks.

THURSDAY, OCTOBER 31, 2002

Back in Princeton, I divided my time between the art department and the Aquinas Institute, which stood only a few blocks from my room on Cleveland Lane. A few of the priests living there were themselves graduate students, and I enjoyed their company. Father Weiser had a phenomenal, if low-keyed, way of empowering students to assume leading roles in the work of the chaplaincy. I started up a weekly newsletter for the institute, distributed at each Sunday Mass. Taking a cue from G. K. Chesterton, I called it *The Dumb Ox* (the title of his classic biography of Thomas Aquinas). We Catholics had fun at Princeton; humor counted high among the virtues. We were anything but earnest and evangelical. (There were other groups that practiced knocking on doors.) Yet, as I look back, the gradual transformation of Aquinas over the first five years of Father Weiser's chaplaincy was astounding.

When I first started going to the 4:45 Sunday Mass at the University Chapel during my sophomore year, there were about thirty of us sitting in the pews of the sanctuary, with a student guitarist or two to accompany us singing the folk hymns of Vatican II ("It's a Brand New Day" and "Turn, Turn, Turn" and "Lord of the Dance"). By this second year of graduate school, the average attendance at that Mass was over 350 students—many of them non-Catholic. We had more students at our Mass than at any other service held there. The influx of Papists must have set those good Presbyterians who built that chapel spinning in their graves. We now had our own organist, acolytes, a processional cross—the works. It all came about through the students who took charge of the liturgy. In some ways, we were quite Protestant—or at least, populist. And we were popular; we never sought to recruit non-Catholic friends to our Mass; they just came.

The highpoint of worship that year was the visit of Cardinal Willebrands of the Netherlands. He said a pontifical Mass in the chapel one Sunday afternoon, and we pulled out all the stops. My friend José Gonzalez, a graduate student in the architecture department, and I served as the cardinal's acolytes. José carried the cross and I swung the incense. José wore red Guccis in honor of the cardinal, and reversed the crucifix to face His Eminence in the ancient fashion (and against the orders of Father Weiser, who was no match for this resident Spaniard). I in turn got so carried away with my task that at the offertory I swung the censer so high it opened and spilled burning embers onto my white cassock: amidst gasps from the long nave, I wondered in that split second whether I had set myself on fire. The danger passed, the embers were extinguished, the Mass went on. I soon retired as acolyte; it would never get better than that.

After the Mass, we took the cardinal to Firestone Library next door for a reception of wine and cheese among an exhibition of medieval manuscripts. At the time I was preparing my seminar report on Bernini's three great altar works at St. Peter's—the baldacchino, the *Cathedra Petri*, and the Sacrament Chapel. I had no trouble getting into a proper Baroque spirit as I concluded my report with a *son et lumière*: a rapid sequence of interior shots of St. Peter's set to recorded choral music by Corelli. My fellow graduate students were bemused and confused: they expected footnotes, not trumpets.

FRIDAY, NOVEMBER 1, 2002

Christmas 1974 offered a unique variation on a confusing theme. My grandmother Sunderland had died the past spring so our excuse for staying in New York to spend Christmas lunch with her was, in the Watergate lingo of the year, "inoperative." So we lured my Scribner grandmother into the city. The day would have been filled as usual with early morning stocking openings—yes, even at our ages—followed by breakfast and then the pilgrimage down Park to the marathon service of music at St. Bart's.

By evening my mother and I had a legitimate escape from the Christmas unraveling at home: two subscription seats to the Met Opera that night. Off we went to a confectionary *Don Pasquale*—frothy, sweet, and light in the best tradition of bel canto. Then, at the very end, one of the singers came back onstage and set up a small lighted Christmas tree to everyone's delight. I'll always remember that moment as the perfect grace note for the feast of our Lord's birth: a small, charming gesture at the end of hours of exquisite singing and music in the service of comedy. Christmas is divinely comic: it resolves new order out of disorder. The manger of animals and straw dissolves through an epiphany into a throne room for Kings from afar to offer their gifts of tribute to the newborn King. All through childhood, the evening that caps Christmas Day was always a letdown. For this one Christmas, it was the opposite: a true lifting of spirits to the holy, through music and a sacramental tree however dwarfed by the vast proscenium of the Met stage.

SATURDAY, NOVEMBER 2, 2002

By the time I passed my exams in May of 1975, and went through graduation for a second time with my parents on the lawn in front of Nassau Hall, I was ready for a break. That weekend, back in Far Hills, my father happened to mention that he had lost an editor at Scribners and was short a hand. Quite impulsively, I piped up that I would like to return to New York and help out at the office. And that is how I followed the family footsteps and became an editorial assistant as soon as I was on the final lap to getting my Ph.D. I was still going home by other routes.

SUNDAY, NOVEMBER 3, 2002

My last day before employment, I went to morning Mass at St. Paul's Church in Princeton, which was being said in memory of my grandmother Sunderland. It was a consoling transition back to the city and to a first job. I took the train to Penn Station and walked northeast through Central Park to the apartment on Seventy-fourth Street. Every time I pass the mall and band shell, I think of that journey home—for good. Yet I had kept my room at Mrs. Humphrey's house and soon reverted to my Gemini life again, dividing my nights between Princeton and New York.

In Princeton that summer, I ran into a past acquaintance from the Aquinas Institute, Ray Keck, a doctoral student in Spanish literature from Laredo, Texas. A young teacher at Hotchkiss School, he was house-sitting for a professor while writing his dissertation on Lope de Vega. We soon became close friends, as inseparable that summer as Lord Sebastian and Charles Ryder. The fact that we were both Catholic converts and passionate about music (he is a superb organist) added layers to a friendship that has not waned to this day, despite the hundreds of miles between New York and Laredo, where Ray is now president of a university. Although we meet only once or twice every ten years, the last time was worth the wait: we were leaving our children off for their first day at Princeton, when we all met quite unexpectedly in the cafeteria of Forbes College. When he later told me that his daughter had gone to a swing dance as Charlie's date, I finally had all the proof I needed that God's sense of humor is indeed boundless—as God only knows.

That summer I decided to reward myself extravagantly for my modest paychecks: I wrote to Heim Gallery in London and said I wanted to buy the Bernini crucifix I had seen there the previous summer, one of the series of bronzes Bernini had designed for St. Peter's in Rome. I liquidated some childhood savings (rationalizing that it cost less than two new cars—and would last several hundred years longer) and arranged to have it shipped to the office. It arrived in a crate that looked like a small coffin, much to the bemusement of my publishing colleagues.

MONDAY, NOVEMBER 4, 2002

Nineteen seventy-five was a Holy Year, the first of my lifetime, since the previous one had been in 1950 (not that anyone in my good Protestant family would have noticed it). As soon as I heard that I was to go to the

Frankfurt Book Fair in October as part of our small delegation representing Scribners, I made plans for my pilgrimage to Rome, which granted more
indulgences than I ever got around to counting. I wanted to study Bernini's
Sacrament Chapel in St. Peter's, for which he had designed the most magnificent tabernacle in the world in honor of the Holy Year of 1675, a mere
three centuries earlier. Father Weiser at Princeton suggested I write to our
leading American prelate in the Vatican, Cardinal Wright, who was head of
the Congregation for the Clergy—and so I did. He invited me to meet him
after a pontifical Mass he planned to celebrate under Bernini's baldacchino,
and thence retreat to his office overlooking Bernini's colonnade.

Wright was magnificent, though a little unsteady on his feet, and his
young aide (now Bishop Wuerl of Pittsburgh) and I helped him walk along
the long aisle from the sacristy to his car outside the basilica. I was so pre-
occupied by having a cardinal on my arm that only at the last second before leaving St. Peter's toward his parking space did I look up and realize
we were walking through the door (actually a false door) of Bernini's tomb
of Pope Alexander VII: over our heads, the gilded bronze skeleton of
Death held aloft an hourglass. The juxtaposition of that Baroque memento
mori and the cardinal's Fiat in the dazzling light of day was more than even
a Bernini could have envisioned. As the three of us talked in the cardinal's
rooms, he gestured toward the huge crowd of pilgrims below in St. Peter's
Square and announced in his sonorous baritone, "And they say this pope is
unpopular!" He also told me a story that left an indelible impression about
the allure of Rome I had felt so strongly down to this day.

The cardinal's longtime physician in the States, a Jewish doctor, had recently retired from his American practice and had settled in Rome. Cardinal Wright was puzzled by this choice of cities. Why, he asked, did the
doctor choose the center of Catholicism, a city so steeped in ecclesiastical
trappings and culture? The doctor pointed to St. Peter's as he replied:
"Well, you see, we no longer have our Temple of Jerusalem. Your St. Peter's,
its successor, is the closest thing to it, along with your priesthood, and tabernacle, and Holy of Holies." The response struck a deep chord, for a constant
theme both in Rubens's Eucharist tapestries and in Bernini's baldacchino
was the notion of "topographical transfusion" (Irving Lavin's inspired
term) from the Temple of Jerusalem to the New Temple of Christendom,
the new Holy of Holies where God truly dwelt, now in the form of his

sacramental body, transubstantiated bread. I have longed to make the return trip and visit the remains of Solomon's Temple in Jerusalem. Where better, in the words of our St. Paul's anthem, to "pray for the peace of Jerusalem"? I suspect that my pilgrimage will indeed come well before that peace—but not this year.

TUESDAY, NOVEMBER 5, 2002

Later that fall, after decades of delay, Scott and Zelda were finally reburied in the Catholic cemetery of Rockville, Maryland. I had been unable to attend the ceremony, but instead had arranged for a memorial Mass to be said in the once exclusively Protestant Princeton chapel that noon, a few steps from the library where I was at work. No doubt Fitzgerald smiled at the delicious ironies of both liturgies. His daughter, Scottie, wrote to me the following account of her experience in Rockville, along with typically gracious words of our small efforts in Princeton:

> *Surely it was the Princeton prayers which made our little ceremony go so smoothly. The day was perfect; a mild breeze rustling the fallen leaves, and there were just the right number of people, about 25 friends and relatives, 25 press, 25 county and church "officials" and 15 admirers who just popped up from nowhere. As most of the guests had never before had Bloody Marys in a church basement, the party afterward was a jolly affair, too. I'm sorry you weren't there but loved knowing we were having a backup ceremony in his real spiritual home.*

Was it any surprise that I thereafter volunteered myself as the Fitzgerald editor at Scribners? My father could deal with Mary Hemingway, Ernest's last wife and now professional widow. He had his hands full with her. I had been left the better portion, if by default. Besides, I was already eager to spend more time in Princeton, and soon made plans to cut my workweek down to three days, so that I might spend long weekends in Princeton and get to work at last on a dissertation.

THURSDAY, NOVEMBER 7, 2002

I prepared to commute back and forth across the Hudson. I took the
Bernini crucifix with me to Princeton, and put it temporarily on loan in the
Art Museum, where I gave some gallery talks on it. But on Good Friday I
reclaimed it and carried it over to the chapel for the liturgy of the veneration of the cross. I liked the idea that Bernini's crucifix had returned to an
altar—and a service of Catholic worship—however briefly, before I took it
back to my room on Cleveland Lane.

SUNDAY, NOVEMBER 10, 2002

This afternoon as I sat looking at my father's memorial Rosary Altar during the final Mass I realized that this was the eve of the anniversary of his
death—tomorrow, Veterans Day. Soon after, I saw that there was a short-
age of priests to give out Communion to such a large congregation, and after some back-and-forth sign language with the pastor, I took my place at
the altar, relieved that at the last moment before leaving for church I had
ditched my blue jeans for something more respectable. During the process
of handing the Host to the long line of communicants, the very repetition
of the simple gesture and words ("The body of Christ") struck me deeply,
in a way hard to describe other than by contrast: receiving an award, giving
a speech, singing in public—these all resonate within, but in an ephemeral
and hollow manner. They may leave happy memories, but they do not touch
the soul. The simple act of serving is something anyone can do, yet this repeated handing of the sacrament to a neighbor—for the most part, an
anonymous neighbor—is an honor more far more humbling and precious.

The same distinction may apply to teaching. When I look back over the past twenty-five years of giving public lectures, none of these—however well attended or received—compares with the memory of those small classes of eight to ten students around a table, four times a week in that last term before I finally earned my doctorate at Princeton. I loved every minute of it. By the end of the term, I wanted to be sure that every one of them passed the course (may our Lord feel the same way about us at the Last Judgment). I remember going to one boy's room late at night; he had missed most of the classes that term. I was certain he had given up on the course but told him that if he would only take and pass the final exam he would pass the course: I did not want to fail him. He passed—much to my relief.

My own turn to face my judges at the dissertation defense was far more ceremonial as they sat around a seminar table in academic gowns—like Supreme Court justices. They had all been my teachers at various points before—except for the dean of Rubens scholars, Julius Held, who had by then become my newest if eldest mentor. I, too, passed—which meant that my next task was to order for my last graduation the following June that brightly striped Ph.D. gown I had so long envied on others—and to plan what I was going to do with it.

MONDAY, NOVEMBER 11, 2002

Today is the seventh anniversary of my father's death. I used to mark it by visiting his grave at Woodlawn Cemetery. But today I decided instead to mark it by going to the five-thirty Mass at St. Vincent's and sitting before his restored Rosary Altar; it is there I now find him—with the saints and our Blessed Mother, not in the ground of the Bronx, with bones and dust of bygone Scribners.

Tonight I find it hard to muster the enthusiasm with which, twenty-five years ago, I leapt at the chance to apply for a full-time position as an assistant professor—tenure track—to continue to teach Baroque art with Professor Martin. As part of my campaign for the job, I arranged to have my paper on Caravaggio's *Supper at Emmaus* accepted for delivery at the College Art Association meeting in Los Angeles that February, to be followed by its publication in the *Art Bulletin*. The next month I flew to Sarasota, Florida, to give my first full-length public lecture—on Rubens's Eucharist tapestries—and a gallery talk on the large-canvas cartoons there, the glory of the Ringling collection. Both segments were televised as part of an arts series, and I still have a copy of the videotape. Those twenty-five years have miraculously vanished in a blink; only the art remains unchanged. *Vita brevis, ars longa.* Art endures.

I failed on my job application. The senior faculty wanted me, but I was anathema to the junior members of the department. I was the homegrown boy, the one with inside tracks, a friend of the department chairman and, worse, of the university president. My father was a charter trustee. No wonder they wanted me out; and out I went, back to publishing by default. At least I had a summer interlude in Rome, Antwerp (for the four hundredth Rubens anniversary), and finally London, before returning to the States and my office.

Be careful what you pray for, they say: you may get it. I did not—and I have been blessed. Had I got that post at Princeton I would never have returned for good to my beloved zip code in New York. I would not have spent most evenings the next couple of years at the Metropolitan Opera, where I met both Francis Robinson, who soon became my mentor and guide through that musical paradise, and Mary Costa, the definitive Musetta who became my musical muse. My Princeton years concluded not with a final graduation, but with Mary's encores under the stars, backed up by the New Jersey Symphony, for ten thousand entranced listeners at a summer concert on the lawn behind Palmer Stadium—among them my parents and grandmother Scribner.

Mary's spiritual depth and perception matched her luminosity as a star who knew how to sparkle. There can be no doubt as to the reason the President has just chosen her to serve on the National Council on the Arts: in a realm of pretense, she offers reality. She also has a rare gift of insight: she once told me out of the blue that I would marry my childhood sweetheart, Ritchie Markoe. When I asked why, she replied, "Because you are always speaking of her." Within the year, Ritchie and I were married.

Mary was not alone in that perception. One evening at home, several months later, my father told me in earnest jest that it was about time I got married (I was just about to turn twenty-eight). In fact, I had been secretly pursuing Ritchie, trying every trick in the trade to lure her away from her imminent fiancé (I used the movie *High Society* as my textbook, as I tried to emulate Bing Crosby's moves to reclaim Grace Kelly.) So, with feigned innocence, I asked him whether he had anyone in mind. His reply: "Well, you'd make your mother very happy if you'd marry Ritchie Markoe."

After our Far Hills wedding on the hottest August day of the year, we retreated to England, where, one evening in the Cotswolds, we ran into my grandmother Scribner and her boyfriend (forty years her junior) at the inn where we were staying. My grandmother was suddenly speechless—a new phenomenon. But the next day the four of us went for a motor trip. At one point at lunch, the thought occurred to me that were this a Noël Coward comedy, my bride would now sneak off with Granny's beau, leaving grandmother and grandson alone to commiserate, and perhaps continue the trip according to Greene's *Travels with My Aunt.*

In London, Ritchie and I had dinner with my favorite author-friend, P. D. James—now Baroness James of Holland Park—who turned to Ritchie, bride of two weeks, and said in her most earnest voice, "You know, my dear, you have married a very complicated man." The subsequent years have done little to disprove that assessment. But now, as I am long past my deadline to retire for the night, I hear a silent echo of those brief words of comfort *"Requiem aeternam dona ei, Domine, et lux perpetua luceat ei."* May my father rest in peace, this Veterans Day, Armistice Day, and—long before—feast of St. Martin of Tours, who divided his cloak to clothe a beggar. As my dad would say, "These are the people our Lord came to save."

TUESDAY, NOVEMBER 12, 2002

Tonight I watched a documentary on the Jimmy Carter presidency. While I vaguely recall the towering inflation and the long gas lines of that year, I had forgotten the grim national backdrop against which Ritchie and I set up house in my old bachelor apartment on Sixty-eighth Street, just five blocks from her new job at Buckley, where she was beginning as a teacher of Beginners (Buckley-speak for kindergarten). A few months earlier, before we were officially dating, she had asked me to write her a letter of recommendation. I wrote the most Baroque one I could conjure up, and they hired Miss Markoe (quite on her own merits), who eventually arrived for work as Mrs. Scribner. I remember thinking as I wrote: If she is this good, why are you just writing about her? It was a new and happy experience that September to return to my old school now as a faculty spouse.

For the past academic year, I had already been returning to Buckley once a week for a piano lesson with Paul Rotella. A few months after the lessons had begun, he helped me choose the processional and recessional marches for our wedding: the march from *Rigaudon* and Handel's "See the conquering hero come," from *Judas Maccabaeus*, which I had first heard played in the coronation scene from the film *The Prisoner of Zenda*, shown at Buckley prior to our learning to sing it in Glee Club. I had even purchased a second Baldwin upright piano to install in my office at Scribners (where Max Perkins had once kept his sofa). It was pure self-indulgence, for in fact I had little opportunity to play it after hours. Yet it more than paid for itself—and during office hours.

One day, not long after our wedding, Scottie Fitzgerald arrived at the office along with her two daughters, to have a meeting with my father and me over a proposed contract for all the Fitzgerald books. The new copyright law had given her the right to reclaim them and take them to a new publisher; she had no dearth of aggressive suitors. Her agent, lawyer, and literary adviser had all been pressing her to leave us—for their own interests more than her benefit. But she had a sense of loyalty and tradition, and those were our strongest cards to play. She arrived bearing a wedding gift for Ritchie and me, but as soon as she caught sight of my new office piano, she asked me to play her something. So I sat down and played my favorite Chopin waltz (thank God, I did not then know its nickname—the "Adieu"!). Halfway through it, I had the chilling thought that Fitzgerald's future at Scribners might depend on this waltz. But somehow I made it through, without a hitch, and Scottie sighed, "It's all so romantic ..." That same day she told us to proceed with a contract—which remains in effect for the life of the books.

After that impromptu office performance, my next assignment—playing for Ritchie's class Christmas party at Buckley—was a dream ranging from "Silent Night" to "Rudolf the Red-Nosed Reindeer" and "Jingle Bells." I also got to read two of my favorite Scribner books from childhood: *The Duchess Bakes a Cake* and *Plum Pudding for Christmas*, both by Virginia Kahl. I had succeeded at last in returning to a classroom—however briefly—by a most unexpected route, one that took me full circle. It was a fitting way of approaching our first Christmas.

SATURDAY, NOVEMBER 16, 2002

Today, after exercising, I stretched out on a chaise outside the steam room at the Racquet Club and read the most unlikely of books in that setting—a book about dying. The author is a distinguished Catholic scholar and priest, who has written about his skirmish with death during a near-fatal illness. It is a strong candidate this year for a Christopher Award, and several weeks ago I volunteered to review it. Today was as good a time as any, although I did my best to conceal the cover of the book from others around me. Reading a book about dying in a health club seems a sacrilege. I had looked forward to my assignment; I was certain—on the basis of a few random snippets here and there—that I would find it intellectually dazzling and spiritually inspiring. Instead, I found it annoying: too many self-conscious citations from great writers, too egocentric, too critical.

I wondered whether a professional celibate is in the best position to pontificate about sex as a denial of death. But his assertions that "death with dignity is a delusion" and that "death is always the final indignity" prompted a silent yet insistent protest from this reader stretched out in a white-tiled room that might have been a morgue—but for the comings and goings of athletic bodies. I thought back seven years to the day of my father's death. He died with the same dignity with which he lived. His death marked the saddest day of my life, yet at the same time an epiphany that I have finally come to appreciate only after reading the denial of everything

I witnessed during those last precious moments. The priest's book did not illumine—for me, at least—the darkness of death. But the memory of my father's does, and I see that it must be recorded here while it still remains vivid. It is now past midnight, a new day—and I must catch some sleep before reliving that death.

SUNDAY, NOVEMBER 17, 2002

It was a Saturday, November 11, which we now commemorate as Veterans Day, but which my father knew in his youth as Armistice Day. Pope John XXIII said that every day is a good day to be born and a good day to die. But I think that Armistice Day is especially good—after my dad's long, debilitating illness, twice the length of the Great War. Death can be, at the least, an armistice, a cessation of battles, an extended truce.

In my father's case of Alzheimer's, as a result of an experimental operation called an omental transposition to the brain—the first ever to be performed in the United States—he never lost the higher functions of the brain: he enjoyed listening to books on tape, to classical music, and to family and friends who came to visit. His vision was a kaleidoscope of confusion; he had lost a sense of time and place; he walked with great difficulty and had increasing problems swallowing; yet he never failed to recognize his wife, his three sons, and two grandsons by their voices. He never mixed us up, right to the day he died. And he never complained. But a few days earlier, following several days of fever and pneumonia that had been beaten back with a bombardment of antibiotics (with my reluctant capitulation, against my better judgment, to the pleadings of his night nurse), he said to me simply and quietly, "I'm not happy." I agreed that he had every reason not to be, until he felt fully recovered, I hoped in a few days. At the same time, I vowed that if the pneumonia returned—as it did a couple of days later—it would not precipitate another battle. It would, rather, be accepted as "the friend of the dying," as one of his doctors had described it to me a couple of years earlier. At that point my mother and I agreed that when the time came, he should be protected from ambulances, hospitals, invasive tubes, and machines. Fortunately, we were in a Catholic nursing home run by an order of nuns who placed the dignity of the dying person above the cause of a hopeless medical campaign.

Early that Armistice Day, I came into my father's room and found him very weak, his breathing labored, as though he were running a slow-motion marathon. But he did not appear in any distress or great discomfort. I explained that the rest of the family would be coming by during the day, and that I would be back by evening, after taking son Christopher out to Long Island for his last soccer game. Before leaving, I asked him whether he would like to listen to some Richard Strauss or Mozart. He loved them both—as do I—and he made his choice, which I followed by setting the CD on the player before leaving the room. I only wish I could now remember the composer, since it was the last word he spoke to me.

When I got to our weekend house, an hour away, with Christopher, I saw that the wooden lamppost along the driveway had fallen down and lay on the grass. Its base, unbeknownst to us, had been rotting away over the years; the tall crossbeams finally broke off and fell. But for the lantern at the end, and the electric wires running from the ground, it resembled—to my eyes—a fallen, life-sized cross. As I carried it off on my back to place it up against a tree in the woods, I thought of all those paintings I had studied under the label *The Ascent of Calvary* and thought, So this is how you carry a cross. The bizarre event and its iconography drove me straight to the phone inside the house, where I called my father's aide, Ingrid, who confirmed my sense of foreboding with perfect German practicality: "I think you should return here as soon as you can." So I explained to my eight-year-old that we would have to skip the soccer game, but would stop by the field on the way and pick up his trophy for that season. He considered that an acceptable compromise. He held his trophy, and I held a cell phone to keep a line of reports coming to me from my father's room; then, halfway there, the phone went dead—another coincidence I relegated to the shelf of bad omens.

I rushed over to our apartment to drop off Christopher, and then sped back to the nursing home; my brothers had just left after many hours to go back home for a while; my mother was reported to be on her way back to his room. By now his breathing was very shallow and as mournful as basset horns. But except for the sense of exertion required for each breath, he seemed beyond pain and the distractions of discomfort. Still, the hollow, labored breathing bothered me, and leapfrogging from the mystical to the pragmatic I started inquiring as to whether he had been given any pain medication or sedation; someone suggested Tylenol with codeine; I raised the stakes: "What about some morphine or Demerol?" His aide, Ingrid, responded in Teutonic clarity: "What are you trying to do to your father, Charlie, kill him?" Gratefully I took the Tylenol with codeine option as Ingrid lovingly wiped his brow with a cool cloth, and combed his hair with a solemnity that can only be called sacrament. During that week, one or two priests from St. Bartholomew's came to visit and offer prayers of healing (for the soul if not body); but at these final moments, there was never a thought of calling in a priest to administer last rites. The CD had been changed to one of his favorites—*Show Boat*. To the background of that beloved score by Jerome Kern, we supplied a counterdialogue: "You are breathing more easily now; it must be to the rhythm of the music. Let your eyes close, and get the rest you so deserve after such a long ordeal. You've earned the right to fall into a good, comfortable sleep by now. Let yourself relax, just sink softly into the music."

When my mother returned to the room, *Show Boat* was in its final act; she went over to stand by him; then she sat in a chair at the foot of the bed. I stood at the head, repeating the words about the approaching sleep he so long deserved. My mother asked if I thought his breathing seemed fainter. I replied that, yes, he was finally relaxing and on the verge of drifting off. I felt his heartbeat with one hand and listened intently: it was like a slow movement of music—one of Liszt's *Consolations*—that gradually fades into silence as the tempo retards toward the final, still note.

As my father's breaths grew weaker and farther apart—in expanding measures of silence—I knew the end was at hand. My sole concern at this point was that nothing interrupt the peaceful rhythm of this drawn-out diminuendo: no startling sound, no movement, no note of panic. I had once read that our sense of hearing is the last to leave us at death. So our whispered words and the familiar music—the recording of *Show Boat* in the background—seemed a sacrament, his last rite. (Of course, only my father may hereafter confirm or refute such speculation.) In the meantime, I cling to one final fact: at the moment the horns sounded their triumphal finale to that musical he had loved since childhood, he stopped breathing. The

CD finished, the room was silent; I felt for a heartbeat or even partial breath. There was none. I waited a few minutes that stretched into eternity. Still, nothing.

Very quietly, I asked Ingrid to go and find the nurse who was to bring my father's medication at five, explaining that I didn't think he would need it. I was buying time. The nurse came in and placed her stethoscope on my father's heart, then looked at me as I looked back at her and at Ingrid with a slight nod. It was like that harrowing moment in the last act of *La Bohème* when everyone in the room, in near silence, looks around and reads in each other's eyes that Mimì has just died (on cue to the music)—except for her beloved Rodolfo, who thinks she but sleeps. At this moment, the one I dreaded most, I could think of no move or gesture better than the one that tries gently to break the unspeakable news to the beloved. I went over to my mother, put my arm around her shoulder, and whispered: "He's gone." At that point, the floodgates of grief open swiftly—and safely. For he is indeed gone: not from our hearts, or minds, or prayers—but from a world of suffering, sadness, and loss.

The process, as much as that final image of stillness, offered the most unwelcome yet oddly consoling epiphany of my lifetime. It all seemed so entirely fitting for a man who had maintained a steadfast sense of irony about the inevitable end of every human life. My father loved to say, "People are dying today who never died before," and, "He has passed into the nearer future." He gave a gentle twist to the pompous formulations of sages. He eschewed melodrama; he quietly slipped out of this mortal theater to the last chords of *Show Boat*.

MONDAY, NOVEMBER 18, 2002

After I took my mother home, the work began. My father had agreed that his neurologist at New York Hospital–Cornell could perform an autopsy on his brain for Alzheimer's research, in particular to determine the effects of the experimental operation two and a half years before. I tracked down

Dr. Relkin at his home in New Jersey and he guided me through the steps necessary to arrange the transfer of my father's body to the hospital. It was already Saturday evening, most people had gone home, and time was of the essence. The hospital was right across the street, and faced with a bureaucratic nightmare, I was sorely tempted to wheel my father over there myself, an idea Dr. Relkin discouraged—to say the least. An hour or so later, out on the street rushing back and forth in the worst pelting rain and wind I'd ever felt (my umbrella blown to bits by the northeaster), I remember being struck by a strange sense of déjà vu. I couldn't figure it out: it all seemed so fitting and familiar, yet I couldn't remember ever being caught in such a storm.

A couple of days later, that piece fell into place as I happened to reread Hemingway's condolence letter to my grandmother upon my grandfather's death: "It was a lovely trip from Monday until Saturday evening. Then came this news and a big storm came the same night with thunder and lightning (like in the Bible) and the surf pounding on the reef outside of where we lay and the Norther started to blow . . ." I had read this description fifteen years earlier, when my father published the collection of Hemingway letters, and now it had come back to me as an elusive memory in that second Saturday evening storm. Beyond forging a final link between father and son, my grandfather and father, that symbolic storm offered a literary epiphany: our memories are shaped by what we read as much as by what we see. Déjà lu, déjà vu.

Just as "The Battle Hymn of the Republic" will always evoke RFK's funeral at St. Patrick's, so my father's favorite anthems—Parry's "Jerusalem," Brahms's "How Lovely Is Thy Dwelling Place," and Knox's "O, Pray for the Peace of Jerusalem" from St. Paul's School—will forever echo his funeral at St. Bart's. We followed his coffin out to the singing of his favorite hymn, "Onward, Christian Soldiers." Several years earlier, as warden of the vestry, he had proposed a single-word slogan for the church's 150th anniversary: "Onward." It summed up his attitude about everything. Returning home from the burial at Woodlawn, where my father joined the three Charleses before him, our eight-year-old, Christopher, turned and said out of the blue, "Dad, I can't wait to be dead." Suppressing a laugh, I replied that it was worth the wait—there was plenty to do in the meantime. But I was as pleased as consoled by the thought that, despite the sadness, rain, and cold, the message of Easter had dawned on our child.

TUESDAY, NOVEMBER 19, 2002

"Amazing Grace"—that was the hymn scheduled today at St. Patrick's. If someone had suggested a year ago that I would be leading a congregation at the Roman Catholic cathedral of New York in singing this Evangelical Protestant classic, I would have burst out laughing. The hymn was but the prelude to a still more amazing grace at the end of the Mass.

Monsignor Clark arrived five minutes late for the Mass: the suspense somehow added a new level of meaning to the phrase "how sweet the sound" once the hymn finally began. Nothing fazes Monsignor; he finished on time, right to the minute. I usually leave the cathedral by the back door immediately, but this time I lingered a bit, perhaps thirty seconds, at the organ to tell Donald how much I liked the hymn. Just long enough: when I turned to go, I heard my name called, and looked up to see a striking blond woman approaching along the side aisle. It was Eileen Relihan, my father's private nurse at New York Hospital for the two months he lingered at death's door after developing pneumonia from a blood transfusion. She refused to give up on him; had it not been for her, he would never have had the final two years (and more) of his life. The last time I had seen her was seven years ago, two blocks away, at St. Bartholomew's the day of his funeral. And here she was again, looking not a day older, and just twelve hours after I had written about the funeral late last night. Amazing grace.

WEDNESDAY, NOVEMBER 20, 2002

Late last night I read some more of Andy Greeley's prayer journal. It is starkly honest and often searing as he strives to reconcile suffering, loss, and death with faith. Often he speculates about that heavenly reunion when "we all shall be young again." It is a joyous, redemptive image. Do I believe it? I don't know. On the subject of the hereafter, or what my father whimsically dubbed "the nearer future," I am literally agnostic—that is to say, unknowing—yet strangely untroubled by the absence of clarity. It is God's business, after all, not mine. There was a recent mention in the *Times* of scientific speculation about "precreation," the time before time. What did God have to do before the existence of his universe? Wondering about the time *after* time seems equally paradoxical and meaningless. It is like asking what happens to music after it is played: Where do the notes, melodies, and harmonies go? Is every performance, every sound somehow recorded for eternity—or only the rarities, those of ethereal beauty? Or is it enough that it was played, perhaps to perfection, only once?

As we approach Advent in the Church year, the Bible readings at Mass focus on last things, the *eschaton*, or Apocalypse. I confess to finding the book of Revelation anything but that: its apocalyptic imagery is rich in poetry and visual images for artists, but it seems more a kaleidoscope than a mirror of eternity. On this subject, the two readings chosen for my father's funeral seem more than sufficient—that beautiful passage from the book of Wisdom, "The souls of the just are in the hand of God, and no torment shall touch them . . . they are at peace," and those reassuring words of our Lord in John's gospel: "Let not your heart be troubled; you believe in God, believe also in me. In my father's house are many mansions. If it were not so I would have told you. I go to prepare a place for you." To be with God, with Absolute Love, would be reward enough—beyond pain, longing, suffering, separation, anxiety, or need. The rest I leave to him.

Today I read Teresa McGee's beautiful book *Jim's Last Summer: Lessons on Living from a Dying Priest*, her account of the time she spent visiting this Maryknoll missionary who approached his terminal cancer with the same honesty and courage with which he had earlier conquered his alcoholism. His death had more than dignity; it had grace. If any book this year deserves a Christopher Award for "lighting a candle," this is the one. I sent in my report today, sparing no enthusiasm for his lessons on living. It reminds me of Sir Thomas Browne's inverted, Platonic image of life as "the shadow of death." We live amongst shadows; the light we know is but "the shadow of God." In my eyes, that image eclipses even heaven itself.

SUNDAY, NOVEMBER 24, 2002

Ordinary time is drawing to a close: in four days Thanksgiving will be upon us, and three days later the Church begins a new year with Advent. I like the Feast of Christ the King—I suppose because it always reminds me of my first, at Princeton, with Archbishop Sheen in the pulpit of the chapel. It's an anachronistic feast, to be sure: how many kings are more than figure-heads at best these days? But somehow Christ the president, or Christ the chairman, sounds senseless. And so much of Judeo-Christian imagery is anachronistic, rooted in another time and place: temples, sacrifices, taber-nacles, priests, and demons. But who would claim that our time is any more rational—or benign? No pagan horrors can rival those of the past century, and the past two years of the present one, in the degree of devastation. Hu-man suffering has held its place on our assembly line of mass production. As Archbishop Sheen said, "Christ the King rules from a cross." I shall be grateful for Advent and the expectation of a Child.

WEDNESDAY, NOVEMBER 27, 2002

Tomorrow is Thanksgiving. Today the scaffolding came down, row by row (it must have been five or six stories high) on the Rockefeller Center tree in preparation for the ceremonial lighting next week. The Christmas decor is already in place in the store windows, and the crowds have begun to gather in midtown. This year I capitulated to the timing of the marketplace. When I got home, I took out my fiber-optic tree that Charlie had found so amus-ing, and set it in place on the piano of the music room. Of course, this tree was made in China, with layers of irony beneath the irresistible price. But then, we sing of the Three Kings from the Orient—so why can't this bargain tree come thence as well? I see that Saturday, the eve of the first day of Advent (also the first day of December, as Father Andrew pointed out to me with poetic glee), is also the first day of Hanukkah. I am tempted to make a final, if less orthodox, purchase: a menorah.

I saw a beautiful, also bargain, silver-plated antique menorah (in best Baroque spirit) last night at Bombay and Company, where I also found to my amazement picture frames of simulated leather spines of Scott Fitzgerald's *The Great Gatsby*. After seventy-five years, our greatest novel of the past century has been adapted to frame family photos. I think I'll buy the menorah. Then I'll have to figure out the protocol for lighting a candle each day of Hanukkah, something I've always wanted to do ever since I read that Father Greeley does it. No priest better appreciates the potential of such symbols and rituals to nurture a sacramental imagination: I shall follow his lead. The festival of lights seems a proper prelude to Epiphany.

As for Thanksgiving, we shall be minus one more Charles, in addition to my father, whose last Thanksgiving meal with us was nine years ago. Our son is staying at Princeton to work on his junior paper. I once told him of my senior-year Thanksgiving of a deli turkey sandwich alone in Princeton, exactly thirty feasts ago, as I stayed there to work on papers soon due. He is following suit, so Ritchie reminds me that I have no one to blame but myself. Yet I don't blame myself—or him. I believe in movable feasts: let Hallmark cards set the magic dates; I see no reason to be slave to them. Any day is as good for thanksgiving as the next. The word in Greek is "Eucharist," and that of course is celebrated every day of the year—in the Mass. Perhaps I'll get Chris to go with me—to humor his earthly, if not heavenly, father.

SATURDAY, NOVEMBER 30, 2002

The last day of November: the last day of ordinary time and the last day of the present Church year. Tomorrow brings Advent, a new year, and the final stretch to Epiphany. None too soon. Today Ritchie went off with her

friend Josie, a brave 9/11 widow, to see the new Broadway production of
La Bohème while I stayed home and practiced the first hymn of Advent for
next week at St. Pat's—"Come, thou long expected Jesus." I could not bring
myself to buy tickets to a theatrical production of *Bohème*, complete with
body mikes and amplification. Nor have I any desire to update Musetta after twenty-five years of seeing and hearing perfection in the form of Mary
Costa. So, too, every Marschallin and Mozart countess makes me yearn for
Schwarzkopf, and I find myself taking refuge in recordings. Perhaps this in-
transigent nostalgia is but a reflection of autumn, lengthening shadows, approaching solstice and year end. I need a festival of lights. I shall seek it in
music, in *Messiah* or Bach's *Christmas Oratorio*, and in the first candle of the
Advent wreath tomorrow. I miss those Advent calendars of my Buckley
days, with a window to open each day before Christmas.

SUNDAY, DECEMBER 1, 2002

Today I walked across the park to meet Father Andrew on the West Side;
past the Museum of Natural History, another landmark of those years, I
stopped into a small toy store to look for an Advent calendar. They were
all wrong—too big, too abstracted, no silver sprinkles. Then, in the middle of a pile, I stumbled upon a traditional, sentimental scene of a young
girl in bed, with angels above bearing gifts, and a sleeping dog below—with
lots of silver sprinkles. There was no wrapper, no price tag—it was clearly
a lone leftover from another year—but exactly what I wanted for Ritchie. I
asked the puzzled salesclerk what I should pay: he suggested fifty cents.
Much too low, I said (it was printed in Germany; its *Tannenbaum* was the real
thing). So I paid him four times his price and still felt I had the bargain of
the season.

After meeting up with Father Andrew, who was having coffee with
some of his younger parishioners, we stopped in a card store in hope of
finding one more calendar, this time for myself. Again, they were all wrong,
except for one small calendar on the shelf, no bigger than a Christmas

card—a scene of the three Magi at the manger, almost Rubensian in its magical Baroque vision, complete with sparkles—and yes, made in Germany. I had found my calendar and my own miniature Epiphany.

MONDAY, DECEMBER 2, 2002

Yesterday's Old Testament reading was from the book of Isaiah; though it was not as familiar as many from my favorite prophet-poet, I took it as a good sign and did not resist the temptation to peek ahead in the missal. There I discovered over the next few weeks those very passages set to music by Handel in *Messiah.* I am grateful that this year, the second in the Church's three-year cycle, follows Isaiah through the weeks of Advent, which gives me an excuse to play *Messiah* sooner and often. I wonder whether those verses of the prophet would resonate so much, even when spoken or read haltingly, if not for the inner voices singing Handel. Yes, the words came first—by a few thousand years—but it is through music and the composer's alchemy that they reach an exalted level of emotion and of the spirit.

Today the responsorial psalm (122) had the same effect: I heard not only the psalmist's words but, in silent counterpoint, the organ and choir of St. Paul's singing the school anthem. Alas, our New American translation has lost the rhythmic grace of the King James Version. "I was glad when they said unto me, 'Let us go into the house of the Lord.' Our feet shall stand in thy gates, O Jerusalem" has been diluted to "I rejoiced because they said to me, 'We will go up to the house of the Lord.' And now we have set foot within your gates, O Jerusalem." Fortunately, the phrase "Pray for the peace of Jerusalem" has been left intact.

I now wish I had bought that silver menorah last week when I saw it in the store window. I returned there tonight, already four days into Hanukkah, but they were all sold out. The salesman gently pointed out that I was a little late. So I bought a Christmas nutcracker instead. But I refuse to give up on my candelabrum; I saw a replica of an antique one in the Metropolitan Museum Store in Rockefeller Center as I passed by today on the way to St. Patrick's. Tomorrow I shall buy it: I may have missed lighting the first four days, but if I wait another year I shall miss all eight. I wonder why it seems so important this year; perhaps it is the constant image of terror and destruction in the Holy Land. Each photo of another suicide bombing oddly recalls that relief on the Arch of Titus in Rome, showing the Roman soldiers looting the Temple of Jerusalem and carrying off the menorah. "O pray for the peace of Jerusalem." But that is only a part, and perhaps even a small part, of the impulse to share the experience of these lights. Somehow it seems inseparable from Advent itself: like the readings from Isaiah, it links us to the people and faith that awaited—and await—the coming of the Messiah.

TUESDAY, DECEMBER 3, 2002

Today began with the bitterest cold of the year, or so it felt. What has happened to global warming? Walking down Park Avenue, I soon caught sight of the dome of St. Bart's and remembered that I wanted to send my goddaughter Carola Pease a new tree ornament from that church. I was tempted to postpone the detour and head straight for the warmth of my office, but I heard my father's inner voice: "No rush—just do it immediately." So I headed for the narthex gift shop. Each year St. Bart's creates a new gold cross from one of the many adorning that church. This year it is the altar cross in the memorial crypt chapel. The last time I saw that chapel was for the prayers around my father's casket an hour before his funeral. But this miniature version of the cross is bright and shining, more befitting Christmas.

After the purchase I went inside the church and savored its stillness and dim light, a refuge from the bustle of business outside. A huge Advent wreath hung suspended from the high barrel vault of the nave. Off to the side, in the north porch, just beyond the marble angel in the baptismal chapel, a bank of blue flickering votive candles burned brightly—a welcome addition that would have been anathema, much too Roman, in the days of my youth. Beyond it burned a single silver lamp suspended beside a new icon of Virgin and Child. The highly stylized, Byzantine features of both Mother and Son and their dark complexions seemed an inspired abstraction for this city of such diversity of race and nationalities. But then Byzantium was ever at the crossroads of cultures; its icons still speak to us, and perhaps open a window into divinity. I was glad to have taken the detour.

Before my next detour at noon—to St. Patrick's—I decided to seek via the Internet the original German verses to "Silent Night," and found far more than I had imagined: a *Stille Nacht Gesellschaft* Web site, a cornucopia of information about the world's most famous carol. With dictionary in hand, I reverted to the schoolboy forging a word-for-word translation until every sound of the original made sense. Perhaps there is still more magic in that carol than meets the eye, for never have I enjoyed singing at St. Patrick's so much, or so effortlessly.

On the way home, I finally found a small brass Hanukkah lamp—at Hallmark, of all places. It took me a while to get all nine candles to stand straight, and I managed to light them without setting our dining room table on fire. Ritchie seemed bemused by this addition to the Christmas decor. I tried to explain the biblical source of the candles and the fact that Jesus and his family and disciples would have celebrated this feast; but in the end I fell back on the indisputable point that they gave off a cheerful glowing light at dinner—before being relegated to my Music Room. I cannot figure out exactly how these disparate pieces—Carola's cross, "Stille Nacht," the Mass, and the menorah—fit together, but today was one of those rare days when everything falls into place.

THURSDAY, DECEMBER 5, 2002

Today was filled with *musikalische Zufall*—musical serendipity. First a call to Elisabeth Schwarzkopf and a promise to send my practice tape of Schubert lieder. It's still not good enough, but I realize that if I wait much longer I may never have the nerve to send it. I quoted my father's admonition "No rush, just do it at once," which brought forth a laugh of approval and her instant translation into German. More surprisingly, Elisabeth told me that she had never heard her recording of "Stille Nacht" as a duet with herself, which is included as a bonus track on her reissued *Christmas Album.* So I promised to send her my copy of the CD in time for Christmas, which then prompted a visit to HMV for its replacement. I ended up ordering a half dozen—I'll give them as Christmas presents.

Last night, I caught sight of Maria and Byron Janis waiting for a car as I walked home; it brought back memories of Jack Hemingway's memorial service two years ago, which concluded with Byron's performance of Chopin's "Adieu" waltz in A-flat, a moment that lured me back to the keyboard—and to that first waltz I had ever learned. Today I unwrapped two early Christmas gifts: one was Dinu Lipatti's recording of all the Chopin waltzes; the other, a collection of Schubert impromptus played by Krystian Zimerman. So in my office, facing the computer screen, I may hear two masters play those pieces I still practice from time to time; they suggest a New Year's resolution to return to that other keyboard when I am finished with this one at Epiphany.

As I passed St. Patrick's this afternoon, with snow falling around the newly lit Rockefeller Center tree, I had an immediate sense of transience— an unexpected memento mori. I wondered whether this approaching Christmas might be my last. The thought was, strangely, not the least morbid; it was devoid of anxiety. As our government tells us to expect another attack like 9/11, it is hard to imagine anything as permanent. Each time I sit in St. Patrick's, I look up in wonder at the soaring vaults and stained glass—but always with the background image of it all crashing down. These days, every monument casts the shadow of a ruin. But more than that, each one, indeed each flicker of beauty and grace, reflects a "simple gift," in the words of the Shaker song—a gift to be treasured, today. I knew that as soon as I got home I wanted to play again Flicka von Stade's incomparable singing of "Simple Gifts," together with Mary Costa's "Shall We Gather" and Dame Elisabeth's "Stille Nacht." These are my magical touchstones as I myself struggle with the notes and words. I finally understand why I do it: to appreciate more fully the great artists who illumine our world through sound, word, and image.

What I did not expect was a "Christmas Message" from Mason Senft

on the hall table, words that finally gave shape to the shadows and flickering lights of the day's musings. Announcing his move to a new home and
reflecting on the year following 9/11, he writes: "Perhaps the most important lesson of all is the knowledge that there are no guarantees. Life is
meant to be lived one day at a time. There may never be a tomorrow. So
each of us has to learn to live in the 'now,' with hope for the future, but not
the daily worries which pollute our very existence. If there is a tomorrow
we'll be prepared for it. If not, we will have lived today to its fullest." Tomorrow is the Feast of St. Nicholas—but today has been feast enough.

FRIDAY, DECEMBER 6, 2002

Thanks to a flyer in St. Patrick's I am better informed this St. Nick's Day than
ever before: I had never realized that the saint who became our Santa Claus
was originally a bishop in present-day Turkey at the time of the emperor
Constantine. He was famous for performing anonymous works of charity for
the poor and for his devotion to children. The tradition of Santa delivering
his gifts to children down a chimney derives from a story of how once the
good Bishop Nicholas, in order to save three daughters from being sold by
their debt-ridden father into slavery as prostitutes, secretly delivered three
bags of gold coins—a dowry for each daughter—down the chimney pipe of
their home one night. I am grateful that as a child—or as a parent—I never
knew this dark backdrop for our quaint tradition of "stockings hung by the
chimney with care, in hopes that St. Nicholas soon would be there." The
bishop apparently attended the Council of Nicea, which wrought our Creed
recited each Sunday—but that is another story. I had always thought of this
Nicholas as European, probably because he is known as Nicholas of Bari, the
Italian town to which his remains were transferred after the Moslems overran
Turkey. I am sure that the Eastern bishop of Myra was a holy and able shepherd of his flock, but I am all the more grateful to the accretions of colorful
mythology—like the Herculean figure on my St. Christopher medal. Myths
and poetry triumph over bare facts for good reason. I long to return to my *Tall*

Book of Christmas to revisit these tall tales in the weeks ahead: I only wish that I had a credulous child on my knee to listen, as I once did, with widening eyes.

SATURDAY, DECEMBER 7, 2002

At eight o'clock this morning, Aunt Patsy attended a private memorial Mass at St. Dominic's for her husband and son. It had been arranged by a devout and generous friend, but the church's scheduling of it early on a Saturday morning was less than inviting. Even less welcome, in my eyes, is the church policy of not inviting a fellow Christian, in this case the wife and mother of the two people being remembered, to the altar at Communion. Aunt Patsy, a faithful Episcopalian who raised all her children in the Catholic faith of her husband, is far more tolerant of these Roman traffic rules than am I. They remind me of the story of St. Teresa of Avila, whose cart got stuck in the mud during one of her trips to the many convents she founded in Spain; shaking her fist heavenward, she shouted, "No wonder you have so many enemies if this is how you treat your friends!" *Ecclesia semper reformanda*—the Church is ever in need of reforming itself. Perhaps the current crisis will bring forth a church that follows the example of our Lord—who turned away no one—not a codification of rules worthy of the IRS.

SUNDAY, DECEMBER 8, 2002

Today should have been the Feast of the Immaculate Conception, except that this year the eighth of December falls on a Sunday, and so the second Sunday of Advent takes precedence, as it should, over a new doctrine declared by a nineteenth-century pope. The feast, however, is not forgotten, but simply postponed a day. I can wait.

At lunch, Aunt Patsy asked me whether I believed in Masses said for the dead—or rather, whether I believed that they convey any special benefit to the dead. I answered truthfully that I do not: the dead are already with God and need no special Masses. The benefit of these Masses is for the living relatives and friends who partake of them, who derive from them a sense of comfort, and even solidarity with the dear departed, through prayer and the sacrament. I added that I do not envision God as some Forty-seventh Street diamond merchant who barters and strikes deals with us, rewarding the dead for Masses commissioned by the living. Medieval Catholicism has left us many treasures, beginning with Romanesque and Gothic cathedrals; but its contorted economy of grace is not one of them.

One medieval image, though, did strike a chord today—literally—as I drove back into the city this afternoon from Long Island: the image of the Virgin Mary as Queen of the Stars. One of the musicians in a concert of Advent music being broadcast live on the radio from the Botanical Gardens was explaining the slightly off-kilter harmonics of a choral work invoking the Virgin. It had to do with the medieval notion that there is a resonance and consonance in the "music of the spheres"—what we might call celestial music—when we find ourselves in the right spiritual and physical place within the universe, under the stars. At that conclusive point in the piece, all the voices finally come together, in synch. One of the popular representations in art of the Immaculate Conception is the image of Mary standing in the heavens, amidst the stars, with the crescent moon at her feet—a vision of John in his book of Revelation that was soon equated with Mary. The imagery reached its apex during the Baroque era, just as astronomers were turning their telescopes heavenward and confirming the revolutionary theories of Copernicus and Galileo. I'll try to think of those masterpieces by Rubens, Murillo, Velázquez, and Giordano tomorrow at Mass. In the meantime, I confess to being transfixed by the Spielberg sci-fi miniseries *Taken.*

I have never had the slightest interest in science fiction or extraterrestrial beings. But this television drama is different. Perhaps I am simply caught up in the very human soap-opera elements that propel the story. It reminds me of the time Hemingway teased my father by saying that he had started reading the New Testament and couldn't put it down since he had to find out how it ended. But there may be another element as well, an extraterrestrial one. At this darkening time of year, in the Advent season of expectation, the heavens assume a new aura. The stars shine a bit brighter, even for us, as one of them did once for three Wise Men.

MONDAY, DECEMBER 9, 2002

I played the Dinu Lipatti CD of Chopin again, and this time I read the biographical note. I vaguely recalled that this pianist had died young. But I had forgotten how young. He had leukemia and died at the age of thirty-three, the same as our Lord. This recording had been made the very year he died. Its producer, Walter Legge (Elisabeth Schwarzkopf's husband), had this to say about the young Romanian pianist he had signed up four years earlier in Switzerland, while Lipatti was already suffering the early stages of that terrible disease: "God lent the world His chosen instrument, whom we call Dinu Lipatti, for too brief a space."

Somehow that comment by the very worldly, perfectionist producer seemed more apt than any homily from the pulpit on this Feast of the Immaculate Conception, which is, in fact, a theological formula for biological and spiritual perfection—that is, the notion that Mary was preserved from all stain of sin from the moment of her creation (or conception) in order to serve as the perfect instrument in bearing God's Son. I am not sure that I have ever really grasped the meaning of "free from original sin." Did she have the capacity, the free will, to commit sin? Can anyone, even our Lord, be considered fully human without that freedom? Perhaps it is enough to say that she never sinned in fulfilling her special calling. It's like saying that a musician never hit a wrong note, or that Mozart never wrote a bad one. It stretches our imagination, but that is precisely what good authors do— so why not the original Author?

TUESDAY, DECEMBER 10, 2002

The advent of solstice, of shorter and colder days as we approach the official start of winter, seems to be reflected in the daily newspaper accounts
of the deepening crisis—both financial and spiritual—in the Catholic
Church in America. The lawsuit-plagued archdiocese of Boston is flirting
with the legal shield of bankruptcy to cover its past sins and future reckoning. Angry Catholics are demanding the resignation of its ironically sur-
named archbishop: Law. My devotion to the faith and its sacraments
remains undimmed, but my regard for the earthen vessel—the institutional
Church—is sorely tested; I take some small comfort in the certainty that I
am in good company. But just when I begin to look back nostalgically on
the Church of my youth, someone—or Someone—sends a timely reminder that perfection is not to be found next door.

One of my favorite churches—God knows which—has become so
caught up with fund-raising that money now seems the sacred element for
consecration. Its rector got up in the pulpit not long ago and announced to
his congregation, "The good news is that the money is there; the bad news
is that it is still in your pockets." I don't think that even Evelyn Waugh could
have invented a better parody of preaching. But for me, often susceptible to
the lures of memory and nostalgia, it reminded me of another lesson. Father
Greeley once wrote that if you are disillusioned with the Catholic Church,
then join another one that looks perfect, and you will discover the moment
you join it that it has already ceased to be perfect. As St. Paul reminded us
almost two thousand years ago, we have our treasure in earthen vessels.

WEDNESDAY, DECEMBER 11, 2002

Last night I decided on impulse to bring home a Christmas tree in time for dinner. Ritchie had wanted a full one, tall enough to touch a ten-foot ceiling. Two avenues eastward, a quarter mile from our front door, I found just the one. But with both sons still away at school I realized I'd have to carry it home alone. In the past, with smaller trees, I had carried them at one side, like a kayak, or perched on a shoulder. But this one was too unwieldy, and so I found myself dragging it along the street, to the bemusement of rush-hour passersby. I tried to imagine I was taking it home through woods unobserved. If only there had still been a layer of freshly fallen snow on the ground.

Once it was set up in the dining room, the red walls provided the perfect Christmas contrast with the evergreen. I got up on a chair and draped three hundred small white lights on it, then crowned it with the angel with hue-changing fiber-optic illuminated wings, a traditional figure imbued with psychedelic powers. Gazing upon this new addition to the room—the largest tree we have ever had in twenty-four Christmases together—I expressed the wish that we could just leave it as is for a while, at least until the boys come home in a week. I wanted to delay the addition of ornaments and gaudy tinsel. Why? Partly out of laziness, no doubt, yet also from some vague aesthetic impulse.

The simpler, bare, lush evergreen, its outline illumined by the bright white lights, seemed to convey the joyous expectation of Advent better than a fully decked tree with branches weighed down by glittering ornaments. There is something evocative in a tree evolving toward the full splendor of Christmas. But also something more, something I had not grasped until late this afternoon at the final Mass at St. Vincent's, to which I arrived a few minutes late. The celebrant, Father Kevin, was already in the midst of a brief homily that described the setting up of a tree today at the Dominican priory. That tree, too, had yet to receive its ornaments, but Father Kevin explained the obvious that had eluded me. Before all those accouterments are introduced, the innate beauty of the tree itself may be grasped: the underlying form, the beauty that grows from the limbs and needles themselves, without human intervention. It is the essential, elemental beauty that holds the most power.

I thought back to all those examples from New York childhood: the line of lit trees along Park Avenue, in the sanctuary of St. Bart's, and later at St. Vincent's—all sans baubles and tinsel. But then, turning to my favorite childhood book, *The Tall Book of Christmas*, I found the earliest source of this joy—a few apt illustrations of the "Story of the First Christmas Tree." The story is about a poor woodcutter who gets lost in the woods on a snowy Christmas Eve, but is guided home by benevolent wood fairies that light up a series of fir trees to mark the path for him to follow. Thereafter, he places lights on a fir tree each Christmas Eve—thus establishing a worldwide tradition down to this day. Perhaps our tree, bare but for its lights, still evokes in my mind's eye the image of those magical trees that bring the woodcutter safely homeward. Another case of nature imitating art? Soon enough the ornaments will have their day, but not before I savor our *Tannenbaum*—a powerful symbol for the living essence of Christmas, free of all dazzling, distracting glitter.

THURSDAY, DECEMBER 12, 2002

This afternoon I delivered Ritchie's portrait of John Powers's dog Blagard to his apartment on the way home. I was planning to stop off at St. Vincent's for five-thirty Mass, but I got so engrossed in conversation that I realized I would never make the extra mile in time. John was completing his application to enter the seminary program to become a permanent deacon and asked me to write a letter of support to the rector of the seminary. I suggested that perhaps I should omit the story of how I once suggested throwing his crucifix out the window—at age six—to "watch Jesus fly." He concurred. What I really wanted to write was simply that if the Church had

had more priests and ministers of the gospel like him it would not be in the present mess, from which no honorable exit yet appears in sight. But I shall write all the Homeric formulas of piety the occasion demands. The substance will be easy and genuine, only the phrasing will be wrought with Baroque artifice—and, I pray, persuasive passion.

We went around the corner to the modern Church of St. John the Evangelist, in the corner of the building that houses the offices of the archdiocese. On my way east on Fifty-sixth Street I had passed several design stores filled with ultramodern, minimalist furniture, and wondered who would ever want to sit in such chairs or recline on such sofas. The church was their ecclesiastical cousin—all 1960s contemporary, a prefab hybrid of Le Corbusier and Mies. Yet I found a strange beauty in its ugliness: all the liturgical objects were conceived in a *Star Trek* mode for the next century—that is to say, our present one. The message transcended the prosaic design: a church is not a museum; it is a living presence that, rooted in the present, looks as much to the future as to the past. The first Catholic church that I visited almost thirty-three years ago, St. Paul the Apostle, was equally striking in its departure from my Gothic expectations. Yet it preserved the faith—old wine in new wineskins—as does this one. Sometimes the common vessel heightens the ineffable power of the sacrament it holds—or so it seems tonight. I shall be glad to be back inside the neo-Gothic mystery of St. Vincent's tomorrow, but I am grateful for today's taste of chiaroscuro, the shadows that enrich the light.

FRIDAY, DECEMBER 13, 2002

This morning I was back at St. Vincent's. The words of the Mass and the priest's homily were muted, soothing background music to the constant wandering of my eyes—over carved wood, polychrome statues, geometric patterns of colorful marble in the new floor around the altar. The sanctuary gleamed like gold in half-light.

Once in the office, I decided to follow my father's maxim. As I watch the page count mount, with only a few weeks to go before Epiphany, the need to find an editor suddenly looms on the horizon. All along I have had one imprint in mind, Doubleday, which published Bishop Ahern's beautiful book on St. Thérèse and also Bill Buckley's autobiography of faith. (It also has the best line of Catholic paperbacks in America—Image Books.) But as soon as I called its publisher of religious books, the operator told me he was no longer there. My heart sank. I asked a colleague to find out whom I should now call: she sent me an e-mail explaining that Eric Major had returned to England and that the new publisher was now Michelle Rapkin. I couldn't believe my eyes. Michelle was the young editor I first sought out in 1985 and finally lured to Macmillan the next year to revive our Scribner and Macmillan religious publishing programs. She soon became my favorite colleague and worked wonders in breathing new life into our religious classics and finding many new authors before she was recruited by another firm in time to miss the hostile takeover battle that subjected us to Robert Maxwell's doomed empire.

As we caught up on old times over the phone, I tried to explain to Michelle my "Epiphanies" journal and the expert editorial help I would soon need. She asked whether I had ever read Henry van Dyke's *The Story of the Other Wise Man*. Yes, I explained, it was long after I had first heard that story from the pulpit of St. Bart's as a child: "*You* sent me a copy of the paperback you published at Ballantine Books, months before you crossed Third Avenue to join us at Macmillan." It had been Michelle to whom I owed the pleasure of reading that short masterpiece by the venerable Scribner author. I read it on a plane to Palm Beach in the summer of 1985—a most unseasonable route for the journey of the Magi! What I had not recalled until just now was the name on its spine, the very imprint Michelle had launched at Ballantine/Random House: "Epiphany Books." Now I wonder what is the more unexplainable: the timing of my recollection and reconnection, or the fact that I forgot it in the first place? On top of my desk I catch a glimpse of a book I have never opened: Schacter's *The Seven Sins of Memory—How the Mind Forgets and Remembers*. Perhaps I should read it; in the meantime, I am satisfied with yet another coincidence attributable to God the Anonymous.

SATURDAY, DECEMBER 14, 2002

The Book of Common Prayer has an especially memorable pairing of generalities in its general confession, recited at the beginning of each service of Morning Prayer: "We have left undone those things which we ought to have done, and we have done those things which we ought not to have done." How strange that the former, those sins of omission, seem to weigh the heavier as time goes on. But then, the author has placed them first, doubtless for good reason. In the twilight of Advent, those "should have's" arise more frequently and urgently than at any other time of year.

A couple of days ago I called my oldest living mentor, Professor Julius Held. Now in his ninety-eighth year, he is living in a nursing home a few miles from his house in Old Bennington, Vermont. I last visited him a year and a half ago, on my way to pick up Chris at the end of his school year at Eaglebrook. Although a refugee from the Nazis in the 1930s, when he came to America and was spared the terrible fate of so many friends and relatives, Julius never abandoned his love for the German language, culture, and heritage of his youth and his Jewish ancestors. I'll never forget the justifiable pride he felt when after years of persistence he succeeded in having the site of the destroyed synagogue in his hometown, Mosbach, rededicated in the mid-1980s as a memorial park for the town's victims of the Holocaust. Julius embodies that largeness of spirit and humanity that illumines the paintings of those two seventeenth-century geniuses Rubens and Rembrandt, about whom he is the greatest living expert. I could never calculate, much less repay, my enormous debt to him over almost thirty years. I never wrote anything about Rubens without first seeking his advice—and imprimatur.

At the end of my last visit to Julius, I played him a few pieces on the baby grand in the lobby of the nursing home and promised to return to play more. But too much time has already passed, and when I recently called his room to discuss a visit, his aide told me that he had just returned from the hospital, very weak from recurring bouts of pneumonia and unable to speak over the phone. It took me back suddenly to my father's last days; all I could suggest was that they set up a tape or CD player to fill his waking hours with classical music.

Today I went to Mason's new studio with a new intention, and impatience. "No rush, just do it" was my mantra as I sought in these last two Saturdays before Christmas to get something recorded, however flawed, to send to Elisabeth (to whom I had promised a sampling of efforts) and now to Julius—I pray not too late. This past week I had been close to giving it all up: the curse of the perfectionist. But, dazzled by Mason's new home and studio, my spirits immediately lifted and I told him I wanted today just to forge ahead and see how much I could get on tape. By the end of the hour, we had three Schubert lieder. The mistakes were plentiful, yet as I listened to the playback I heard for the first time my own voice and not some manufactured attempt to find a better one. It was more honestly imperfect than imperfectly honest. Mason agreed and explained the oft overlooked obvious: the greatest enemy to singing is the ego. (Thus birds and babies are spared.) With the layers of ego stripped away like yellowed varnish on an old-master painting, the original colors may yet have a chance to shine through. It is a chance worth taking, a journey worth continuing. I wish only that I had started out sooner. But even van Dyke's fourth Wise Man eventually arrived in time to see our Lord—on the cross.

SUNDAY, DECEMBER 15, 2002

Today is known as Gaudete Sunday—a brief respite of rejoicing during the penitential preparation of Advent. As I listened to the radio, driving into the city this afternoon, I heard a rendering of Handel's "Rejoice greatly, O daughter of Zion." For all its welcome familiarity, it had a freshness and originality that I had not recalled from countless hearings at this time of year. As the days draw closer to Christmas, the burden of organizing annual tips and presents begins to crowd the more spontaneous moments of gathering joy—the sparkling lights and sounds and smiles of the season. It is time to pull out the recordings of Bach's *Christmas Oratorio* and Handel's *Messiah* to recapture the wonder amidst the worldliness and world-weariness.

Thanks to the Internet and St. Paul's School, I have some timely help from one of my grandfather's authors, Sir Winston Churchill. The "Quote of the Month" for the first electronic issue of my school's newsletter is attributed to him: "We make a living by what we get; we make a life by what we give." We know the Magi only by what they gave—and how far they traveled to deliver their gifts. Their images are beginning to appear all around, inside and in front of churches—and in God's good time. I used to see the manger and, first and foremost, the Holy Family. Now it is the visitors, especially those three exotic ones, who catch my eye. Angels and saints and our Savior seem part of the supernatural order. The all-too-human pilgrims, from shepherds to kings, who made their way to that manger—these are the greater source of wonder.

MONDAY, DECEMBER 16, 2002

As I sat down today at last to write a letter to Julius Held, I recalled in an instant that he was the one who first explained, in great detail, my favorite Rubens *Epiphany*, the High Baroque masterpiece now in the Antwerp museum. It was he who had first connected the wonderful camels dominating the top of the altarpiece with the words of the prophet Isaiah appointed to be read at the Mass on Epiphany: "The multitude of camels shall cover thee, the dromedaries of Midian and Epha." From those exotic beasts of burden the artist painted a host of worshipers descending in a graceful reverse S-curve toward the Virgin and Child.

Only Rubens could have reflected the liturgical elements of the Mass in a biblical backdrop with all the joie de vivre of a Flemish Baroque feast. The foremost king offers not gold, but robed in vestments of ecclesiastical splendor, he swings a censer of frankincense as if he were a priest kneeling before the sacramental body exposed on the altar. Mary displays her infant Son, the original body of Christ, whose reclining pose prefigures a pietà.

Rubens has retained the close association of Nativity and death so common throughout early Netherlandish altarpieces, which likewise employed "disguised symbolism" in the mundane details of straw (bread), the ox (sacrifice), and the wooden crate covered with a white cloth (altar), all adding up to the supreme sacrifice of the Mass. Ancient Rome is represented by the two soldiers standing beside a Corinthian column entwined with ivy, symbolizing its supplanting and renewal by the new Roman Church; the universality of this Catholic empire is embodied in the assembly of witnesses—including an Asian, an Indian, and an African—from the knight on horseback to the beggar below. All it lacks is the resounding chorus of Handel's "For unto us a child is born." How it all brings back so many happy memories of my visits to Old Bennington in the 1970s while Held was finishing his work on his "Rubens Bible," as I call his magnum opus, a critical catalogue of the artist's more than four hundred oil sketches.

On one of those visits I learned that Julius—like my father and me—had a special affection for *Der Rosenkavalier*, which he said he had first heard in Vienna in the 1920s as a graduate student, with Lotte Lehmann as the Marschallin. Strauss had been well served by his librettist, von Hofmannsthal. Last year as I prepared a Scribner Classic of our English translation of Buber's *I and Thou (Ich und Du)*, I was sorely tempted to share with the reader in a preface my private theory that Buber may have been influenced by von Hofmannsthal's opening dialogue in *Der Rosenkavalier.* I resisted the temptation to go out on that limb in print, but today I finally decided to share this wishful thinking with my longtime mentor.

As the curtain rises at the breaking of dawn, Oktavian sings to his beloved Marschallin: *"Du, du!—Was heisst das 'Du'? Was 'du und ich'? Hat denn das einen Sinn? Das sind Worte, blosse Worte, nicht? Du sag! Aber dennoch: Es ist etwas in ihnen, ein Schwindeln, ein Ziehen, ein Sehnen und Drängen, ein Schmachten und Brennen: Wie jetzt meine Hand zu deiner Hand kommt, das Zudirwollen, das Dichumklammern, das bin ich, das will zu dir; aber das Ich vergeht in dem Du."* ("You, you! What does 'you' mean? What about 'you and I'? Does it make any sense? They are words, empty words! No? Tell me! But in spite of that, there is something in them, a delirium, a magnetism, a longing and urging, a thirsting and burning: as now my hand finds your hand, the desire for you, the holding of you, I am that that desires you, but the 'I' is lost in the 'You.' ")

It sounds like an anticipation of Buber's mystical treatise, written a

decade after the premiere of this opera. By the time Buber wrote that theological book in Vienna, *Der Rosenkavalier* was already famous. I have tried to
find some connection between von Hofmannsthal and Buber—there is
some evidence that Buber admired his poetry—but I can come up with
nothing specific. As in my long-standing pairing of Rubens and Bernini,
the influence, perhaps subconscious, of the former on the latter was never
publicly acknowledged. But I like to believe that our beloved *Rosenkavalier*
had just such an influence on our small religious classic, especially since my
father's introduction of the opera to me as a youngster included an insight
that approached sacred ground.

When the Marschallin wistfully reflects about the passage of time, gazing into a mirror, she begins with regret and sadness as she traces its course
through the new lines in her face. But she finds a new source of equanimity and acceptance in something that qualifies as one of the most poignant
musical epiphanies of all time. Singing now to her beloved Oktavian, she
concludes that, after all, there is no reason to fear time: *"Auch sie ist ein
Geschöpf des Vaters, der uns alle erschaffen hat."*—"Time, too, is a creation of the
Father, who has made us all."

TUESDAY, DECEMBER 17, 2002

Graham Greene once wrote that "in every childhood there is a moment
when a door opens and lets in the future." This enchanting quotation graces
the brochure for the new Carle Museum of picture-book art in Amherst,
Massachusetts. Its director, Nick Clark, who sent it to me, gave me enormous help as curator of the Chrysler Museum in Virginia, where I traveled
a dozen years ago to study and photograph Bernini's last sculpture, a marble bust of Christ the Savior, on which the eighty-year-old Bernini was
working at the time of his death. But this past year's journey has been in
the opposite direction—back to youth, back to those elusive doors. They
remind me of a recurrent dream my father used to have; he described it in

his memoir, written—or rather dictated—toward the end of his life, after he had lost the ability to read and write:

> *I often dream of my grandparents' house in New York City—poignant, vivid dreams. Oftentimes it involves my finding a room that goes off a staircase with a hidden door. There is a delightful room filled with books on the shelves and furniture that I didn't know was there. In another dream, I am again in my grandparents' house in the city and the little study opens on to the countryside, so that the city dissolves into a rural landscape with a farmyard and all kinds of bucolic sights.*
>
> *I have thought much about what role such dreams may have. I call them romantic dreams, because they suggest that there are doors in familiar places that you haven't known were there, showing that reality has a way of opening up doors beyond the walls that confine us in life. These dreams express the romantic impulse for the unknown and also for literature, the yearning that fuels the creative imagination and scholarly curiosity alike.*

Our earliest memories are inevitably colored and shaped by the intervening years; often we seek some external confirmation of the images and sensations they leave imprinted on us. My recollection of that concert of a lifetime—the Van Cliburn *Emperor* at Tanglewood—was undermined by recent listening to the tape, for I was seeking in that recording a door through which to reenter that time and place, to relive the original experience in a renewed flush of adolescence. Fortunately, I gave a copy to a more detached and discerning listener, Jim Wood, and this is what he wrote in return: "That Van Cliburn recording is just out of this world! Thanks a million for it—it is on more than I'd like to admit (poor Connie thinks I've flipped). But he is spectacular in this and was obviously an inspiration to Leinsdorf.... And to think he had the generous thoughtfulness to encore the entire last movement! If nothing else happens this winter I'll wear out that to keep my focus on this still gorgeous artistry that we humans are capable of showing."

Jim has rescued a precious epiphany from second-guessing—just in time for Christmas. I took a long detour home tonight—all the way to Lincoln Center to buy more copies of Elisabeth Schwarzkopf's *Christmas Album.* As I walked back east across Central Park at dusk, I passed the meadow on which I had listened to so many Met Opera summer concerts, then the empty band shell, passing a young man wearing a red Met Opera cap while he listened to his headphones. Was he a member of the orchestra, a singer, or just a fan like me? Emerging from the park on my street, Seventy-second, I caught sight of my grandmother's apartment house. The windows on her floor were dark. I pictured that one door I would give almost anything to reenter; but of course, only if I might find what exists in memory alone on the other side. I shall have to settle for the brass door knocker of High Sunderland Hall in Yorkshire I salvaged after her death; it now hangs on my son Charlie's door. Yet I am grateful to both Greene and my father today, for I may yet pass through that door again—if only in a dreamscape.

WEDNESDAY, DECEMBER 18, 2002

Handel's *Messiah* is everywhere these days—in churches, cathedrals, schools, concert halls, music shops. Today in an article about an upcoming performance by the St. Thomas Choir, the music director confessed that one year, not so long ago, he experimented by performing Bach's *Christmas Oratorio* instead, saving Handel's masterpiece for the season for which it had originally been intended—Easter. The audience stayed away in droves, so *Messiah* is back—but not yet in my Music Room: Bach's oratorio still plays in the background tonight. It is more ecclesiastical than operatic; it glows with the flickering of church candles, not the blaze of chandeliers (or footlights). There is a magic to the Bach that never stales; it becomes more miraculous at each hearing. He is the master of all sacred music.

Handel was, like Verdi, essentially an opera composer, which may explain why his *Messiah*—like Verdi's *Requiem*—tops the charts of popularity. But Handel was also a master recycler of themes, a pragmatic composer in those days before recordings. As Professor Knapp once explained in his choral music course, the grammatically bizarre emphasis, with strong downbeat, on the insignificant conjunction "for" in Handel's chorus "For unto us a Child is born," has a simple explanation and nothing at all to do with the sacred text of the King James Bible. This theme had originally been written for one of Handel's Italian operas, where the downbeat fit the libretto like a glove. But does any listener—or singer—today notice, much less mind, that we hear "*For* unto us a Child is born"? Of course not. In the contest between words and music, the latter will always win the day—at the hand of a great composer.

"And unto us a Son is given." Today both our sons came home from their respective schools—cause enough for rejoicing. Charlie, who is embroiled in historical controversies of race and politics far beyond anything I had to reconcile in my ivory tower of art history, at least had the chance to audit a course in medieval art. And Chris just announced that over this holiday he must learn all his lines as the lead in Shakespeare's *The Comedy of Errors*, the one comedy of the Bard's I have never read (or seen performed). At least the title sounds familiar enough—the story of my life as a parent, if I dare be so optimistic and stress its first word: at this point in life I want only *comedy*, whether divine or profane, I don't care, so long as it ends in happy resolution.

Charlie insisted I retire my newly acquired menorah, claiming it would be only a source of confusion (mainly about his dad's convictions, or even sanity) among his visiting friends from all religious traditions; but at least he allowed the angel with wings of changing fiber-optic colors to stay atop the tree; for him, high-tech kitsch is redeemed by the comic spirit of Christmas, as may, I pray, we all be in God's own time.

THURSDAY, DECEMBER 19, 2002

This morning at the nine o'clock Mass at St. Vincent's, I spent most of the time gazing at the crèche set up at the Rosary Altar: the stable was there and the straw was on the ground, with fresh evergreen spruce trees framing it—but no figures, no animals. The manger was empty, awaiting the arrival—or in this case, placement—of the Holy Family, animals, angels, shepherds, and eventually the Kings. To the left of the evocatively empty manger was the liturgical tabernacle-tomb of Christ in the stone wall, framed by two carved angels. Both manger and tomb awaited the body of Christ, the first in the form of an infant figurine for Christmas, the second in the form of the sacramental Hosts to be transfered there on Holy Thursday, when the altar is stripped and the tabernacles emptied until Easter. How close birth and burial are found in this transept, as in life.

When I arrived at the office a phone call from Julius Held's daughter informed me that her father was slipping away into a final sleep and that there was no point in my sending Buber's book since he was now beyond reading. Yet, my letter faxed on Monday had indeed arrived in time, she said, the last letter he had read. How grateful I felt for my father's saying, and I wondered whether my preoccupation with an elusive German translation had not, after all, been responsible for keeping it foremost in mind. "*Keine Eile . . . aber sofort*"—that's as close as I'll get to it. Yet it conveys none of the humor of my father's English, which is why some things are indeed untranslatable, and why we may need all the languages the Tower of Babel produced.

The next call was from my college roommate telling me that his eldest son, who is the same age as Christopher, was almost killed by his roommate a few days ago at St. Paul's. The doctor called the sudden, irrational attempted murder by an otherwise amicable boy "a psychotic break." Fortunately the victim was saved by two guardian angels in the form of hockey players who came to the rescue in time to avert the greatest of human tragedies—the death of a child.

This news took me back to the day we got a call saying that our son Charlie had been awakened early one Sunday morning (in the very same dormitory) by a similar angel, that time in the form of a teacher on his way to buy the morning paper, who evacuated Charlie and his fellow students sleeping directly below a smoldering fire in the attic. The fire department was called and arrived (by their calculation) only a matter of minutes before the attic and entire third floor would have exploded in an inferno. A few months later, after both shock and gratitude had settled deep, I read Charlie's account of his experience; it was his answer to a question on the Princeton admissions application about a "life-transforming" experience:

*After narrowly escaping death in a fire this year, I learned not to take anything for
granted. . . . I consider myself extremely lucky to have survived. While watching the
smoke pour out of the building, I immediately realized that I held a common false
assumption—that fire alarm systems always work. Additionally, I realized how
quickly and unexpectedly one can become deprived of all one's possessions, not to
mention one's life. Hitherto, I had never considered fire to be a likely threat to my
well-being. I had been wrong . . . almost dead wrong. Despite all the material setbacks
that the fire caused, I did gain some valuable wisdom. Since I could easily have died
that morning, without warning, it dawned on me that one should never postpone
extensions of gratitude, apology, or affection, because any day could be one's last.
Indeed, "Thank you," "I'm sorry," and "I love you" cannot wait another day. I now
know how rapidly such plans can go up in smoke.*

Rereading these words of the eloquent eighteen-year-old, I wonder
whether it is not the perfect message for the final week of Advent—and
perhaps, as well, the perfect translation into practice of his grandfather's
witty saying: "No rush . . ."

SATURDAY, DECEMBER 21, 2002

Tonight at St. Jean's, with Ritchie and both sons, we heard what I considered the best summary of the Christian faith ever delivered from a pulpit.
After tracing the prophecy of a Messiah and eternal restoration of the
kingdom to God's people through its multiple misinterpretations, the priest
raised the central question: Why has Christianity seemingly made so little
difference to peace on earth? (The question resonates as another war with
Iraq looms on the horizon.) The answer he gave was that believers so often—and so widely—assume that God works out his purpose on his own:
we have only to witness and worship. But that is not the message of the
gospels: everything about Jesus, from the moment of the Annunciation to
Mary (today's gospel reading), points to God requiring human consent and
cooperation in each act of salvation. The Incarnation itself was predicated

on Mary's assent to the angel: "I am the handmaid of the Lord, be it done unto me according to thy word." (In another moment of divine coincidence, Christopher turned to me during that gospel reading and whispered, "Dad, this is what I read at Eaglebrook's Christmas service a few days ago.")

Before coming to church, Charlie had asked me to explain the origin of the Peace Corps. I mulled over all sorts of strategic, Cold War motives of JFK and his advisers striving to save impoverished countries from the lure of Communism. But after the homily, a much simpler answer came to mind—the concluding words of the first Catholic president's inaugural address: "Here on earth God's work must truly be our own."

MONDAY, DECEMBER 23, 2002

Late last night and early into the wee hours of the morning I revived a personal tradition of my own, which I had begun almost twenty years ago: playing tapes of my beloved friend Francis Robinson's radio broadcasts called *A Collector's Christmas*. It's my annual Christmas gift to myself. No one was better at introducing the musical treasures of this holy season than Francis, so many years the public voice—and soul—of the Metropolitan Opera. He wrote his own warm and illuminating commentary and delivered it in his inimitable, rich Tennessee baritone. As I listened to these familiar introductions and recordings of Sutherland, Corelli, Pavarotti, Price, Schwarzkopf, among the many Met stars in Francis's pantheon (and he knew them all well), I felt a sudden sadness and nostalgia I had not recalled from years past. It was not only the sound of his voice and the reminder of how much I missed his company; there was something more, but I could not guess what.

By the end of this *Collector's Christmas*, a title repeated time and again throughout the broadcast, I was mulling over my status as a notable noncollector: the very idea of collecting has never engaged me. I have no collections of stamps, coins, rare books, or assorted memorabilia for display.

But as Francis signed off, I realized how wrong I was. I have been an avid collector from my earliest days to the present; my collection is of memories—a rich, even priceless (if unmarketable), collection. It sometimes takes only a tape, a book, or a photo to open it, which must be the reason I return to these reliable staples so regularly.

Today I learned that Professor Held died yesterday; his daughter, Anna, called with the news. He had died peacefully. He was ninety-seven. He deserved no less. Was his passing perhaps what I had felt, but not yet realized, last night? God knows. This same morning a fax from Dame Elisabeth mentioned the Monet book I had sent her as a Christmas gift. She said it would help her to enjoy again "the visible blessings of the past." Her graceful phrase reminds me also of audible blessings, as well as those others preserved and kept alive by memory, imagination, and dreams. In his last months, weeks, and days, Julius told his family that he spent more and more time in his childhood town of Mosbach, in Germany. Memories may be the only collection we can take with us on our final journey.

TUESDAY, DECEMBER 24, 2002

Today has been a Christmas Eve of the unexpected. The hymn chosen for the noon Mass at St. Patrick's was the most appropriate "Come, thou long expected Jesus." We were all ready—priest, deacon, lector, and I—to begin our entrance procession to the front of the sanctuary, but there was no organist. We waited. Still no organist. I could see the priest's eyes begin to brighten at the prospect of a brief musicless Mass; so I decided to make a preemptive strike: "No problem, let's just go; we'll sing the hymn a capella. The church organ was broken on that Christmas Eve when 'Silent Night' was first performed; it will be an adventure, and Christmas Eve is the right time for an adventure."

I had run all the way from the office to get to the cathedral on time; I was not about to turn back now. The priest made no reply. And so we pro-

ceeded. By the time I got to announce the hymn I saw the substitute organist dash into his seat, and prayed he would know what hymn to play. (I
would have preferred a capella to this chasm of suspense.) After the first
verse, he stopped playing; I began the second verse alone; he eventually
caught up. By this time I had been so distracted that I found myself singing
not the words on the sheet but the words to the old Episcopal Church version (a far more poetic one) I had sung so many times as a schoolboy. And
so the rest of the Mass continued: the organist repeatedly disappeared from
his console, wandered along the aisle, and returned only just in time to play
the next section of music. I had had my Christmas Eve adventure—or so
I thought. At the end of the Mass, I went up to him and said with all the
cheerfulness I could muster for this day, "Well, you really arrived in the St.
Nick of time."

When I got home to ready everyone for the afternoon service at St.
Bart's, I discovered that the fiber-optic angel on top of our tree had burned
herself out; her light gone, she was now just another figurine. More serious
was Christopher's sudden attack of stomach pains, which took him to his
bed while the rest of us went to join my mother at church. She arrived in the
pew, beaming, just as the congregation began the processional hymn "O
Come All Ye Faithful." (She had run most of the way.) When we got to the
Communion hymn, "Silent Night," I sang the three verses *auf Deutsch*, to
honor the original composer. It was worth the look of amazement and
amusement on my mother's face as we proceeded back from the altar: *"Christ
der Retter ist da!"* I sang along with the congregation—"Christ the Savior is
here." Less approvingly, Charlie turned to his mother and whispered, "Has
anyone told Dad we are in America?"

Originally I planned to get to the midnight Mass at St. Jean Baptiste, as
I did last year, once everyone was in bed. But tonight I found myself instead
keeping an eye on our younger son, sick in bed. His doctor had called us
back within a minute of Ritchie placing the emergency call to his answer-
ing service. Yesterday, I had questioned Ritchie's sanity in sending his office
such a sumptuous Christmas plant. "You'll see," she replied; "someday,
we'll have an emergency and be glad we remembered them." But the very
next day? Is this what is euphemistically called a mother's intuition? Or did
the God of coincidences have yet another lesson to teach me—the night
before Christmas?

WEDNESDAY, DECEMBER 25, 2002

Last night was a horrific variation on that early childhood theme of staying up as late as possible to catch a glimpse of Santa arriving to fill the stockings. I was up for most of the night—first out of concern for Chris, on whom I checked regularly; he, in turn, just as regularly told me to go back to bed. Finally I turned on the bedside radio softly and was entranced to hear Puccini's *La Bohème*. A strange choice, I thought at first, until the obvious dawned on me several hours before sunrise: the opera opens on Christmas Eve!

"Stille Nacht, heilige Nacht . . ." It was holy, but far from silent. When dawn finally broke, I wondered whether any of us would make it through the Christmas Day celebrations. But as soon as Chris announced he felt much better, my own symptoms receded, and we all made it over to my mother's for our family Christmas lunch. This year represents the eighth without my father, and yet it still feels odd to sit at his place at the table. Through shared stories, jokes, and reminiscences he is still very much the central presence.

By the time we left to return home—all of one block away—the streets, sidewalks, and rooftops were covered with snow, and glimpses out the windows evoked those wonderful wintry sets of Zeffirelli's *La Bohème* at the Met. Before all the presents had been opened I knew I had to dash off, leaving my wife, sons, and brother alone to secular entertainments while I caught the five-thirty Christmas Mass. At first I thought to go to my regular St. Jean Baptiste, but then changed my course and raced a block and a half east on Seventy-second Street to the little Church of St. John the Martyr. Originally built for the local Czech community, it is hardly more than a large chapel— an odd mixture of imagined medievalism and functional modernity. Half the Christmas greens were artificial, half the statues were painted plaster, and yet the overall effect was one of charming authenticity. There is a naive intimacy about the interior that captures the message and atmosphere of that first Silent Night. Besides, I have a special bond to this church through my father.

For his last two and a half years Dad lived down the street at the Mary

Manning Walsh Home, where Ritchie, our boys, and I would descend upon him each Sunday evening. This was the church we stopped in for Mass on the way back home. Today, on Christmas afternoon, with the streets hushed beneath several inches of new-fallen snow, I cherished the links between this sacred space and those final visits with my father. There was nothing grand about the village of our Lord's birth on the first Christmas: "O little town of Bethlehem, how still we see thee lie . . ." That was the image this homely—and homey—miniature parish conjured up this afternoon. The architect Mies was right: "Less is more." That is the message this blessed Christmas has left imprinted on snow and soul.

THURSDAY, DECEMBER 26, 2002

On the flight south to Florida today I began to read my Christmas present from Chris: *The Bible Unearthed: Archaeology's New Vision of Ancient Israel and the Origin of Its Sacred Texts.* I can't put it down. It juxtaposes the historical narrative of the early books—from the journey of Abraham through the triumphant reigns of Kings David and Solomon—with the most up-to-date archaeological findings. The result is, so far, a picture of a biblical Camelot rooted in history but magnified through literary inspiration and myth. It is the kind of study that would raise the hackles of any fundamentalist or literal reader of scripture. But I find it, so far, as consoling as it is engrossing. The idea that the early books of the Bible should be taken at face value as a record of historical facts would be a tougher test of faith than the notion that they reflect, through a prism of poetry and myth, a journey of theological discovery—in other words, a series of epiphanies leading to deeper experiences of God through history.

In a unexpected way this Christmas present has taken me right back to where I was at its giver's age: in a third-form "Ancient History/Sacred Studies" class at St. Paul's. I was a more literal reader of scripture then, but so were we all. Yet this new adventure poses no problems of faith. On the contrary, it suggests that the greater threats come with taking the Bible as a science text (as in the Church's battle with Galileo three centuries ago, and the current cultural war over creationism in public schools) or as a legal document, a divine grant of land (prompting endless battles over the borders of Palestine and Israel). The gospel of Matthew begins by tracing the ancestry of Jesus through the carpenter Joseph to King David and then all the way back to Abraham. This lineage explains why Christ was born in Bethlehem, the city of David, but not why he lives in the hearts and lives of his followers two millennia later. That is the mystery beyond the power of any earthly author to explain. In the meantime, I look forward to returning to the archaeology of the Bible as I spend the last week of this year on an island named after the greatest of the pagan Roman gods—Jupiter.

FRIDAY, DECEMBER 27, 2002

I have finished the book. I had not realized—or remembered—how much brutality, violence, bloodshed, and utter destruction was chronicled in the Hebrew Bible we call the Old Testament. Despite the poetic license of the biblical authors, the historical reality they rewove into sacred texts was no less coarse or harsh. The real miracle is that out of such a messy cauldron poured forth ideas (and ideals) of divinity and human community that continue to nourish us thousands of years later. Their familiarity never stales. Archaeology has stripped the scriptures of layers of historical claims, but at the same time lays bare the more arresting fact of human creativity and imagination—the miracle we label inspiration and attribute to a source beyond our experience.

The sculptors Michelangelo and Bernini described their miracles wrought in stone as ultimately products of God: they wielded the chisel and hammer, but God sent the ideas, directed their hands, and shaped the final expression. They saw themselves as tools in the hands of God. Perhaps the biblical writers and editors, the prophets, priests, and scribes who cobbled together the scriptures, saw themselves in such a light. We can never know: they remain anonymous; they have left only their words. I thought often during this provocative and brilliant deconstruction of biblical sagas and myths that I would become literally disillusioned. Quite the opposite; the authors, Finkelstein and Silberman, sum up the reason why: "It is only when we recognize when and why the ideas and events described in the Bible came to be so skillfully woven together that we can at last begin to appreciate the true genius and continuing power of this single most influential literary and spiritual creation in the history of humanity."

SATURDAY, DECEMBER 28, 2002

Ending the year in Florida, as we have for the last decade, is an otherworldly experience. Yesterday I tried to stop by St. Christopher's Church here in Hobe Sound, and found it locked. The beautiful sunny day somehow made the impenetrable sanctuary seem even more incongruous, an affront to the Christmas season. Already I miss those city churches, never more than ten blocks apart, and open all day to pedestrians. Of course, there are no pedestrians here: everything is surrounded by a parking lot. But for people who choose never to leave their sofas, religion has found its prime place—on television. It is hard to decide which main branch of Christianity, the Protestant Evangelical or the Roman Catholic, has better perfected self-parody via the airwaves. Each has its own cable network. One is hosted by polyester preachers; the other by a formidable nun in an overstarched habit: Evelyn Waugh would have had a field day down here.

SUNDAY, DECEMBER 29, 2002

Today is the Feast of the Holy Family. St. Christopher's was open at last, and I found myself there for the noon Mass. The sanctuary was filled with

Christmas decorations, and the priest in his otherwise unmemorable homily advised us to look closely at them and enjoy them for the one remaining week of Christmas, before they are taken down and packed up for another year. He also informed us that the crèche scene in front of the altar owed its origin to St. Francis of Assisi, who no doubt would have appreciated the prominence given to the animals—ox and ass, sheep and camels *(Se non è vero, è ben trovato)*. The Old Testament reading is one of the most beautiful all year. Taken from Genesis, it recounts God's covenant with Abram, who as the renamed Abraham is promised to become the father of generations of descendants as numerous as the stars in the sky.

Today's feast reminded me of a retort I used to offer when, during our son Charlie's first six years as an only child, I was sometimes teased by friends about the discrepancy between our number of offspring and my Catholicism. Where are the rest of the brood? they would ask. "Well," I'd reply, "we take the Holy family as our model." Perhaps it was sitting in a church bearing the name of our younger son that reminded me of that time. But as the priest aptly reminded us, the Holy Family serves as a model of all families, however unconventional in configuration: it is their binding love we are all called to regenerate.

TUESDAY, DECEMBER 31, 2002

The last day of the calendar year. The elaborate, festive decorations have been set in place at the beach club for the big New Year's Eve bash tonight. The entrance has been planted with a menagerie—if that is the term—of plastic pink flamingoes; I'd like to kidnap a pair for the front lawn back home. Otherwise, the preparations leave me cold, even in this warm tropical climate. Tomorrow is a holy day of obligation. I suppose it reflects the church's wisdom in attempting to moderate the drunkenness of the evening before by reminding the faithful that they must be able to stagger to Mass the next day, the first of the new year.

Instead of going to one of the two anticipatory Masses at St. Christopher's this afternoon, I decided to stop by and visit the Episcopal chapel here on the island, which rises tastefully, in Spanish Mission style, in the midst of the golf course—where else? Inside, it has all the old-fashioned warmth and sublime familiarity of childhood churches that the postwar St. Christopher's lacks. The luminous stained glass window above the altar, the carved wooden pulpit, the oak pews and needlepoint kneelers—it might have been a miniature St. Luke's in Gladstone. There is no reserved sacrament, no tabernacle lamp to signify the sacramental presence of God within; yet it feels no less a holy place. In front of the lectern stands a small manger scene, with three good-size Kings from the East, a reminder of next week's feast. I recalled that this was the church to which my childhood rector of St. Bart's, Dr. Finlay, retired a quarter century ago, before his failing eyesight ended his active ministry. Later, the retired headmaster of Choate took the post. I wonder whether it will someday house a former rector of St. Paul's. If I could slip in a Catholic priest sometime during off-hours, this would be the place I'd most like to attend Mass. Perhaps someday ... if the winds of ecumenism blow again with the force that followed Vatican II.

The ball on Times Square has dropped. On this day my father used to go around our old offices on Fifth and ask his colleagues how Scrooge celebrated New Year. "I like the way he used to handle Christmas," he'd add with a twinkle.

WEDNESDAY, JANUARY 1, 2003

I awoke to find that the first day of this new year was more than half over—a few minutes past noon. Mass had already begun at St. Christopher's; I threw on my clothes and sped down the road to the music of Johann Strauss, courtesy of National Public Radio's broadcast of the New Year's concert in Vienna. His "workers polka" was good wake-up therapy. The church was not overcrowded and I slipped into a seat near the front, with a prime view of the crèche under the altar just as the words of the Creed were recited. Having missed only the liturgy of the word—the scripture readings—I was able to catch up by glancing through the pages of the missal for this feast of Mary. The gospel passage from St. Luke described the visit of the shepherds to the manger on that first Christmas morning. After the surprising recessional of "Auld Lang Syne," I spent a moment before that crèche and noticed that there were several more shepherds and sheep there than at its Episcopal counterpart on the island. Perhaps, I mused, Catholics identify more closely with shepherds, Episcopalians with kings—at least among the corporate titans of Jupiter Island.

Tonight was a retrospective New Year. CNN featured an account of Nixon's historic visit to China, hosted by his daughter Julie. Afterward I watched a program on Archbishop Sheen, which took me back again to our first meeting in Princeton. For a moment I might have been persuaded that today was the first of 1973, not 2003. Another show took me back even further—to the Holy Land at the time of Jesus's birth—a series of illustrated meditations on the joyful mysteries of the rosary. Decades of time and decades of beads have more in common than I ever suspected: both are cyclical, soothingly familiar, forever old, and forever new.

FRIDAY, JANUARY 3, 2003

Coming home on this cold, drizzly first Friday of the new year—and the last Friday until Epiphany—was like an unexpected cadenza by Mozart. Familiar themes resurfaced in the most refreshing ways, from earliest childhood to adulthood. First, a letter from John Powers recounted in glowing highlights the high Christmas Mass at St. Vincent's I had to miss; then, a propos a letter I had agreed to write in support of his vocation to the permanent diaconate in the Church, he reminded me that we had been friends for forty-five years—far longer than any friend I may claim today—and that he was consequently declining my request to tell me what to write. So, a new evening assignment—and one I soon felt was as much a grace as an honor to be asked to do. I recalled that he had shown me my first crucifix at age six, and then a dozen years later advised me to think carefully before leaping into the Roman faith, as it was not something to be taken lightly. John never took his faith lightly, but he did take himself lightly as he combined true holiness and piety with modesty and humor. Who knows—only God—how many souls he has touched over the years? Spending almost a year at this date in composing, by fits and starts, this spiritual journal of epiphanies, I find in these last days a special gratitude and poignancy for the moments of reflection on people who have shone their faith on others. John is one such star—his faith never has failed to sparkle. During the past months as a cantor at St. Patrick's I have come to know several permanent deacons there and their special ministry of service. John will be an outstanding addition to their ranks. He was my obvious and instant choice as godfather to our firstborn, and he went the extra mile. He was no less a role model as son: both our fathers were at the Mary Manning Walsh Home together for a year, and died a year apart. Then he became the son every mother should have. He has just taken her off to Guatemala for their latest adventure—one set of footsteps I shall decline to follow!

There followed a card and letter from our first au pair, Rosie, who arrived on the scene two years after my baby brother, John. Now the grandmother of two picture-perfect *Knaben*, she wished me *"Frohe Weihnachten und viel Glück und Gesundheit für das neues Jahr."* And for the first time, since age eight, I was finally able to reply, *"Mit herzlichen Wünschen für ein glückliches neues Jahr!"* My remaining New Year's resolution is to lure her here to see herself once again, through the miracle of video, at our family picnic in 1960.

A card and gracious note from Jack Martin's daughter reminded me that thirty years ago this month I was busy writing my senior thesis for him on Rubens. Had it not been for Professor Martin, I would never have pursued a graduate career in art history, but might instead have been reclaimed by my first love, music. Yet, as it turned out, it was his widow, Barbara's, memorial service that took me back to the piano.

Finally, a more formal but no less poignant card from my Princeton classmate the now-dowager queen of Jordan shows the pensive and radiant and too-young widow between her teenage daughters. She looks not a day older than thirty years ago, when we both started our last term toward graduation. It was a terrible year for the Middle East, devastated by the Yom Kippur War. May this anniversary prove the opposite, despite the gathering storm. The message on Noor's card reflects a very different face of Islam, and of its God of Abraham, Jesus, and Mohammed—the Father we all claim as wayward children: *In the name of God, the Compassionate, the Merciful . . . "Peace shall be the greeting from the Merciful Lord"* (Sura Yasin: 58). May that be the prayer we all share on this first Friday, just two days before the eve of Epiphany.

SATURDAY, JANUARY 4, 2003

The sidewalks of New York are already punctuated by dry, discarded Christmas trees. Our own, equally dry and brittle, still gleams with white lights and ornaments and tinsel. As a child I recall how our family tree usually was taken down by New Year's Day—probably a sound idea, for the colored lights burned hot, and dry evergreens are a notorious fire hazard. But now I am loath to shortchange the twelve days of Christmas even by a day. The tree shall stand in full glory until Epiphany. But by whose count? Tomorrow my Roman Church celebrates the feast, since the new Catholic calendar requires that it fall on the second Sunday after Christmas. But for most of Christendom—and most visibly the Episcopal Church of my childhood—Epiphany is still January 6, the day after Shakespeare's *Twelfth Night*, that play celebrating changes in all but "the constant image" of the beloved.

Is not the star such a constant image? And if so, how dare these latter-day ecclesiastical calendar makers change an immovable feast, which Father Andrew O'Connor tonight reminds me was even older than Christmas itself? Last year was a temporal, if not celestial, blessing—the sixth fell on a Sunday. Father Andrew has called to say that he is busy making crowns for the children to wear for the feast at his Church of Holy Trinity tomorrow.

I wonder now whether those Three Kings who are scheduled to arrive at the manger in two days, by the old reckoning, arrived back home to empty thrones. Perhaps some enterprising novelist may yet broach that question: how were their lives changed, both externally and internally, in the rival currencies of power and of spirit? "My kingdom is not of this world," Jesus announced late in the gospel—too late to alter his fate. Eliot's magnificent poem "Journey of the Magi" suggests that their realms and their rule may have been forever altered—as indeed was the world in the millennia that followed that first Epiphany. Eliot wrote his poem in 1927—the year my mother was born, Lindbergh crossed the Atlantic, and the poet's own journey from agnosticism led him to a baptismal font in the Anglican Church. He concludes—in the voice of one of the Magi—that although it all happened so long go, he would make the journey again, but with this question to be answered: were they led to that manger for a birth, or a death? There was certainly a birth, but this one was "hard and bitter agony for us, like Death, our death." They returned to their kingdoms, yet no longer at peace with their old dispensation, "with an alien people clutching their gods." He would, he adds, welcome "another death."

Perhaps my clutching to the original date of Epiphany reflects more than the white Christmas lights I yearn to see sparkle for an extra day. Perhaps it signifies a late reluctance to reach the destination that may mark yet another death to the past. After a year of journey through a journal—of memory, sounds, and images—will I find I have arrived back home by another route, or instead that my journey will have only just begun? Perhaps a priest's homily tomorrow will provide a clue, in which case I shall be grateful for the Church's premature celebration, and for the chance (like Scrooge's) to relive a precious day.

SUNDAY, JANUARY 5, 2003

I am grateful. The five-thirty evening Mass at St. Jean's proved to be the perfect anticipation of Epiphany: all the candelabra on that tiered wedding cake altarpiece of neo-Baroque extravagance were lit, flickering in red and white glass beside the most blazing poinsettias I have ever seen. The Christmas trees still twinkled with lights, while off to the left, in the transept, three life-size statues of the Magi presented their gifts to the Child in the manger, beneath an electric five-pointed star.

From the first moments I found myself taking in every sight and sound of the Mass, as if it were the first—or last—of a lifetime. The first reading, Isaiah's prophecy of the Messiah, resounded with luminous imagery I had never quite appreciated before today. *Non nova, sed nove*—words heard in a new light: "Rise up in splendor! Your light has come, the glory of the Lord shines upon you. See, darkness covers the earth, and thick clouds cover the peoples; but upon you the Lord shines, and over you appears his glory. Nations shall walk by your light, and kings by your shining radiance."

This Sunday, overcast and gray, was bathed by evening in the light of that distant star and reflected in the gilded glory of the church interior. Then, and not for the first time, the obvious stuck home: how dependent we are on our senses—our eyes and ears—to begin to recognize even the faintest outlines or echoes of the divine in our midst. From the burning bush before Moses to the star rising in the East to the transfiguration of our Lord—light has forever been God's shadow. We hear his voice through the limitations of our human language and, more clearly if less literally, in the resonance of music, the holiest of arts.

The homilist today made two simple points about this ancient feast of revelation. The first is that the gospel account of the Three Magi and their confrontation with King Herod (and the best and the brightest of Jerusalem's religious authorities) should serve as a warning never to assume that we truly know God: the priests and Pharisees and scribes were all experts on Isaiah's prophecies, but they missed the Messiah's epiphany in Bethlehem. It was a group of itinerant foreigners who found Truth in that most unseemly setting of straw. God was then, and remains, a God of surprises.

The second point was that our search for him requires a journey, an active participation on our part, perhaps even a pilgrimage that may take a lifetime (and more) to complete. I have wondered through these past several days how this journal will end. It was the wrong question; I should have known better. Tomorrow, the Feast of Epiphany, marks only the end of one journey, one I set out on a year ago. The more important question is what tomorrow will begin.

MONDAY, JANUARY 6, 2003

Today was one of lights and small pilgrimages, beginning with the walk to work after a week's vacation. Entering Rock Center, I rejoiced to see the lights of the huge Christmas tree still blazing, together with the sequence of illuminated angels along the promenade. The secular city still follows the old calendar, thank God. Today is the true feast, at least for the eyes. On my way home, I decided to pay homage to Rubens's *Epiphany* in the narthex of St. Thomas Church. It was nothing like my first encounter with this Baroque altarpiece almost thirty years ago. Back then, an earnest art scholar in the making, I was absorbed in separating the visible brushstrokes between those of the master and those of his assistants: I saw the studio production, not an original painting. Today, the opposite struck me: the whole ensemble of Holy Family, shepherds, Kings, and beasts ablaze in glory. Rubens's vision, his composition, his genius, and those few retouched strokes carried the day—one of sheer beauty. No matter how much it may be discounted among scholars and dealers, this painting reigns supreme among the larger-than-life adorations of the Magi in our city, thanks to its translation across the Atlantic from a village church in Belgium a century ago.

Onward to St. Vincent Ferrer for the five-thirty Mass: I had not seen my home parish since the Christmas decorations went up. Gothic churches were made for evergreens and poinsettias; the lights and colors transform the dark stone interior of massive columns and soaring vaults as nowhere else. After Communion, I knelt before the crèche; the figures were all in place; each angel had a double, as did ox and ass. Yet only two carved wooden camels accompanied the Three Magi; I wondered whether one had wandered off, or whether those persevering Wise Men had had to take turns. The one proffering gold to the Child held out his own crown—a nice touch I had never noticed. As I left the manger, I heard as my silent words of farewell, not the Ave Maria, or any apt prayer for this conclusion of Epiphany, but rather those words of another young child—my own—

on our first visit there together over twenty years ago: *"Ee-eye, ee-eye, O."* There was no improving upon them.

During the Mass, I couldn't help studying the new additions to the sanctuary—those two massive, ornately carved lecterns (really paired pulpits), which initially had bothered me as unwelcome intrusions into a familiar space. But today they seemed in harmony with their surroundings, a worthy frame to the central mystery of the altar. They have come under particular criticism as being liturgically "incorrect," since the lectern for the reading of the word is supposed to be grander than the cantor's stand. But as this Mass without music progressed, I wondered: Who is to say that what we read is more important than what we sing? The angels on that first Christmas did not quote scripture to the shepherds: a heavenly chorus, they sang to the glory of God—*"Gloria in excelsis Deo!"*

On my way home, as I passed St. James's Church, I noticed a choir proceeding through the front door. I had not seen it opened since that church had been shut for over a year of renovations. But inside the candles burned and a small congregation gathered to celebrate an evening service of lessons and carols for Epiphany. I took a seat near the rear and heard the Nativity passages from St. Luke, followed by St. Matthew's account of the visit of the Magi. Each was interspersed by a carol or anthem. The last one I heard, before leaving for home, was an anthem ("Say, where is he born") from Mendelssohn's unfinished oratorio *Christus.* I had never heard it before. The music was set to St. Matthew's words of the star appearing in the East and the Wise Men who followed it. What was sung was precisely what had been read—only elevated by the magic of music. So much for the critique of those identical lecterns a few blocks south: words and music are twin creations of the Father who has made us all. We are the ones who complicate creation, who delay—and sometimes deny—the simple epiphanies around us.

It was Evelyn Waugh, through his beguiling, eccentric character Lord Sebastian, who first captured for me the beauty of that story of the Three Magi, the first Epiphany, and put it in perspective. But it was a later novel, much less celebrated than *Brideshead Revisited,* that finally filled out the picture: *Helena.* I had first heard of it over twenty years ago from P. D. James one night at dinner in London, when quite out of the blue she quoted its concluding prayer from memory. Ten years later, I hear it quoted again by a young priest, Father Paul Tabor, during his sermon on the Feast of

Epiphany. (Today he reminds me that it was the first time I ever spoke to him at the church door, teasing that "it would take a Jesuit to quote Waugh in a sermon!") But it took me almost another decade before I finally found a copy of the book and read it for myself.

The last chapter of *Helena*, about the sainted mother of the emperor Constantine, is called "Epiphany." It follows her discovery in Jerusalem of the cross on which our Lord died. On Twelfth Night, old and infirm, she arrives at the shrine of the Nativity in Bethlehem, her final pilgrimage. An hour before dawn, she is taken to the stable-cave for the celebration of the feast.

> *The low vault was full of lamps and the air close and still. Silver bells announced the coming of the three vested, bearded monks, who like the kings of old now prostrated themselves before the altar. So the long liturgy began.*
>
> *Helena knew little Greek and her thoughts were not in the words nor anywhere in the immediate scene. She forgot even her quest and was dead to everything except the swaddled child long ago and those three royal sages who had come so far to adore him.*
>
> *"This is my day," she thought, "and these are my kind. . . . Like me," she said to them, "you were late in coming. The shepherds were there long before; even the cattle. They had joined the chorus of angels before you were on your way. For you the primordial discipline of the heavens was relaxed and a new defiant light blazed amid the disconcerted stars.*
>
> *"How laboriously you came, taking sights and calculating, where the shepherds had run barefoot! How odd you looked on the road, attended by what outlandish liveries, laden with such preposterous gifts!*
>
> *"You came at length to the final stage of your pilgrimage and the great star stood still above you. What did you do? You stopped to call on King Herod. Deadly exchange of compliments in which began that unended war of mobs and magistrates against the innocent!*
>
> *"Yet you came, and were not turned away. You too found room before the manger. Your gifts were not needed, but they were accepted and put carefully by, for they were brought with love. In that new order of charity that had just come to life, there was room for you, too. You were not lower in the eyes of the holy family than the ox or the ass.*
>
> *"You are my special patrons," said Helena, "and patrons of all late-comers, of*

all who have a tedious journey to make to the truth, of all who are confused with knowledge and speculation, of all who through politeness make themselves partners in guilt, of all who stand in danger by reason of their talents.

"Dear cousins, pray for me," said Helena, "and for my poor overloaded son. May he, too, before the end find kneeling space in the straw. Pray for the great, lest they perish utterly . . .

"For His sake who did not reject your curious gifts, pray always for all the learned, the oblique, the delicate. Let them not be quite forgotten at the throne of God when the simple come into their kingdom."

Someday, I pray, I too may make that journey, kneel within that grotto, and offer that perfect prayer of all latecomers to the manger.

CODA:
NOTES ON THE TITLE

I have given some long overdue and needed thought to the source and meaning of the phrase "Light is the shadow of God," from which I have taken my title. My father, the classics major, had introduced me to it in Latin, *Lux Umbra Dei*, as an inscription to post (for inspiration?) on my senior thesis study carrel in the art library in 1972. But I don't recall him ever telling me where he got it. Decades later, thanks to the Internet, I was led to Sir Thomas Browne, for the English version. Then I found its source, not surprisingly, in Plato. But long before Plato, the anonymous author of the book of Genesis reflected on the special relationship between light and God the Creator. The very first command of God is "Let there be light." The first act of creation. "And he saw that it was good." In the New Testament, Jesus calls himself the "Light of the world." The Nicene Creed is even more explicit about the divine identity: Jesus is "God from God, Light from Light." But this Light is not a creation, not the light we know around us and described in Genesis. It is what Saint Paul calls "unapproachable light." Too bright for our imagination, much less our eyes. The English Renaissance philosopher Sir Thomas Browne framed this mystery as a paradox worthy of the metaphysical poets:

> *Light that makes things seen, makes some things invisible, were it not for darknesse and the shadow of the earth, the noblest part of the Creation had remained unseen, and the Stars in heaven as invisible as on the fourth day, when they were created above the Horizon, with the Sun, or there was not an eye to behold them. The greatest mystery of Religion is expressed by adumbration, and in the noblest part of Jewish Types, we finde the Cherubims shadowing the Mercy-seat: Life it self is but the shadow of death, and souls departed but the shadows of the living: All things fall under this name. The Sunne it self is but the dark simulacrum, and light but the shadow of God.*

THE GARDEN OF CYRUS, CHAPTER 3

I am reminded of the similar paradox expressed by my favorite poet of that period, John Donne. In his sonnet "Death Be Not Proud" he concludes, "One short sleep past, we wake eternally, and Death shall be no more: Death, thou shalt die."

Then through my day's journey into literary sources, I stumbled upon a Victorian author, critic, and poet I had never before read, John Addington Symonds (1840–1893). He wrote a beautiful sonnet titled "Lux Est Umbra Dei" that sums it up in the most chastely romantic and ecstatic way:

> Nay, Death, thou art a shadow! Even as light
> Is but the shadow of invisible God,
> And of that shade the shadow is thin Night,
> Veiling the earth whereon our feet have trod;
> So art Thou but the shadow of this life,
> Itself the pale and unsubstantial shade
> Of living God, fulfilled by love and strife
> Throughout the universe Himself hath made:
> And as frail Night, following the flight of earth,
> Obscures the world we breathe in, for a while,
> So Thou, the reflex of our mortal birth,
> Veilest the life wherein we weep and smile:
> But when both earth and life are whirl'd away,
> What shade can shroud us from God's deathless day?

No wonder my father had given me that motto as I began to write my thesis about Rubens's *Triumph of the Eucharist*. For that artist, as for Bernini and the other giants of the Baroque age, light was infused with metaphysical meaning. The sacrament in its golden monstrance always blazes as a beacon of light, just as the Gloria explodes into golden shafts and gilded angels emanating from a stained glass window in Bernini's masterpiece for the far apse of St. Peter's, Rome, above the Chair of Peter. Caravaggio included no painted apparition of Christ in his *Conversion of Paul* for Santa Maria del Popolo: for that revolutionary naturalist, light alone was sufficient to explain the divine source of Paul's blinding conversion on the road to Damascus.

I am by now used to God's use of coincidences as humorous prompt-ings. Even so, I was startled when the lector, at the beginning of Mass to-day, announced that the theme of the day's Mass was "God's divine light." In Paul's epistle to the Ephesians we are told to become "children of light, for light produces everything good." In the gospel reading, Jesus grants sight to a man blind from birth. The priest in his homily observed that light was to be identified not only with sight, but with love. This notion of light as a medium of divine love, as a moral force, brings to mind that lovely poem written by Cardinal Newman during a sea voyage when his life seemed threatened by storms:

THE PILLAR OF THE CLOUD

Lead, Kindly Light, amid the encircling gloom
    Lead Thou me on!
The night is dark, and I am far from home—
    Lead Thou me on!
Keep Thou my feet; I do not ask to see
The distant scene—one step enough for me.

I was not ever thus, nor pray'd that Thou
    Shouldst lead me on.
I loved to choose and see my path, but now
    Lead Thou me on!
I loved the garish day, and, spite of fears,
Pride ruled my will: remember not past years.

So long Thy power hath blest me, sure it still
    Will lead me on,
O'er moor and fen, o'er crag and torrent, till
    The night is gone;
And with the morn those angel faces smile
Which I have loved long since, and lost awhile.

AT SEA. JUNE 16, 1833

No wonder these verses cried out for music. Today we sing them.

ABOUT THE AUTHOR

CHARLES SCRIBNER III has spent his life among books. A great-great-grandson of the founder of Charles Scribner's Sons, one of the most distinguished American publishing houses, he worked as an editor and publishing executive for nearly thirty years. He received his Ph.D. degree in art history from Princeton University, where he taught in the Department of Art & Archaeology and serves on its advisory council. An expert in the field of Baroque art, he is the author of biographies of Rubens and Bernini. He and his wife, Ritchie, an artist and museum educator, reside in New York City.